Individualizing Educational Objectives and Programs

Individualizing Educational Objectives and Programs

110637

A Modular Approach

Peter J. Valletutti, Ed.D.

Dean, Division of Extension and Experimental Programs
and Professor of Education

and

Anthony O. Salpino, Ph.D.

Assistant Professor of Special Education

Coppin State College
Baltimore, Maryland

University Park Press
Baltimore

UNIVERSITY PARK PRESS
International Publishers in Science, Medicine, and Education
233 East Redwood Street
Baltimore, Maryland 21202

Typeset by American Graphic Arts Corporation.
Manufactured in the United States of America by The Maple Press Company.

Library of Congress Cataloging in Publication Data

Valletutti, Peter J
  Individualizing educational objectives and programs.

  Includes bibliographies.
  1. Individualized instruction.   2. Handicapped
children—Education.   I. Salpino, Anthony O.,
joint author.   II. Title.
LB1031.V35   371.39′4   79-10724
ISBN 0-8391-1265-3

Contents

Acknowledgments

We are grateful to three great women for their cogent comments, constructive criticisms, and insightful suggestions: Billie B. Valletutti, Florence Christoplos, and Mary Strawhorn.

to my brothers, Drs. Angelo and Joseph Valletutti

p.j.v.

to my beloved parents, Oscar and Rose

a.o.s.

Individualizing Educational Objectives and Programs

Introduction

This series of modules is a guide to implementing diagnostic/prescriptive teaching. The term *diagnostic* refers to understanding pupils as total human beings. The term *prescriptive* refers to working out ways of helping pupils realize their greatest potential. The diagnostic/prescriptive process is not mysterious or esoteric, if initiated with acceptance of the pupils *as they are* with unknown potential for development. The teacher's role is to provide understanding and supportive guides for individualizing instruction in the development process.

Individualizing instruction is not complicated. The process includes simple ideas applied to each part of the total individualization of instruction. The simplicity may frighten many of us who have been conditioned to favor approaches that are highly structured and unnecessarily complicated. Educators have been brainwashed to denigrate their own talents and unique insights and to rely on the wisdom of presumably more sophisticated professionals who carry testing materials from school to school. Unfortunately, the results of psychological tests rarely bring enlightenment to teachers because they are seldom translatable directly into teaching practice. The absence of translation and the use of impractical jargon reinforces the dependence of teachers on others and prevents them from utilizing common-sense approaches to evaluating the educational skills and needs of pupils. The modules herein are presented to help and convince teachers that they possess the necessary skills and can acquire further knowledge and skills needed to individualize instructional programs. Occasional help from other professionals is needed, but this should be on request and for specific and relevant information.

These modules are meant to stress the critical role of the pupils themselves in the total diagnostic and prescriptive process and to emphasize the crucial role parents must play as well. A three-way communication with mutual respect and cooperation underlies the relationship among teachers, pupils, and parents. This team must value open communication throughout the instructional process, respecting each one for the special perceptions they bring to the educational planning and implementation processes. The orientation throughout is on maximum participation and democracy so that the process of education reflects the basic tenets of this society.

Attempts to individualize a diagnostic/prescriptive approach have already become mandatory for handicapped children and are equally applicable to all children. The requirements of PL 94-142, The Education for All Handicapped Children Act, has at its conceptual core the development of a written individualized education program (IEP)[1] for all handicapped children.

The content of the written education program must include a statement on:

a. The pupil's present level of educational functioning
b. Annual goals, including short-term instructional objectives
c. The specific educational services to be provided
d. The extent to which the pupil will be able to participate in programs with the nonhandicapped
e. The projected initiation date for each service and the anticipated duration of each service
f. The evaluation criteria and procedures for ensuring that instructional objectives are being realized

Central to the development of the so-called IEP is the role played by parents in the *formulation, approval, review, and redesign* of the IEP for their child. Also, when appropriate, pupils participate in those meetings during which the content of the written program is determined.

With slight modifications, the model mandated by PL 94-142 for the handicapped may serve as the model for individualized planning for all pupils. Granted, the problems are many and difficult in interpreting, implementing, and funding the IEP requirements stated in the law. Nevertheless, the desirability and appropriateness of the general intention are not diminished by these problems. From the laudatory work with the handicapped, benefit may accrue to the nonhandicapped as well if well-written and well-documented individualized education programs are mandated for all pupils at all levels in all of the schools.

If teachers possess and/or acquire the skills and knowledge set forth in the 12 modules of this book, they will have begun the process of becoming professional educators who value the individual worth of each pupil and have the competencies to make that goal operational. The modules are presented as a comprehensive beginning toward the development of diagnostic/prescriptive skills. Their acquisition is a never-ending process that brings continuous excitement and challenge to the profession.

---

[1] For an excellent review and summary of IEPs see Torres, S. (ed.). 1977. A Primer on Individualized Education Programs for Handicapped Children. Foundation for Exceptional Children, Reston, Va.

FORMAT OF THE BOOK

A modular approach was selected in order to allow readers to proceed through the modules at their own pace. The readers must judge for themselves those areas to be stressed and developed. A modular approach emphasizes self-evaluation and self-instruction within the structure and direction of the program.

Each of the 12 modules is structured as follows:

1. Statement of Modular Objective
2. Pretest
3. Introduction and Overview
4. Activities and Experiences
5. Concluding Statement
6. Posttest
7. Literature Cited and/or Suggested Readings
8. Test Answers (located in the special section at the end of the 12 modules)

After reading the modular objective, readers proceed to take the *Pretest*. If, on completing the *Pretest*, the overall mastery criterion is met as specified in the *Test Answers* section, the module may still be read for additional information. The *Activities and Experiences* should be completed in areas of demonstrated weakness. If the overall mastery criterion has not been met on the *Pretest*, the module should be completed and reviewed until the *Posttest* is successfully taken indicating that the criteria are met.

THE MODULAR OBJECTIVES

Module 1

The teacher will demonstrate knowledge of the prevailing educational goals and objectives of the school district and the general community. The teacher will apply this knowledge to establish individual educational objectives (IEOs) for each pupil.

Module 2

The teacher will demonstrate knowledge of the possible inter-effects that may develop between the expectations and values of the school, community, and family, on the one hand, and pupil behavior and learning on the other.

Module 3

The teacher will demonstrate knowledge of the possible effects of the classroom's physical environment on pupil behavior and learning.

Module 4

The teacher will demonstrate knowledge of perceptual, motor, language, cognitive, and social developmental milestones.

Module 5

The teacher will demonstrate knowledge of the possible effects of sensory, neurological, physical, and mental disabilities/dysfunctions on pupil behavior and learning. The teacher will list those behaviors that suggest the possible presence of medical problems in pupils.

Module 6

The teacher will recommend for diagnosis and/or treatment those pupils suspected of having medical or paramedical problems. The teacher will follow an appropriate referral process and will carry out those recommendations that have implications for classroom organization, instruction, pupil management, and continuing evaluation. Whenever feasible, the teacher also will carry out those suggestions that will assist in meeting therapeutic goals, reporting relevant classroom behaviors to those professionals providing various therapeutic interventions.

Module 7

The teacher will identify individual educational objectives for each pupil based upon an analysis of that pupil's knowledge, skills, concepts, interests, and needs. Toward this end, the teacher will engage in several informal assessment procedures, including: 1) the development and administration of test inventories, 2) the observation and documentation of pupil behaviors as they occur during teaching/learning experiences, 3) the sampling and analysis of pupil behavior and work products, and 4) the interviewing of the pupil and the pupil's parents.

Module 8

The teacher, in concert with the pupil, will establish mastery criteria for instructional tasks. The teacher will assess pupil performance relevant to the achievement of mastery and will provide experiences and techniques that will encourage pupils and assist them with self-evaluation.

Module 9

The teacher will analyze educational tasks in order to establish prerequisite concepts and skills and will arrange these task elements in a sequential order for diagnostic and program sequencing purposes.

Module 10

The teacher will identify alternate subcategories of subject matter in each curriculum area. Based upon available subcategories, in concert with the pupil and other significant individuals, the teacher will make programming decisions appropriate and motivating to the instruction of the individual pupil.

Module 11

The teacher will evaluate the effects of classmates and of himself/herself on the attitudes, behavior, and learning of each individual pupil in the classroom and will modify these interactions when necessary.

Module 12

The teacher will accommodate educational programs to pupil temperament and learning style characteristics.

Module 1

The teacher will demonstrate knowledge of the prevailing educational goals and objectives of the school district and the general community. The teacher will apply this knowledge to establish individual educational objectives (IEOs) for each pupil.

PRETEST

1. List six steps to be employed by the teacher in determining the individual educational objectives that will most benefit each pupil.
2. Give the reasons why the hierarchical ordering of educational objectives are difficult tasks.
3. Teacher preparation programs emphasize two objectives: "what to teach" and "how to teach." For diagnostic purposes, which of these two objectives is more important?
4. Teachers should play a significant role in the development of a school district's curriculum goals and objectives and in the selection and/or creation of curriculum guides. List several ways in which teachers can participate in these processes.
5. Community educational goals and objectives can be communicated unofficially through what groups, individuals, and agencies?
6. What condition is necessary before teachers can work toward alternate objectives that conflict with community- and/or school district-supported ones?
7. When teachers, as public servants, attempt to change curriculum goals, they are particularly subject to pressures from whom?
8. List several groups, individuals, and organizations to whom teachers owe a degree of responsibility and allegiance.
9. List several official sources that identify school district and community educational goals and objectives.
10. List several unofficial sources that influence community and school district educational goals and objectives.
11. List the major educational goals and objectives for the school district in which you teach, or are student teaching, or in which your college or university is located, or in which you plan to teach or student teach. List the goals and objectives in order by priority.
12. List those community educational goals and objectives that are in conflict with those of the school district reported in your answer to Question 11.
13. Based upon your responses to Question 11 and 12 and your own educational philosophy, how would you modify the school district's priority listing of educational goals and objectives?

INTRODUCTION AND OVERVIEW

Identifying Individual Educational Objectives

The primary goal of the overall diagnostic/prescriptive process is the determination of individual educational objectives (IEOs) for each pupil. In order to arrive eventually at IEOs, a teacher should engage in a number of sequential processes designed to culminate in the identification of teaching objectives that are pupil centered and behaviorally stated (see Module 9). This basic diagnostic procedure should be performed with as much precision as possible so that the selected teaching activities are consistent with the needs of each pupil. The process by which IEOs are established is shown in Table 1.

This module is concerned with applying knowledge of prevailing educational goals and objectives of the school district and the general community in order to establish IEOs for each pupil. The primary diagnostic/prescriptive goal of deciding "what to teach" precedes a determination of "how to teach" and, therefore, assumes hegemony over programming methods and materials.

National (Universal) Priority Listing of Educational Objectives

While agreement often is possible on effective and efficient methods and materials of instruction, national consensus on priorities in educational goals is virtually impossible. National goals are usually stated in amorphous terms with no attempt made to establish goal hierarchies. Unfortunately, in social service and government-supported institutions, the number of goals to be institutionally incorporated is expanding in unordered and indiscriminate proliferation. The American public school system, in particular, due to its vulnerability to public pressure, has accepted as pertinent to its functions innumerable vague goals. Attempts to establish a working hierarchy among these goals are rare except, perhaps, in philosophical meanderings remote from the possibility of implementation.

Society has changed much since Spencer classified human activities that were to him a self-evident order of human importance:

1. Those activities which directly minister to self-preservation;
2. Those activities which, by securing the necessaries of life, directly minister to self-preservation;
3. Those activities which have for their end the rearing and discipline of offspring;
4. Those activities which are involved in the maintenance of proper social and political relations;
5. Those miscellaneous activities which make up the leisure part of life, devoted to the gratification of the tastes and feelings (Gross, 1963, pp. 84–85).

Table 1.   Establishment of individual educational objectives (IEOs)

(1) National or universal priority listing of educational goals and objectives	$\longrightarrow$	(2) School district priority listing reflecting community educational goals and objectives	$\longrightarrow$

(3) School district and community goals and objectives as filtered through the individual teacher's perceptions and value system	$\longrightarrow$	(4) Teacher modified priority listing of educational goals and objectives	$\longrightarrow$	(5) Various teacher- directed diagnostic strategies	$\longrightarrow$

(6)
Individual (pupil)
educational
goals
and
objectives
(IEO)

Spencer stated "that these (activities) stand in something like their true order of subordination, it needs no long consideration to show" (Gross, 1963, p. 85). Radical social changes following in the wake of burgeoning technological advances have undermined Spencer's "true order of subordination."

The American school system's present adherence to a multiplicity of goals has led to an obsessive restriction of professional attention to either methodological processes or narrow-range priorities. Educators are preoccupied with atomized goals and the evaluation, dissemination, and implementation of nontheoretically based methodological innovations. Specific materials, methods, and units of instruction are disproportionately emphasized to the neglect of general objectives and principles. The proliferation of information centers, e.g., Educational Research Information Centers (ERIC), regional educational laboratories, and regional materials centers, further encourages educators to avoid identifying educational goals and to concentrate on accumulating a variety of instructional media and data on short-range accomplishments.

The lack of clear principles and priorities among educational goals has led to curriculum practices employed in a philosophical vacuum, practices that are thereby inconsistent, inefficient, and indefensible. Educational practice without principle and design has engendered mindless flitting from program to program and diagnostic approaches that are irrelevant, unscientific, and unnecessarily complex.

In any profession in which diagnosis or evaluation plays an essential part, the diagnostic focus must be circumscribed by that profession's role and scope. Therefore, a physician examines a patient in terms of goals relevant to physical and mental health. A teacher "examines" a pupil relevant to goals and objectives deemed of value to educational growth and development. The more specialized the profession, the more its basic theoretical underpinnings have been defined and the narrower and simpler is its diagnostic function. Unfortunately, educators, especially at the early childhood and elementary school levels, are expected to be supreme generalists possessing diagnostic and programming (prescriptive) skills ranging over a broad spectrum of student knowledge, skills, attitudes, values, and behaviors. In the absence of consensus in national or universal educational goals and objectives, an awesome burden is placed on the individual teacher.

> Answers to the problems of ranking educational goals cannot be found in educational research and technology. The values and beliefs, including myths of the society determine such priorities. Determining priorities is particularly difficult in societies that are complex and profess a pluralistic philosophy of development. The difficulty is evidenced by the bypassing in much of the professional literature of discussions of educational goals in favor of methodological discussions. This neglect occurs despite the obvious futility of arguing how best to accomplish something without clearly understanding what is to be accomplished (Christoplos and Valletutti, 1977, p. 81).

Despite the lack of national goals, teachers through the years have been urged to "teach the *whole* child." Depending upon level and type of assignment, teachers may be responsible for teaching "*all* things to *all* of the *whole* children" in their classes. As laws and judicial decisions mandate the integration of the handicapped into the educational mainstream, the *all* (children) acquires greater significance.

Without a clear understanding of "what to teach," a teacher cannot arrive at a precise determination of "what to diagnose." "What to diagnose" is, however, shaped by what a teacher is expected to teach (or expects to teach). The decision of "what to diagnose" is a critical one since that judgment will determine the direction of the pupil's future learning experiences.

What a teacher is expected to teach is determined, in part, by national or panhuman perspectives. Before one can develop a pertinent list of learning objectives for each pupil, an appreciation for national or universal goals is prerequisite.

Even though national lists have been compiled, those few that exist are written typically in amorphous, general, and idealistic long-range terms requiring the subsequent identification of subordinate, short-term objectives possessing greater behavioral specificity. For example, the Commission on Reorganization of Secondary Education (1937) has identified the seven main objectives of education as follows: health, command of fundamental processes, worthy home membership, vocation, citizenship, worthy use of leisure, and ethical character. Characteristically, a local school system selects such a list of general objectives, which it may or may not modify. It then may proceed to establish a priority listing and supplement the list with those specific educational objectives that, when accomplished, will assist the pupil in progressing to the valued, long-term goals inferred from the generally stated objectives. This refining, objectifying process in progressive school districts is based in part on community goals and expectations and involves the active participation of the teachers of the district.

School District Listing of Educational Objectives

While a teacher may play a limited role in the establishment of national or universal educational goals and objectives, teachers, in cooperation with other educators and the citizens of a school district, should identify those educational objectives that are specific to the community. Community educational goals and objectives, while they invariably reflect more universal ones, more intensely mirror parochial interests, values, and attitudes. As is to be expected, these values frequently result in the revision of those more catholic educational goals and objectives established for societies in general. The teacher's role in selecting and ordering by priority educational objectives for the community in which he/she teaches is an essential professional responsibility. Therefore, this module explores the various procedures through which teachers may determine and assess community educational goals and objectives and explains the relationships existing between school district and community educational goals and objectives and the development of individual educational objectives.

In the more enlightened school districts, teachers are given a primary role in the development of goals and objectives for that district. Systemwide steering committees can be organized to oversee the development and continuous review of curriculum objectives and arrange for their dissemination throughout the district's schools. At times these committees or appointed subcommittees may be responsible for the creation and/or selection of curriculum guides for the system. In many school districts, teachers have been given or have achieved the right to vote on the system's educational goals and objectives, and, in some cases, the teachers, with or without consultants, develop the curriculum guides through committee assignments and/or in inservice workshops. Active teacher involvement in the above processes tends to minimize the metamorphosis that sometimes occurs when teachers examine the school district's prescribed goals, objectives, and experiences designed by others.

Even in those cases where teachers do not play a part in the evaluation of educational goals for the school district, teachers, nevertheless, influence goal development as these objectives are filtered through the perceptions, interests, and idiosyncracies of individual teachers. When teachers are passive observers in discovering the educational goals and objectives of a specific community, they must analyze and synthesize these objectives, whether officially or unofficially expressed. (Goals and objectives are likely to be unofficially communicated when they deviate from the national or state goals or if they are not subject to ready measurement.)

In the process of filtering community and school district goals and objectives through their own value systems, teachers usually arrive at a list of educational goals and objectives by priority. In striving to attain these objectives, however, teachers must be especially careful not to ignore those priorities sanctioned by the school district and/or community, nor work toward alternate objectives that antagonize the community and/or school district authorities unless they have already created a power base of their own, i.e., a powerful segment of the larger community. When teachers find that school district/community goals and objectives contrast with their own philosophy of education, they must decide either to surrender or face censure. It should be remembered that teachers, as public servants, are particularly vulnerable to both internal (school and school system) and external (community) pressures.

Conflicts are not resolved easily since teachers, by the very nature of their profession, have multiple responsibilities and allegiances. The diverse and potentially adverse allegiances include, but are not necessarily restricted to, the following (the list arrangement does not imply a ranking by priority; rather, the order of importance shifts in each school district, in each school, and for each teacher):

1. Panhumanistic needs and values
2. National goals and objectives
3. State goals and expectations
4. Local governmental goals and expectations
5. Community goals and expectations
6. Local board of education values and objectives

7.   School districts' central administrations' goals and objectives
8.   Regional administrators' goals and objectives
9.   School principals' values and objectives
10. Other school administrators and supervisors
11. PTA and other parent-sponsored advocacy groups
12. Parents of their pupils
13. Students' needs, interests, goals, and values
14. Goals and objectives of the profession
15. Goals and objectives of professional associations or teachers' unions
16. The teachers' own needs, interests, goals, attitudes, and values

The handling of these sundry forces demands much of teachers as they attempt to filter school district and community goals and objectives through their own interests, goals, attitudes, and values and as they teach their pupils and interact with parents.

Problems especially arise when a teacher's philosophy of education idealogically clashes with that of the school district and/or the community. In those cases, teachers must be especially skilled in techniques of effective human relations and in acting as adroit change agents. Often a teacher, for example, feels that he/she must introduce curriculum objectives and materials that are threatening to the school district and/or community and he/she is not able to handle the task with ease. These conflicts, however, may not always be avoided with facility. For example, the teacher may find that he/she is compelled to teach a unit on pollution and, in all good conscience, must indict a local factory that sustains the work force of the community for the hazards created.

Teachers may not always possess philosophies of education that conflict with community goals. On occasion, despite romaticized versions of the heroic teacher fighting regressive community attitudes and standards, one finds teachers and school administrators who fail to uphold democratic principles in a democratic society. Note how some teachers were content to sit idly by and relinquish the leadership and allowed the courts, parental groups, and various advocacy agencies to bring about signficant democratic changes in education. Individual teachers may possess values and behave in ways designed to subvert progressive legislative and judicial action. One wonders, for example, whether a substantial number of teachers (and school administrators) will continue resisting the full integration of handicapped pupils in the educational mainstream. Will some teachers circumvent the requirements of PL 94-142, which mandates the development of IEPs, i.e., individualized education plans, by specifying unrealistically low instructional objectives? Will the fear of accountability result in spuriously low conditions in the IEP contract? Will bigoted and burned-out teachers persist in providing inferior educational opportunity to minority students in order to support their belief of racial/ethnic superiority?

While a teacher's educational philosophy appears to be tangential to the individualization of instruction, it remains an omnipresent factor that continuously influences and controls both edueational diagnosis and educational prescription (programming).

Since a teacher's understanding of community educational goals and objectives is necessary before a focus is given to diagnostic strategies and processes, this module serves to assist both teachers and those preparing to become teachers in assessing school district and community educational goals and objectives and in incorporating those elements into a listing by priority (see Table 1, Stage 4) from which to decide upon specific diagnostic techniques in order to establish individual educational objectives (IEOs) for each pupil.

How to Determine School District and Community Educational Goals and Objectives

As teachers work toward deciding "what to teach" and, consequently, "what to diagnose," they must be cognizant of both the official and unofficial sources that set forth school district and community educational goals and objectives.

Official Sources

1. Community Board of Education directives and other publications
2. School district selected or developed curriculum guides
3. State Department of Education (Instruction) directives and other publications
4. State Department of Education (Instruction) curriculum guides
5. Local teacher associations and/or union publications
6. Board of Education meetings
7. PTA meetings

Unofficial Sources

1. Local newspapers and magazines
2. Local radio shows (especially news, public interest, and talk shows)
3. Locally produced television shows (especially news, public interest, and talk shows)
4. Social and community groups
5. Churches, temples, and other religious organizations and meetings
6. Meetings of political organizations
7. Fraternal and social groups
8. Meetings of special interest groups
9. Public symposia (especially those that feature local politicians since

these individuals invariably gain their power because they mirror or reinforce community views)

10. Informal and formal meetings with parents and other family members of their students

ACTIVITIES AND EXPERIENCES

1. Select a community within your home state with which you are familiar. Based upon research, describe that community in detail. Include in your description such characteristics as:
   a. Population size
   b. Religious/ethnic/racial composition
   c. Socioeconomic group distribution
   d. Age and sex distribution
   e. Business and industries
   f. Health services
   g. Social services
   h. Recreation and leisure facilities
   i. Transportation facilities (including accessibility)
   j. Employment/unemployment levels
   k. Landmarks
   l. Geographic features

2. Once you have described this community in sufficient detail, write to its Board of Education for copies of publications that specify its educational goals and objectives. Review these publications and answer, in outline or essay form, the following questions:
   a. What individuals and groups assisted in the formulation of educational objectives?
   b. In what ways do these goals and objectives compare to those identified by national, regional, and local educational associations? Other groups active in the development of social policy?
   c. How do the objectives and goals compare with those stated in generally accepted curriculum guides reviewed in present and past teacher education courses? As an alternative, check with the curriculum library of a local college or university where a teacher education program exists.
   d. How do the objectives and goals compare with those advocated by the teacher's association and/or union in that community? In your community?
   e. How do these objectives and goals compare with those identified by the State Department of Education (Public Instruction)?

f.   How do the objectives and goals differ from those expressed by the Board of Education where you teach or, if you are not teaching, where you live or attend college?

g.   Would you feel comfortable teaching in that community? Explain the reasons for your answer. Cite specific examples of curriculum goals and objectives and their priorities that conflict and that are congruent with your philosophical approach to education.

3.   Select a communty in another state with which you are generally unfamiliar and in which you might be interested in obtaining a teaching position; carry out the assignments described in items 1 and 2 above.

4.   Obtain a copy of an officially selected or developed curriculum guide from a community within another part of your state. This may be done by writing directly to the local education agency (LEA) or by visiting the curriculum library of a nearby college or university where teacher preparation programs exist. Prepare an outline that presents in order of priority the long-range (generally nonbehavioral) and short-term objectives (generally behaviorally stated) highlighted in the curriculum. Compare these objectives to those expressed in a comparable guide used in the community in which you teach, live, or attend college. Compare them with your own perceptions. How congruent are they with your philosophical orientation?

In obtaining a copy of a curriculum guide, you may want to first select one by the subject and/or level of your assignment or interest. If you do so, work up to a curriculum guide that is more comprehensive (i.e., across subject areas and grade levels).

5.   Obtain a copy of an officially selected or developed curriculum guide from another state where you might be interested in obtaining a teaching position; carry out the task described in item 4 above.

6.   Hold group and individual discussion meetings with the parents of the students in your class. After each of these meetings, write several paragraphs that reveal the insights obtained vis-à-vis educational goals and expectations of parents or parent surrogates. If you are not yet teaching but are preparing to teach, set up a role-playing group with your classmates acting as parents, or ask a community or religious leader to assist you in identifying representative parents from the local area and in setting up several meetings to discuss parental educational goals and objectives.

7.   Obtain copies of the weekend editions of the local newspaper published in the community in which you teach, attend school, or hope to teach. Review these papers thoroughly, especially editorials,

feature articles, special interest, and local news sections. From your readings, prepare a brief paper that presents community educational goals and objectives as extrapolated from the newspaper. In all cases, provide supportive data for your conclusions. Whenever possible cite other, unofficial sources that reinforce your inferences.

8. Listen to several radio and television broadcasts that feature local news and local citizens on talk and public interest shows. Also, attend meetings of several social, community, political, or special interest groups. From these various experiences, suggest, in writing, educational goals and objectives that reflect community educational values and standards. For each observation, provide supportive data, including sources, contexts, dates, names, and quotes. Whenever possible, report on opposing community viewpoints and their sources.

9. Arrange an interview with a community leader who has previously expressed opinions on education. Check local newspapers, talk with parents, a local librarian, and/or a clergyman for assistance in identifying a leader to interview. After the interview has been concluded, prepare a mock newspaper or magazine article reporting upon the interview and its implications for educational goal selection.

10. Attend meetings of the PTA in the school in which you teach or, if not currently teaching, at a nearby school. Also, attend meetings of the local Board of Education (ideally, all meetings should be open to citizens). Discuss these meetings and their implications. Suggest position differences whenever pertinent. If possible arrange an interview with a school board member to discuss present and future educational goals.

11. Invite parents to your classroom to view lessons; after these sessions, hold informal discussions to review parents' perceptions of educational goals and objectives. If you are not teaching, arrange an interview with an experienced teacher and ask him/her to tell you about insights obtained from informal discussion with parents and from visits to their homes.

12. When invited for visits to parents' homes, try to honor these invitations and see what knowledge can be obtained relevant to their educational values. Remember to respect their privacy. You may also gain insight into environmental factors that influence student performance.

13. After completing these 12 activities or suitable variations of them, draw up, in order by priority, a list of educational goals and objectives that you believe most accurately represents the selected community's standards, attitudes, and values.

14. After reviewing the goals and objectives of the school district selected, indicate ways that you would modify them.

CONCLUDING STATEMENT

After arriving at a listing by priority of educational goals and objectives that approximates community expectations and that reflects those of the school district, teachers then usually filter this information through their own perceptions and value systems (see Table 1, Stage 3) to arrive at a modified priority listing (see Table 1, Stage 4). Teachers should then select and carry out a variety of diagnostic stratagems (see Module 7) designed to identify an individual list of educational objectives (IEOs), a cornerstone in the eventual development of an individualized educational program (IEP).

POSTTEST

At this point retake the Pretest.

LITERATURE CITED

Christoplos, F., and Valletutti, P. J. 1977. Education. In P. J. Valletutti and F. Christoplos (eds.), Interdisciplinary Approaches to Human Services, pp. 81–92. University Park Press, Baltimore.
Commission on Reorganization of Secondary Education. 1937. Cardinal Principles of Secondary Education. Bulletin 1918, No. 35. Government Printing Office, Washington, D.C.
Gross, R. (ed.). 1963. The Teacher and the Taught. Dell Publishing Co., Inc., New York.

SUGGESTED READINGS

Benjamin, H. 1939. The Saber-Tooth Curriculum. McGraw-Hill Book Co., New York.
Bigge, M. 1971. Positive Relativism: An Emerging Educational Philosophy. Harper & Row Publishers, New York.
Bredemeier, M. E., and Bredemeier, H. C. 1978. Social Forces in Education. Alfred Publishing Co., Sherman Oaks, Cal.
Charnofsky, S. 1971. Educating the Powerless. Wadsworth Publishing Co., Belmont, Cal.
Coombs, P. H. 1968. The World Educational Crisis: A Systems Analysis. Oxford University Press, London.
Crary, R. 1969. Humanizing the School: Curriculum Development and Theory. Alfred A. Knopf, Inc., New York.
Dahl, J. A., Laser, M., Cathcart, R. S., and Marcus, F. H. (eds.). 1964. Student, School and Society. Chandler Publishing Co., San Francisco.

Heath, D. H. 1971. Humanizing Schools: New Directions, New Decisions. Hayden Book Co., New York.

Hutchins, R. M. 1953. The Conflict in Education in a Democratic Society. Harper & Row Publishers, New York.

Kearney, N. C. 1973. Elementary School Objectives. Russell Sage Foundation, New York.

Keppel, F. 1966. The Necessary Revolution in American Education. Harper & Row Publishers, New York.

Kerber, A. (ed.). 1964. Educational Issues in a Changing Society. Wayne State University Press, Detroit.

Klopf, G. J., and Bowman, G. W. 1966. Teacher Education in a Social Context. Mental Health Materials Center, New York.

Leeper, R. R. (ed.). 1965. Strategy for Curriculum Change. Association for Supervision and Curriculum Development, Washington, D. C.

Magee, J. B. 1971. Philosophical Analysis in Education. Harper & Row Publishers, New York.

Martin, W. O. 1969. Realism in Education. Harper & Row Publishers, New York.

Martin, W. T., and Pinck, D. C. (eds.). 1966. Curriculum Improvement: A Partnership of Students, School Teachers, and Research Scholars. Robert Bentley, Inc., Cambridge, Mass.

McClure, R. M. (ed.). 1971. Curriculum, Retrospective and Prospective. NSSE Seventieth Yearbook. Part 1. The University of Chicago Press, Chicago.

Newman, F. M., and Oliver, D. W. 1967. Education and community. Harvard Educ. Rev. 37:61–106.

Patterson, C. H. 1973. Humanistic Education. Prentice-Hall, Inc., Englewood Cliffs, N.J.

Power, E. J. 1979. The Transition of Learning: A Social and Cultural Interpretation of American Educational History. Alfred Publishing Co., Sherman Oaks, Cal.

Rich, J. M. 1971. Humanistic Foundations of Education. C. A. Jones, Worthington, Oh.

Saylor, J. G., and Alexander, W. M. 1966. Curriculum Planning for Modern Schools. Holt, Rinehart & Winston, Inc., New York.

Taba, H. 1962. Curriculum Development: Theory and Practice. Harcourt Brace Jovanovich, Inc., New York.

Van Til, W. 1974. Curriculum: Quest for Relevance. 2nd Ed. Houghton Mifflin Co., Boston.

Whitehead, A. N. 1957. The Aims of Education and Other Essays. New American Library, New York.

Module 2

The teacher will demonstrate knowledge of the possible inter-effects that may develop between the expectations and values of the school, community, and family, on the one hand, and pupil behavior and learning on the other.

PRETEST

1. List three factors or conditions that have inhibited the individualization of instruction.
2. Cite several examples of ways in which school policies and procedures violate an appreciation for individual differences.
3. Some schools require that pupils spend long periods of time in relative inactivity. List the possible effects that this practice might have on pupils.
4. What possible effect on pupils might occur from ignoring developmental sequences in instructional programming?
5. What possible effect on pupils might occur from ignoring economic backgrounds?
6. What behaviors might a pupil evidence if he/she has had a breakfast consisting solely of junk foods and drinks?
7. What behaviors might a pupil evidence if he/she has not slept all night because of a family crisis?
8. How can a teacher motivate the amotivational pupil?
9. Define what is meant by the halo effect.
10. What characteristics of pupils and their families are used frequently in making judgments about learning and behavior?
11. What are the possible effects on a pupil's behavior when he/she is treated as belonging to an inferior social group?
12. Describe the possible adverse effects of grading pupils and issuing report cards.
13. What are the basic school subjects? What part do they play in a holistic eduation?
14. What is meant by the expression "Students learn best in action settings?"
15. What might happen when family values differ from school values? Cite at least one example that graphically demonstrates how the conflict might seriously affect pupil development.

INTRODUCTION AND OVERVIEW

In Module 1, strategies and procedures were identified and activities and experiences were suggested through which teachers and individuals preparing to become teachers can determine prevailing educational goals and objectives of school systems and communities.

Merely to be conversant with these objectives is insufficient; it is necessary to know how these goals and objectives affect pupils. Therefore, this module is concerned with the possible inter-effects between educational expectations and values' and the learning and behavior of pupils.

A key point for the purposes of this book is that a number of these expectations, attitudes, and values not only have affected the behavior of pupils and the nature of teacher-pupil interaction but also *have militated against the individualization of instruction.* School systems, for most of their history, have denied or minimized the need to evaluate pupils for instructional purposes. For the most part, whatever diagnosis has taken place has followed the medical model, i.e., identify and label for the purpose of separating out and segregating those pupils whose individual differences were so great that they required specialized placement that often excluded them from any form of educational programming. Often, those pupils placed in special classses or special schools received no specialized treatment beyond placement, as if placement ipso facto meant treatment. Separate classes were considered special programming, and the practice of labeling implied a homogeneity of "condition" that was confused with a precise educational prescription.

Unfortunately, teachers of special classes discovered early that every one of their mentally retarded, emotionally disturbed, or physically handicapped pupils had unique skills, knowledge, and needs. Curricula and materials especially prepared by experts for the teachers' assigned groups did not "cure" or remediate the problems of their pupils' educational needs with any notable success.

The concept of individual educational diagnosis or evaluation for the purpose of designing individual educational treatments has only recently emerged as an educational mandate for handicapped learners. For years teachers have been exhorted to individualize or personalize instruction for all pupils despite three key inhibitory factors:

1. The absence of diagnostic skills or diagnostic skill training for preservice and inservice teachers
2. The assignment of diagnosis to other professionals, most frequently psychologists, whose screening techniques and other tests shed little light on instructional needs of pupils
3. Pressures from the school system, from the community, and from

families that subvert, discourage, or penalize attempts by teachers to individualize instruction

The brief discussion that follows examines this last factor and provides a few specific examples that demonstrate how individualized instruction is discouraged. Most communities, school systems, and families expect all pupils (except the most obviously handicapped) to be ready for formal instruction in the traditional academic subjects, such as reading, by the time they are six years of age and in the first grade. This presumption flagrantly violates an appreciation for individual development: many children learn to read by three or four years of age while others do not have the prerequisite perceptual and other preacademic skills necessary to read until the second grade or beyond. Yet it is common practice for *all* first graders to be subjected to reading instruction regardless of level of developmental readiness. Although educators and psychologists from various theoretical orientations often disagree on the basic principles of learning, most do agree on the motivational and therapeutic effects of success: nothing succeeds like success. They also agree on the debilitating, destructive effects of failure. If all pupils, except those obviously defective, are presumed able to learn how to read in the first grade, but in varying degrees of skill, some will be bored, others will progress, and countless others will fail. For those who are bored because they already possess the skill and for those who fail because they lack the prerequisite skills, individualized instruction is a farce.

The same kind of fanciful thinking that suggests the differences in children's cognitive abilities can be easily ignored has led to the belief that all pupils capable of being educated should enter school at approximately the same age, regardless of entering knowledge and skills, and exit from school at the same maximum age, despite the presence of continuing educational needs. Numerous students require a basic, functional education continuing into their adult years. They should not be denied a free public education on the basis of their having passed their twenty-first birthday.

Finally, the misuse by teachers of curriculum guides and standardized texts belies the theoretical commitment to educational evaluation for individual programming purposes. Curriculum guides are meant to be *guides*, not catechism. Assigning the same textbook to *all* pupils within a class for academic instructional purposes is also suspect within the context of individualized education. Common homework assignments also belie a commitment to individualized programming.

School Expectations, Values, and Practices

An examination of some of the expectations, values, and practices of school systems and their possible effects on pupil behavior and learning should help to clarify the role that the school plays in determining pupil behavior.

1. SEP (School Expectation or Practice): The school day frequently is so organized that pupils are expected to spend an inordinate amount of time in quiet activities or seat work. Little time is devoted to activities involving gross motor activities, and teachers seldom alternate quiet periods with active pupil participation.

    PEPB (Possible Effect on Pupil Behavior): Many pupils have been socialized sufficiently to sit for long periods of time, requiring little stimulation beyond the work on hand and the approval of teachers. Others need to self-stimulate and to move about, thus disrupting and distracting themselves and their classmates. For them, a day of endless ditto work can be devastatingly dull.

2. SEP: Learning experiences are not always developmental in nature. Even when known, the hierarchial arrangement of skills often is ignored. The usual situation, however, is one in which the educators involved have not been prepared to think in terms of developmental sequences. Frequently, especially in the early school years, other professionals are hired as consultants (e.g., psychologists, occupational therapists, and physical therapists) to educate teachers on the importance of considering developmental sequences in programming.

    PEPB: Whenever developmental sequences are ignored, some pupils will become frustrated. They are unable to progress easily to the next step in a task since they are, because of inappropriate sequencing, expected to leap over one or more vital, prerequisite steps. Whenever proper sequencing is disregarded, not only does learning suffer but pupils' behavior is likely to deteriorate or regress as well.

3. SEP: Pupils are expected to have similar experiences and come from similar language backgrounds.

    PEPB: Whenever there are pupils from different sociocultural/economic/ethnic backgrounds, materials selected for their instruction and the teacher's language may prove confusing. The pupils may be unable to identify with the instructional materials employed, the teacher's language, and/or the assumed common experiences discussed in the classroom. Any alienation that already exists because of perceived differences will be compounded when individual interests, experiences, dialects, attitudes, and values are ignored.

4. SEP: Pupils are expected to come to school with similar values and from similar economic situations.

    PEPB: Pupils are repeatedly embarrassed because they do not have the money for school field trips and for school lunches. At other times, pupils become confused because the values expressed in the classroom are at variance with those expressed and witnessed in their homes. The impact of pupil embarrassment and confusion on behavior, attitudes, and motivation may result in hostility, bitterness, and various amotivational states.

5. SEP: Pupils are expected to come to school rested, fed, loved, and not abused.

   PEPB: There are pupils who fail to learn and who are restless, distracted, and hyperactive because they are tired and/or hungry. Some pupils attend school after a breakfast consisting solely of a candy bar or bag of pretzels and a cola drink. While these pupils may not be physically hungry, one wonders what the impact of junk foods, especially the caffeine and sugar in a cola drink, has on the behavior and learning of pupils. Certainly, there are those who come to school suffering from the effects of the abuse of drugs, including alcohol. The abuse of substances by pupils and its effect on behavior and learning has been well documented (Brenner, 1979). Then, too, there are pupils who arrive at school after a sleepless night due to family quarrels. Some will be further fatigued by long bus rides to special schools. There is no question that such pupils will be predisposed to problem behavior; they are just too fatigued to learn effectively. The unloved, uncared for, and abused pupils will be in such a state of emotional turmoil and deprivation that their behavior and learning, undoubtedly, will be adversely affected.

6. SEP: Pupils are expected to come to school eager to learn. Perhaps the most exasperating problem facing the schools is the amotivational or reluctant pupil.

   PEPB: Teachers, throughout history, have tried countless strategies in attempts to stimulate apparently unreachable, intractable pupils. Praise, punishment, reinforcement, coercion, enthusiasm, exhortation, appeals (to reason, kindness, good will), love, sarcasm, ridicule, affection, relevant materials, the latest media, the newest machines, suspense, and novelty have been tried. However, no one strategy works with all children or with a single child all of the time. Some strategies, such as sarcasm and ridicule, may work for the moment but have more destructive long-term effects.

7. SEP: Pupils before school admission, are expected to have been taught by their families such social amenities as respect and manners.

   PEPB: When pupils lack the various social graces, they are often subjected to ridicule by teachers and peers. Being laughed at, mocked, and/or ostracized invariably leads to a lessening of the pupil's self-image. A negative self-image, in turn, frequently results in problems both in learning and behavior.

8.   SEP: Parents, generally, are expected to participate in their child's schooling on a highly literate level *and* to have the time and energy to do so.

      PEPB: Pupils are embarrassed, at times, because their parents do not attend PTA meetings, do not visit the classroom during Open School Week, fail to show up for parent-teacher conferences, and do not even bother to sign report cards, much less send in absence notes. A parent may have failed to sign a report card because he/she cannot write. A pupil, in an attempt to cover up for an overworked, harrassed, or illiterate parent, may forge an absence note or a signature on a report card. The apathy that sometimes accompanies poverty and powerlessness is not necessarily an indication of lack of love and concern for a child. Apparent parental interest, on the other hand, does not necessarily indicate either love or genuine concern.

9.   SEP: Pupils are expected to have two natural parents who are married to each other. Educators, textbooks, and a host of other educational materials often disregard the fact that pupils may, indeed, have but a single parent, may be a foster child, may live with one parent and a step parent, may live in an institution, or may be a part of another arrangement.

      PEPB: Educators attempt to use in their curricula topics that are of interest to or relevant to the lives of their pupils. Parents are frequently characters in the stories in readers and social studies books. Some pupils are placed at a distinct disadvantage and cannot relate to discussions about and scenes of a happy home life with both mother and father lovingly present.

10.   SEP: Pupil characteristics such as docility, conformity, politeness, and attractiveness are frequently associated with successful pupil behavior and learning patterns. These assumptions, in and of themselves, help to shape the behavior and learning of pupils because of the self-fulfilling prophecy, i.e., people tend to become what we expect them to become. Moreover, a phenomenon known as the halo effect takes place. Teachers associate those pupils who are docile, respectful, helpful, and/or attractive with other positive personal characteristics, such as intelligence and creativity. Pupils possessing these traits are therefore considered to be brighter and more sensitive, trustworthy, courageous, and reliable. On the other hand, pupils who do not possess these teacher-valued traits and are argumentative, disrespectful, divergent, uncooperative, and/or unattractive are assigned a host of other negative attributes.

      PEPB: Gifted, creative pupils are often not valued by teachers and are subjected to ridicule by peers as well. Less gifted pupils who are smiling, reinforcing of others, and attractive fare far better in schools than do those pupils with greater intelligence, wisdom, and skill. Physically handicapped pupils who have many unattractive qualities, i.e., they drool, have involuntary movements, speak unintelligibly, and eat with difficulty, are frequently viewed as being hopelessly retarded despite normal or above normal intelligence. In a like manner, minimally physically handicapped but seriously retarded pupils with pleasant faces have often confused teachers by performing at a lower level than expected judging from the seemingly intelligent aura they emanate.

11. SEP: Certain pupil characteristics are associated with presumably predictable patterns of pupil behavior and learning. Such characteristics include, but are not limited to:

   a. Racial background (including gradation in skin color, e.g., the darker the skin, the poorer the educational prognosis)
   b. Ethnic background
   c. Religious preference (church attended)
   d. Socioeconomic class
   e. Neighborhood or section of town
   f. Family status and history in community

   PEPB: Pupils who belong to the less valued ethnic and racial minorities, who attend churches less favored, who live in poorer housing or in poorer neighborhoods, and who belong to families who have recently arrived in the country and/or community, are most apt to be treated as inferior. Being treated as unworthy or less worthy characteristically leads to self-hatred, which may lead to apathy, indifference, hatred of others, hostility, and aggression, although, at times, devalued students will try harder, even compulsively, to prove their worth. The bitterness, however, may remain forever.

12. SEP: Schools evaluate and report on pupil progress by comparing their performance to normative data. Grades and report cards are competitive in nature and frequently reflect factors other than pupil progress or achievement.

   PEPB: The competition for grades throughout the pupil's school years can be a most destructive force: witness the increase in suicide rates during late adolescence and the college years in the United States and in those other countries in which admission to college depends heavily on grades and scores on standardized achievement tests. Red marks, crossed out words, written negative comments, Fs emblazoned in the top margins of the pupil's written work are further ways that belittle and humiliate pupils.

Community Expectations and Values

The effects of community expectations and values are idiosyncratic to the community in which the school is located. Nevertheless, there are certain commonalities that appear to be prevalent in the late 1970s in the United States. Just a few of these expectations are offered and discussed in order to impress the teacher or individual preparing to become a teacher that any diagnosis of pupil behavior and learning must consider the impact of the community on pupil attitudes and values.

1. CEV (Community Expectations and Values): The greater community increasingly urges a return to the basics, the fabled three Rs, as if these skills were the only basic skills of import or value. Social and emotional development are downgraded, and there is little money in school budgets for music and art courses, which aid in aesthetic development.
   PEPB (Possible Effects on Pupil Behavior): When the community pressures schools to return to the basics (as if they really had left them), it expects the schools to spend a disproportionate amount of time on academics, thus neglecting other human essentials. For many years, the importance of physical health and safety have been minimized. Physical education received negligible emphasis in the curriculum until President Kennedy stressed the value of physical fitness. Despite the fact that professional educators have championed the education of the "whole" child, major segments of the community persist in thinking of education in narrow terms. The perennial battle over the inclusion of units of instruction in sex education and the recent clashes over curriculum experiences in death education are just two examples of the reluctance of some communities to accept their responsibility for holistic education. The enduring neglect of the "whole" child continues to shape and distort the development of students. The glorification of the three Rs continues to reduce the scope of education for too many in our society.

2. CEV: Communities generally expect schools to be quiet places where learning occurs under the unchallenged leadership and direction of teachers while the pupils are essentially passive reactors.
   PEPB: The fact is that pupils learn best in active settings rather than as passive observers. They learn by doing. For example, the room may be quieter when the teacher conducts a chemical test with test tubes, chemicals, and a burner, but pupils will learn more if they have their own test tubes, chemicals, and burners with which to carry out personally each step in the sequence of physical and chemical events. This alternative in which the pupils participate actively will

probably result in a noisier classroom. However, more learning will be taking place.

3. CEV: The community expects children to become well-functioning, independent, literate, and resourceful adults.

    PEPB: Unfortunately this goal generally means "in the image of the community." While this goal may conflict with the teacher's value system (see Module 1), it may, simultaneously, interfere with the healthful development of individual pupils whose self-directed goals and values diverge from the community's image of responsible adulthood. Those individual pupils who are in conflict with the community may battle, rebel, or drop out. Apathy, indifference, anomie, drugs, and even suicide may result. Should the schools merely serve to maintain the status quo? Should they merely attempt to duplicate the previous generation, failing to meet the needs of those pupils who have keener insights and greater vision?

4. CEV: Communities usually expect their schools to conform and to discourage controversy among pupils. They expect materials that will not be offensive to "good" taste (theirs, of course) to be put in their libraries and on their schools' reading lists. Very often communities will find themselves in the midst of substantial conflict with their school system, e.g., the community's desire to remove books from the school library or its actions to delete or drastically modify sex education policies. Furthermore, community members expect that doctrines alien to the American system of government will not be considered or discussed. They expect the schools to be a vital, vibrant force in promulgating and maintaining the values and attributes of their respective communities.

    PEPB: Pupils who possess a keen sense of democracy, who are alert to needs, desires, and issues that are less provincial and more universal in scope, will frequently be threatened and punished for stirring up controversial issues that upset the equilibrium of the community. Yet most advancements in knowledge and in social welfare have sprung from those select individuals who saw something in a different light and fought for the acceptance of their vision. While the stabilizing goals of communities are to be applauded, one wonders about the means schools use to stifle those pupils with creative, visionary solutions to community and world problems.

5. CEV: Communities traditionally expect the schools to keep a suitable distance from community problems and affairs.

    PEPB: Pupils cannot be developed into full, interested, active, participating members of a community unless sufficient time is devoted to discussing community problems and issues. Unless pupils become actively involved in community affairs through school activities and experiences, they will not be prepared to live effectively in that community as adults. Also, they will not be prepared to assist in effecting the changes through the years that will enable the community to become a better place in which to live and to meet the challenges of the approaching decades.

6.   CEV: Communities expect the schools to foster administrative policies that will maintain traditional values. They often feel endangered by nontraditional approaches such as automatic promotion, diplomas for attendance rather than achievement, and open admissions to colleges, and will exert pressures on the schools to discourage them.

PEPB: For pupils who are not promoted because they are unable to achieve at group-determined, rather than individually prescribed, levels, being "left back" is a traumatic experience with profound psychosocial sequelae. For handicapped learners who are unable to perform at preconceived levels because of motor, language, and/or cognitive factors, the denial of a certificate of completion is a cruel and unnecessary further reminder of their failure as human beings.

Family Expectations and Values

The central issue in any discussion of family expectations and values and their impact on pupil behavior and learning is the recognition that each family is unique. A pupil may be raised by a single (divorced, widowed, or unwed) parent, by foster parents, by a grandparent, by an older sister, by stepparent(s), or by being shuttled back and forth among various relatives. A pupil may have no family, but may be a resident of an institution and attend public school by day. Because of the variety of family and living arrangements and the uniqueness of each, family expectations and values can be discussed only in general terms. Despite the vagueness of the few examples offered, the point being emphasized is that family expectations and values, whenever a family exists, critically affect student behavior and learning.

1.   FEV (Family Expectations and Values): Significant family members may use language that is markedly different in content, structure, logic, and elaboration from that used and taught in school.

PEPB (Possible Effects on Pupil Behavior): In school pupils may be encouraged to use formal language devoid of slang, colloquialisms, and profanity, whereas at home and in the community, the language patterns modeled are informal, colorful, and rapidly communicated. The attempts of pupils to use school-reinforced language are likely to be met with amusement and ridicule. Peers in the community may feel that the pupils are "putting on airs" and make them the butt of verbal and/or physical abuse. Many teachers have despaired of effecting changes in pupils who after school return to environments that reinforce language not valued by the school. Moreover, pupils who come from homes in which a different language than the school's is spoken are also at a special disadvantage.

2. FEV: Significant family members may devalue the importance of book learning and school because of their negative experiences with school. Conversely, in a family of high achievers, school and education may be highly esteemed and of paramount importance.

PEPB: In the first situation, the pupil may feel that academic success and adherence to school rules are rejections of the values held by loved or feared family members. These pupils will, at times, deliberately fail or disobey school rules so that their behavior conforms more closely to family values. For example, a bright male pupil from an anti-intellectual family that values machismo in its males may go to great lengths to hide his intellectual superiority.

On the other hand, there is bound to be conflict when pupils' level of achievement is drastically lower than that of their family. A student, even one with normal cognitive ability, may demonstrate physical ailments in order to avoid school. A handicapped pupil who is born to a family whose vocational standards are far superior may suffer because of the omnipresent reminders that he/she is inferior to other family members.

3. FEV: The family's moral behavior vis-à-vis the use of drugs and alcohol, lying, cheating, and stealing may differ markedly from behaviors being taught in the school.

PEPB: Pupils whose home environment and moral code differ significantly from that of the school may become confused when reprimanded or punished for behaviors that are considered normal in their homes and general environment. Some may have the courage to change their behaviors, risking family ridicule and censure; countless others do not. School, for the latter group remains an alien institution to be suffered through until they are liberated.

4. FEV: Family members may suffer from severe emotional or psychiatric disturbances and model behaviors that conflict with those valued in the school environment. The likelihood of there being a family member with emotional pathology living at home has increased over the years as society continues in its attempt to normalize the lives of adult mentally retarded patients, removing them from institutions, and returning them to the community (Connaughton, 1979).

PEPB: The behaviors evidenced and the values expressed by disturbed family members, especially parents, may be so deviant that their children suffer from similar pathologies. Children reared in homes with markedly disturbed adults are more likely to be predisposed to bizarre, inappropriate behavior, which is apt to create problems in management, and may or may not affect learning.

5. FEV: The family patterns of behavior that may have been passed down from previous generations may include such destructive practices as psychological, physical, and/or sexual abuse.

    PEPB: Abused pupils are likely to be maladaptive students suffering not only physically, but also psychologically, with problems including guilt, fear, heightened anxiety, anger, resentment, and bitterness. In the absence of healthy mental states, student learning and behavior cannot be expected to be satisfactory.

6. FEV: Families' ethnic, racial, and religious backgrounds may be such that restrictions are placed on pupils that exclude participation in some school practices and events.

    PEPB: Pupils may not be able to join in the singing of Christmas carols and may be ridiculed for failing to do so. Other pupils may not be able to join in the Pledge of Allegiance and may be derided for that behavior. Still others may not be able to share in the food prepared for holiday celebrations because of religious codes, and thus feel excluded and different. Ethnic, religious, and racial differences may proscribe certain behaviors that are commonly accepted by the majority, thereby causing the minority group members to feel not truly American, strange, and/or misfits.

7. FEV: The parents' work schedules may not permit attendance at PTA meetings, or at school plays, athletic meets, or art exhibits in which students are participating.

    PEPB: Pupils may become demoralized when parents or other significant family members fail to show an active interest in their work, or cannot because of working late hours or working two jobs. This is especially true when the parents of their peers are present for such events. Although there may be no immediate adverse response or effect, the hurt felt may be expressed in other ways at later times.

ACTIVITIES AND EXPERIENCES

1. Obtain copies of college catalogs that present curricula in teacher education programs that prepare regular classroom teachers. Bring in a sample catalog with an accompanying course description that specifies a required course or courses in educational evaluation or diagnosis.

2. Describe in a brief essay factors and sources that may subvert the

attempts of teachers to diagnose for programming purposes. *Do not* use factors listed in this module. Cite only your own examples.

3. Discuss how the use of a standardized spelling text for a given grade is contrary to an individualized approach to instruction. Suggest alternate ways in which teachers can plan their spelling lessons, ways that allow for individualized programs.

4. Discuss the pros and cons of providing a free public education to handicapped individuals over 21 years of age. What performance criteria would you suggest be used for "graduation" from free public education programs for the handicapped besides chronological age?

5. From your *own* experience, describe and discuss specific school expectations, values, and practices that have profoundly influenced a pupil's behavior. (You may use an experience from your own background as a student, but only if you are not concerned about your privacy.)

6. From your *own* experience, describe and discuss specific community expectations and values that have profoundly influenced your own or another student's behavior.

7. From your *own* experience, describe and discuss specific family expectations and values that have profoundly influenced your own or another student's behavior.

8. What additional school, community, and family expectations and values would you include in this module because you believe that they, too, have a significant relationship to pupil behavior and learning?

9. Visit a state instituion in which there are pupils who attend a public school program during the day. After one or more visits, discuss those factors at the institution that might have a significant effect on pupil behavior and learning.

10. Schedule an interview with a parent liaison specialist (pupil personnel worker), and ask him/her to share special insights acquired over the years pertinent to the modular objective.

11. Discuss in three to five pages the possible inter-effects that may develop between school, community, and family expectations and values, on the one hand, and pupil behavior and learning on the other hand. Use as your frame of reference the school in which you are currently teaching, where you have previously taught, where you are student teaching or involved in another practicum experience, or where you attended school. Please change the names of the school district, the community, and families to ensure anonymity of all individuals and places discussed. Do not in any other way make it possible for a reader to guess the identities.

CONCLUDING STATEMENT

Perhaps there is a natural predilection to engage in a kind of diagnostic process that seeks answers for the behavior and learning of pupils within the pupils themselves. This bias, unfortunately, disregards significant external forces that influence and determine pupil behavior and learning. Certainly most teachers are loathe to seek answers for pupil's lack of academic progress or regression in their own practices or in the modus operandi of the school system itself. As a result of required professional studies in psychology and sociology, most teachers have attained a degree of sophistication in recognizing the possible effects of the family and community on pupil behavior and learning. However, a note of caution must be sounded, since there may be a tendency to rely on stereotypic judgments rather than concrete evidence as support for diagnositc hypotheses. If a pupil comes from an economically poor minority group, do not fall into the intellectual trap of assuming that he/she is, therefore, undernourished, uncared for, and abused. If, on the other hand, a pupil comes from a well-established family in a well-manicured part of town, do not jump to the conclusion that his/her life is idyllic and the reason for lack of academic progress or for behavior/social immaturity can be found in the idiosyncratic quirks of the pupil's diseased psyche or mutated genes. Beware of finding only simplistic answers.

POSTTEST

At this point retake the Pretest.

LITERATURE CITED

Brenner, A. 1979. Nutrition. In P. J. Valletutti and F. Christoplos (eds.), Preventing Physical and Mental Disabilities: Multidisciplinary Approaches. University Park Press, Baltimore.
Connaughton, J. P. 1979. Psychiatry. In P. J. Valletutti and F. Christoplos (eds.), Preventing Physical and Mental Disabilities: Multidisciplinary Approaches. University Park Press, Baltimore.

SUGGESTED READINGS

Bronfenbrenner, U. 1972. Influences on Human Development. The Dryden Press, Hinsdale, Ill.
Dion, K. K. 1972. Physical attractiveness and evaluation of children's transgressions. J. Pers. Soc. Psychol. 24:207–213.
Escalona, S. K. 1968. The Roots of Individuality. Aldine Publishing Co., Chicago.

Gordon, I. J. 1971. Parent Involvement in Compensatory Education. University of Illinois Press, Champaign.

Goslin, D. A. (ed.). 1969. Handbook of Socialization Theory and Research. Rand McNally & Co., Chicago.

Lindzey, G., and Aronson, E. (eds.). 1968. The Handbook of Social Psychology. 2nd Ed. Addison-Wesley Publishing Co., Inc., Reading, Mass.

Lurie, E. 1970. How to Change the Schools: A Parents' Action Handbook on How to Fight the System. Random House, Inc., New York.

Maehr, M., and Stallings, W. (eds.). 1975. Culture, Child and School. Brooks/Cole Publishing Co., Monterey, Cal.

Rist, R. C. 1970. Student social class and teacher expectations: The self-fulfilling prophecy in ghetto education. Harvard Educ. Rev. 40:411–451.

Shinn, R. 1972. Culture and School. Socio-Cultural Significances. Intext Educational Publishers, Scranton, Pa.

Skinner, B. F. 1968. The Technology of Teaching. Appleton-Century-Crofts, New York.

Valett, R. E. 1977. Humanistic Education: Developing the Total Person. C. V. Mosby Co., St. Louis.

Wallace, G., and Kauffman, J. M. 1973. Teaching Children with Learning Problems. Charles E. Merrill Publishing Co., Columbus, Oh.

White, B. L., and Watts, J. C. 1973. Experience and Environment: Major Influences on the Development of the Young Child. Prentice-Hall, Inc., Englewood Cliffs, N.J.

Module 3

The teacher will demonstrate knowledge of the possible effects of the classroom's physical environment on pupil behavior and learning.

PRETEST

Answer *True* or *False*.

1. Behavioral and learning problems that are thought to be endemic to impoverished areas occur, and even flourish, in modern suburban schools.
2. Failure to recognize the effect of the physical environment on pupil performance may lead to a faulty interpretation of pupil behavior.
3. The physical environment plays more of a role than do teachers and families in facilitating pupil growth and development.
4. Noninvolved or nonfocused student behavior may occur in a classroom that is too small or too large.
5. Classrooms that are too large have the greatest amount of random behavior of pupils.
6. All pupils should benefit from placement in open space schools.
7. The reason that broken desks and chairs should not be used by pupils in special education classrooms is because of safety and the reinforcement of a poor self-image.
8. Brightly polished, shining furniture is ideal for visually handicapped pupils.
9. Rocking chairs and armchairs should not be placed in classrooms because they allow pupils to retreat from classroom pressures.
10. Bulletin board and other classroom displays that are too disorganized may be overstimulating to pupils.
11. An effective teacher will design floor plans to include alternative seating arrangements.
12. The typical seating arrangement, with the teacher's desk placed in the front of the room, fosters peer interaction.
13. Pupils seated in the row nearest the wall participate more than classmates in any other row except the first row.
14. Preferential seating should never be provided for the hearing-impaired pupil because it will encourage other pupils to ask for similar preferential treatment.
15. Seating arrangements should be determined by the desired teacher-pupil or pupil-pupil interaction.
16. Pupils with language deficits may become confused as they attempt to interpret auditory clues that are being masked by classroom noise.
17. Loss of teacher vitality because of improper ventilation has little effect on pupil motivation.
18. Heat stress may be particularly debilitating to physically handicapped pupils because they must expend greater amounts of energy than do nonphysically handicapped pupils.

19. Photophobia refers to that fear a pupil experiences when exposed to bright lights.
20. Fluorescent lights have been cited as a cause of hyperactivity in pupils.
21. It has been suggested by a specialist in the field of learning disabilities that windows should be covered with black plastic to completely control lighting.
22. Attention is a nonbehavioral construct that cannot be measured by pupil-teacher eye contact.
23. Wall-to-wall carpeting should be installed in all classrooms regardless of the types of pupils in the classrooms.
24. Some educators have recommended the avoidance of all colors, except gray, for walls because they may be disturbing to hyperactive pupils.
25. Cartoon and storybook characters painted on classroom walls may be frightening to some preschool-age children.
26. Handicapped pupils are usually impervious to their surroundings and consequently the physical environment for such pupils is not as important as for the nonhandicapped.

INTRODUCTION AND OVERVIEW

Over the years society has become increasingly aware of the debilitating effects of drab, neglected, unclean, unhealthy surroundings on human beings but has paid scant attention to the possible effects of the classroom's physical environment on pupil behavior and learning. Since both pupils and teachers spend well over half of their waking hours in the classroom for several years, this is a serious oversight. Undoubtedly, it arises in part from the recognition that the effectiveness of instruction depends far more on teacher-pupil interaction (see Module 11) and family-child interaction (see Module 2) than it does on the classroom's physical environment.

Many parents, however, have become especially concerned with physical environments, particularly since they have achieved a level of affluence that has made it possible for them to move from deteriorating urban centers. New schools built to house and educate their children generally have been modern structures embodying the latest architectural advances and housing the best furnishings and other accessories. Unfortunately, these parents and the educators they hired frequently discovered that new structures, built at great cost, have not necessarily resulted in improved education and, in turn, enlightened, well-educated pupils. Many suburban parents suffered bitter disillusionment when they found behavioral and learning problems, thought to be endemic only to central cities and impoverished rural areas, occurring and at times flourishing in their own newly constructed schools.

Although the physical environment admittedly plays less of a role than do teachers and families in facilitating the cognitive, psychomotor, and affective growth of students, it nevertheless is a significant factor that must not be overlooked when evaluating pupil performance. While dirty, poorly maintained, colorless classrooms certainly need to be replaced, building modern, windowless, factory-like boxes of impersonal, look-alike rooms or open spaces is not a satisfactory replacement. Studies of workers in factories, patients in hospitals, and elderly individuals confined to nursing homes have shown that humans usually respond in many ways, some very subtle, to a cheerful, well-lighted, properly ventilated environment (Barker, 1968; Stern, 1970). It is reasonable to assume that pupils and teachers will also function best in clean, cheerful, well-lighted, properly ventilated surroundings. Poor ventilation may be the reason a pupil is sleepy rather than a host of other possible factors: boredom, malnutrition, drug abuse, or family crises. Failure to recognize the effect of the physical environment on pupil behavior and learning may lead to a faulty interpretation of pupil behavior (Smith, Neisworth, and Green, 1978).

Teachers working in economically impoverished urban and rural areas have intimate daily knowledge of the impact of the environment on the learning and behavior of their pupils. However, special educators are perhaps the most familiar with teaching under adverse physical conditions and thus are more alert to their impact on pupil behavior, learning, and, most especially, pupil self-image and esteem. Special educators who have taught in public institutional settings are probably the ones who have been most impeded by physical environments inimical to learning. Likewise, special educators teaching in public schools have known on a personal level the debilitating and interfering effects of inadequate classroom environments. Even in these enlightened years, there still are special education classes housed in school basements or in makeshift rooms partitioned out of former storage areas; some teachers teach in cramped, windowless rooms converted from supply closets; others teach in portable classrooms located in a lot adjacent to the school. Many of these portables are in such states of disrepair that they appear to be shacks located across the tracks from the main house. Even when mainstreaming of pupils is sought, many special pupils are still segregated in inferior quarters. A visit to basement and portable classrooms will provide dramatic evidence of society's attitude toward the handicapped and of the impact of inferior physical environments on pupils and teachers alike. A stop at a century-old school in the heart of a deteriorating central city area will furnish further support to the notion that teachers and pupils are influenced by their physical surroundings. Another stop at a colorless, barren, stuffy, classroom in a state institution for the handicapped will probably convince the visitor of the devastating impact of a dirty, dank, and dismal environment on teachers and learners.

While a clean, attractive, modern school does not necessarily foster healthy pupil attitudes and behavior, neither does a dilapidated building invariably result in a demoralized teaching staff and pupils. Nevertheless, there are certain conditions that may exist in the physical environment of the classroom, the rest of the school, the school's facade, and the area surrounding the school that may seriously affect both pupils and teachers.

A list of classroom environmental factors that should be considered when analyzing the behaviors of pupils follows. Please note that because the mainstreaming of handicapped students is mandated by PL 94-142 and various state laws, each physical environmental factor listed is discussed within a mainstreaming framework, i.e., each factor in the physical environment is viewed in terms of its possible effect on the handicapped as well as the nonhandicapped.

Room Size

Perhaps the most important physical factor in the environment of students is the size of the classroom. Shapiro (1975), examining the influence of floor space on young pupils' behavior, stated:

> Noninvolved behavior (unfocused behavior) was lowest in classrooms that provided between thirty and fifty square feet of floor space per child. Noninvolved behavior was highest in classrooms where the space was either less than thirty square feet or more than fifty square feet per child. Crowded classrooms (less than thirty square feet per child) had the greatest amount of deviant and onlooking behavior, while larger classrooms (more than fifty square feet per child) had the most random behavior (p. 440).

It should be noted that the size of room or the amount of square feet considered ideal on a per pupil basis must be examined in its relationship to the amount of furniture since the size of the room may meet standards while the amount and size of furniture and equipment may considerably diminish space and contribute to crowded conditions. Teachers who have taught in small classrooms frequently have complained about their rooms having been too crowded, inflexible, and constricting (Sommer, 1969). The absence of clear boundaries between activity areas arising from crowded conditions leads to pupil distractibility, restlessness, and interference with the work of their peers. Hostile behaviors occur frequently and include both verbal and physical aggression. Comparisons to the classroom as a microcosm may be logically made from the body of research that reports on the destructive forces and hostile behaviors occurring in overcrowded and overstimulating urban settings (Srole et al., 1961; Schorr, 1963; Milgram, 1970; Freedman, Klevansky, and Ehrlich, 1971; Glass and Singer, 1972; Fischer, Baldassare, and Ofshe, 1975; Stokols, 1976).

Studies that tell of the desultory and perverse effects on animals caged in close quarters may have implications for pupils similarly constricted in crowded classrooms (Mason, 1960; Harlow and Harlow, 1969).

On the other hand, excessively large classrooms with vacant spaces may have a serious impact on hyperactive and disturbed pupils, who may wander or run about, aimlessly seeking contact, stimulation, or control. Moreover, other pupils who tend to function better in limited boundaries may become anxious and frightened when confronted with large, open areas. Finally, in recent years, open-space classrooms have been championed as a more suitable and effective architectural alternative to traditional classrooms. It has, however, become obvious to teachers, parents, and school administrators that there are pupils who are unable to deal with changing, amorphous, flexible boundaries and require the closure offered by walls and doorways. To conclude, teachers should be especially aware of the possible untoward pupil behaviors that may arise from crowded or too open classrooms (Mitchell, 1972; Innes, 1973; Ittelson et al., 1974).

Classroom Furniture

Classroom furniture should be carefully selected to meet the individual needs of pupils and to provide them with a comfortable, reinforcing, and safe environment. For example, chairs and desks should be bought in various sizes or be adjustable for comfort and ease of performance for all pupils regardless of height or weight. Often, broken desks and chairs have been passed down to special education classrooms; this practice, besides being an unsafe one, can only serve to reinforce the low self-image and self-esteem usually felt by most handicapped pupils. Additionally, brightly shining furniture surfaces that reflect light may, because of the attendant glare, create problems for visually handicapped pupils (Pelone, 1962). It should be noted that some classrooms have been provided with nontraditional classroom furniture, including rocking chairs and armchairs. This type of furniture affords an opportunity to sit in comfort, to move to a special corner to read, and to retreat from the pace of the classroom. Many people require quiet times in which they can be by themselves and quiet places where pressure or stress factors can be diminished. Quiet times may make it possible for pupils to consolidate what they had been taught earlier. Furthermore, if teachers are providing their pupils with a functional curriculum there will be a need for learning areas in which household furnishings and equipment may be used by pupils to practice appropriate functional behavior. Bulletin boards and shelving should also be available to display pupils' art and academic work. The display of pupil work is a reinforcing strategy that is bound to increase pupil motivation and involvement (Bender and Valletutti, 1976). Unfortunately, many teachers use bulletin boards to display their own talents and to impress administrators, supervisors, parents, and their fellow teachers. Simultaneously, bulletin boards designed by teachers denigrate or downgrade the artistic products of pupils and thus deny them the therapeutic benefits that can be derived from the joy and pride of displayed academic and creative works. Bulletin boards and shelf displays that are too busy, disorganized, and overstimulating may be too much for easily disrupted pupils to handle. Finally, the selection of furniture for comfort, reinforcement, and safety must be supplemented by the designing of floor plans to include alternate seating arrangements, display areas, learning stations, space for ease of movement, space for physical activities, and consideration of student safety and psychological well-being (Abeson and Blacklow, 1971).

Seating Arrangements

In the traditional classroom, the teacher's desk is placed at the front of the room with the pupils seated in rows of seats facing it. This typical arrangement suggests that the teacher is the center of the universe. Other physical arrangements, such as a circular or semicircular arrangement, would suggest greater equality, would place the teacher in a less authoritative position, and would encourage peer interaction. Pupils who sit in the front row tend to participate more than those in subsequent rows, and students seated near the wall participate more than classmates in any other row except the first (Sommer, 1969). The participation of hearing-impaired students especially may be significantly affected by seating arrangements.

> Preferential seating helps to minimize the strain of listening while maximizing the opportunity to fill in with visual clues. It is very important that the hearing-impaired child be seated close to the teacher, but, at the same time, as far away from noise sources as possible because ambient noise often interferes with listening even if the child can see the speaker clearly. . . . Another important aspect of preferential seating is visability. The hearing-impaired child will rely heavily on visual clues, speechreading, and facial expressions to assist him in comprehension. He cannot utilize these skills well if he is forced by seating to look directly into a light source such as a window or door. . . . Light that shines from behind the student and illuminates the teacher's face is preferred unless interfering shadows are cast. . . . If the structure of the class is such that the hearing-impaired child can move around to hear better when others are reciting, this freedom will be very helpful to him. This may have to be handled very diplomatically, or the entire class may want to share this activity (Friedman, 1975, p. 47).

Teachers must become increasingly sensitive to the effect of seating arrangements on pupil behavior and learning, whether or not the pupil is handicapped. Perhaps alternative seating arrangements that reflect curriculum goals should be employed. For example, when encouraging group discussions, a circular seating pattern would be preferable. At other times, when wishing to facilitate peer tutoring, clusters of desks and chairs should be arranged as interest/activity centers. At yet other times, the traditional arrangement might be used when the teacher is demonstrating a task or using the chalkboard to illuminate an idea or to graphically present a skill sequence. Then, perhaps, in the final analysis, it is the relationship between the nature of the teacher-pupil or pupil-pupil experience that should determine the seating arrangement. Flexibility should be possible (Russo, 1967; Koneya, 1976).

Noise Level

An active, exciting, dynamic classroom may be a noisy one. However, an excessively high noise level may adversely affect the learning and behavior of students (Glass and Singer, 1972; Cohen, Glass, and Singer, 1973; Bronzaft and McCarthy, 1975). First, too much noise may distract normal learners who find it difficult to hear and/or attend to teachers and classmates. These individuals may find it difficult to concentrate on self-directed and other quiet classroom activities because of high levels of ambient noise. Second, loud and persistent noise may exacerbate the problems of hearing-impaired pupils who are attempting to use their residual hearing to function effectively in the classroom. Pupils with language deficits may become confused as they attempt to interpret auditory clues that are being masked by classroom noise. Furthermore, hyperactive pupils who are easily distracted are more apt to be hyperkinetic and inattentive when bombarded with competing background noise. Thus failure to learn or to perform acceptably in the classroom may be a direct result of a noisy environment rather than a function of faulty instruction and/or pupil indifference or pathology.

Whenever considering the impact of the noise level on the performance of pupils, the interrelatedness of physical factors must be appreciated. For example, teachers who teach in classrooms that overlook the school playground, front a heavily traveled street, or are adjacent to a construction site may face a particularly irksome problem, especially when windows must be opened to provide needed ventilation. Furthermore, the size of the classroom may be a contributing factor in that an increase in noise level may be a function of classroom size: too many pupils in too small an area lead to excessive classroom noise (Sommer, 1969). Classrooms must be examined and acoustically modified when necessary, e.g., provided with sound-treated acoustic tile for ceilings and walls and with carpeting for the floors. These factors must be considered in order to improve the learning and behavior of pupils.

Ventilation

To function normally all humans need a good supply of fresh air and moderate temperature. It seems obvious that we cannot expect pupils to learn or behave well in classrooms that are too hot (or too cold) and improperly ventilated. Stagnant air and high temperatures will not only reduce the energy level of teachers, resulting in a loss of teaching vitality, but will also reduce the pupils' alertness and motivation. Most students, whether nonhandicapped or handicapped, are bound to feel lethargic, inattentive, and irritable in a hot, stuffy room (Griffitt and Veitch, 1971; Baron and Lawton, 1972). Heat stress may be particularly debilitating to physically handicapped pupils, who must expend great amounts of energy in order to perform what for others are simple motor tasks. In many areas of the United States classrooms should be air conditioned if a proper temperature is to be maintained. In all areas proper ventilation must be provided if pupils and teachers are to function at optimal levels.

Improper ventilation and excessively high temperatures in classrooms are likely to increase the negative behavior of pupils with behavioral and learning disorders, who are experiencing daily frustration as they fail to cope with their lives in general and with school in particular (Bryan and Bryan, 1978). Pupils who suffer from asthma, hay fever, and other allergies affecting the upper respiratory system are apt to be extremely uncomfortable and their achievement levels greatly reduced when they are asked to learn in rooms that are poorly ventilated and oppressively hot (Patterson, 1972). Thus it may be seen that various types of pupils will experience serious difficulties with their learning and behavior due to improper ventilation.

Lighting

Reading and other visual classroom activities may be mentally taxing and physically fatiguing when carried on in poorly illuminated classrooms.

> Too much light, as well as insufficient light, may result in a decrease in visual acuity. This is true not only for people with normal eyes but also for those with certain ocular disorders. . . . Individuals with certain types of early cataracts may be dazzled and complain of ocular discomfort when exposed to bright lights. Persons with exophoria (outward deviation of the eye) . . . may also complain of photophobia (abnormal intolerance of light) in the presence of intense illumination (Cross, 1975, pp. 21–22).

Recent research has linked fluorescent lights to hyperactivity in pupils. In two separate studies, behavior change in pupils occurred following conversion from incandescent to fluorescent light and vice versa. Pupils performing in classrooms lit incandescently exhibited fewer somatic and behavioral problems than when they had been in rooms lit fluorescently (Painter, 1976). Ott (1976) found that pupils working under incandescent lights were more highly motivated, performed better academically, and exhibited fewer behavioral problems than when they functioned under fluorescent lights. This research indicated that standard fluorescent light tubes emit harmful radiation producing hyperkinetic and inattentive behavior. Changing to full-spectrum fluorescent tubes with lead shields purportedly produces more natural light and eliminates negative reactions (Valett, 1978). Thus it seems that type and quality of illumination must both be analyzed since both can be factors in pupil performance.

Windows

Several factors, including high energy costs and vandalism, have led to more schools being built without windows or with windows that do not open. The presence or absence of windows has stirred considerable controversy among educators. Some suggest that the presence of uncontrolled light encourages inattentiveness and hyperactivity; they have even recommended that when there are windows, they should be covered with black plastic so there is complete control of lighting (Barsch, 1965). Others believe that windowless schools may inhibit teachers and pupils alike, causing them to feel too detached from the outside world and to respond phobically. Still others see the issue as a tempest in a teapot. However, Sommer (1969) has hypothesized that pupils may be so adversely affected that they might even begin to hallucinate in monotonous and claustrophobic environments. Those who support the presence of windows comment on the enjoyment and learning that take place when pupils are able to see the change of seasons, the hustle and bustle of human and vehicular traffic, and those other sights that at times serendipitously bring enriching experiences to the classroom. However, those who feel that the presence of windows subverts pupil attention have failed to appreciate that attention is a nonbehavioral construct that cannot be measured by pupil-teacher eye contact. Additionally, those educators who argue for windows that can be opened point to the need for ventilation when heating/cooling systems fail to function properly. Moreover, pupils with visual impairments may encounter problems in windowless classrooms because of a total dependence on artificial illumination. Finally, if one believes in the individual needs of pupils and teachers, the effect of the absence or presence of windows cannot be dismissed as an insignificant environmental factor (Karmel, 1965; Salt and Karmel, 1967).

Carpeting

Wall-to-wall carpeting has been provided in many modern school buildings to aid in the reduction of classroom noise, to conserve energy, and to provide comfortable and cheerful surroundings. Carpeting is especially valuable in open-space classrooms, where noise levels must be carefully controlled and where pupils are encouraged to engage in self-selected and self-directed activities. When carpeting is available, pupils are able, for example, to assume comfortable positions during reading and story time activities without worrying about lying on cold and dirty floors. Moreover, pupils who are subject to seizures will benefit when floors are carpeted because of the diminished probability of injury from falls. In the absence of carpeting, physically handicapped pupils with unstable ambulation may need to wear helmets to protect against head injuries. The wearing of a helmet, however, may make such pupils acutely aware of, and sensitive to, their differences. Carpeting, on the other hand, may create problems for pupils who are only able to move about in wheelchairs and for teachers and aides who, sometimes, must move neurologically impaired pupils in wheelchairs and other specially constructed chairs and devices. Finally, carpeting may present a significant hygiene problem when there are pupils in the classroom who are not toilet trained because of physical, cognitive, and/or developmental reasons. While carpeting may provide many advantages, and most teachers would prefer to teach in carpeted classrooms, its potential disadvantages for some special pupils must not be ignored.

Wall Colors, Textures, and Displays

The type of wall construction, the colors that walls are painted, and the ways that walls are decorated may have an impact on pupil behavior. While many educators would tend to minimize the importance of paying attention to these details, teachers of special pupils must explore the various implications. First, the existence of differential psychological responses to color has been documented in several fields of special interest (Abeson and Blacklow, 1971; Heimstra and McFarling, 1974; Smith, Neisworth, and Green, 1978). Educators, however, have not sufficiently investigated the color phenomenon as it applies to classroom walls. A number of teachers and psychologists who have worked with hyperactive, distractible, and impulsive pupils have recommended the avoidance of most colors because they might be overstimulating and have suggested the use of light gray paint instead (Cruickshank et al., 1961). For many pupils, however, the selection of wall coloring appears to be an inconsequential matter, although the selection of paints is related to the total illumination design. Light or pastel shades seem to be the preferred colors for classrooms because they are more restful, both psychologically and visually. Dark colors tend to create problems for visually impaired pupils, who are hindered more than their normally seeing classmates because of the light-absorbing qualities of dark colors. In addition, it has become a common practice to paint cartoon and select storybook characters on the walls of classrooms (and hospital pediatric wings) where there are preschool-age children. While such decorations may provide pleasurable and stimulating environments for most young children, some young pupils with emotional and learning problems may become frightened by these characters because they feed into a private fear or fantasy. Similarly, pictures displayed on walls may, at their best, furnish color and enrich the lives of most students, and, at worst, be innocuous or harmless. On the other hand, they may be disconcerting, overstimulating, or frightening to students with emotional problems. This is not to say that walls must be left bland and undecorated. Attractive, colorful pictures of scenery and/or nonthreatening people can bring warmth and a feeling of well-being to a classroom. The classroom should be as attractive as feasible, just as we expect our homes and work places to be as comfortable and pleasant as possible.

An additional factor to be considered by the teacher is wall texture; some classrooms have walls constructed of roughly textured cement blocks. These walls present a safety hazard, especially for pupils with mobility and visual problems. They may hurt themselves by brushing or falling against these rough surfaces. Autistic and other disturbed or severely retarded pupils may hurt themselves seriously when banging heads or extremities against cement block walls during self-destructive episodes.

ACTIVITIES AND EXPERIENCES

1. Visit a portable classroom located in a lot adjacent to a school. Then visit a classroom in the main building. In a brief essay describe the differences in the physical environment that you believe have directly affected pupil learning and behavior.
2. Visit a special education classroom that is located in a school basement. In a brief essay discuss the impact of the classroom's physical environment on pupil attitudes and behavior.
3. Visit the oldest and the newest school buildings in an urban setting. Contrast the behaviors and attitudes of teachers and pupils in both of these schools. Include in your comments a brief discussion of the *total* physical environment (i.e., the classrooms, the overall school building, and the area surrounding the school) and its impact on teachers and pupils.
4. Conduct an interview with a teacher who is teaching in a school in which handicapped students are being mainstreamed, i.e., are attending classes with nonhandicapped students. Determine the modifications made in the classroom and the school's physical environment that have been made to facilitate the integration and positive mental health of handicapped pupils. Prepare an outline of the key ideas.
5. Visit a state institution for the handicapped. Describe your sensory impressions of the general facilities, paying special attention to school buildings, classrooms, and other learning areas. Describe the possible impact of the setting on a hypothetical pupil entering the institution after living in the community for several years. Include in your comments a description of the possible impact on parents.
6. Select at least two of the following environmental factors, and discuss, in a paragraph for each, the possible effects on pupil attitudes and performance:
    a. School cleanliness and general maintenance
    b. Accessibility to the school building for physically handicapped pupils

    c. Accessibility of drinking fountains, lavatory facilities, elevators, sinks, and coin telephones for physically handicapped, visually impaired, and/or functionally illiterate pupils

7. If there is an open space school in your community or one nearby, visit it and describe the ways in which you believe the physical environment in the open space school differs from the traditional school. Include the open space school's impact on its pupils.

8. Select at least two of the following factors, and discuss briefly their possible impact on pupil attitudes and performance:
    a. A large sign on the school building stating, "The _____ School for the Physically and Mentally Handicapped"
    b. Evidence of much vandalism, e.g., broken windows, graffitti, and a scarred facade
    c. A well-equipped playground area with special play equipment for handicapped pupils

9. Write a 3- to 5-page paper justifying the importance of including in a teacher's diagnostic armamentarium an assessment of the classroom's physical environment and its possible impact on student performance. In your position paper, cite specific examples that illustrate and support your position.

CONCLUDING STATEMENT

While this module has emphasized a number of classroom environmental factors that impact on pupil attitudes and performance, teachers should be alert to factors in the physical environment existing outside the classroom and within the school as a total entity. For example, physically handicapped pupils may require handrails throughout the school building to assist them in traveling throughout the building. In addition, pupils with learning and/or cognitive problems may require legible signs and other visual clues, i.e., rebuses, arrows, and different color floors (walkways), as aids to finding their way around the school. Elevators may be necessary for nonambulatory pupils and braille legends on elevator floor buttons and floor landings may be needed for blind riders. Facilitating the movement of handicapped pupils throughout the school is essential to the development of motor skills, social skills, and to the growth and development of self-worth and self-image.

It is extremely important that the impact of the physical environment on pupils be recognized. It should be kept in mind that physical, emotional, or mental handicaps do not make pupils impervious to their surroundings; the handicapping condition may make them ultrasensitive to the environment. It is important to recognize that nonhandicapped pupils may learn well in spite of negative surroundings, but the handicapped need as much reinforcement in all areas as is possible to provide.

While key classroom factors are identified and discussed, there are countless others that are too obvious to detail and, perhaps, a multitude of others that are too subtle to be recognized.

POSTTEST

At this point retake the Pretest.

LITERATURE CITED

Abeson, A., and Blacklow, J. (eds). 1971. Environmental Design: New Relevance for Special Education. Council for Exceptional Children, Arlington, Va.

Barker, R. G. 1968. Ecological Psychology. Stanford University Press, Stanford, Cal.

Baron, R. A., and Lawton, S. F. 1972. Environmental influences on aggression: The facilitation of modeling effects by high ambient temperatures. Psychonom. Sci. 26:80–82.

Barsch, R. 1965. A Movigenic Curriculum. Bureau for Handicapped Children, Madison, Wisc.

Bender, M., and Valletutti, P. J. 1976. Teaching the Moderately and Severely Handicapped. Vol. I. University Park Press, Baltimore.

Bronzaft, A. L., and McCarthy, D. P. 1975. The effect of elevated train noise on reading ability. Environ. Behav. 7:517–528.

Bryan, T. H., and Bryan, J. H. 1978. Understanding Learning Disabilities. 2nd. Ed. Alfred Publishing Co., Sherman Oaks, Cal.

Cohen, S., Glass, D. C., and Singer, J. E. 1973. Apartment noise, auditory discrimination, and reading ability in children. J. Exper. Soc. Psychol. 9:407–422.

Cross, H. E. 1975. Educational implications of visual disorders. In R. H. A. Haslam and P. J. Valletutti (eds.), Medical Problems in the Classroom, pp. 15–31. University Park Press, Baltimore.

Cruickshank, W. M., Bentzen, F. A., Ratzeburg, F. H., and Tannhauser, M. T. 1961. A Teaching Method for Brain-injured and Hyperactive Children. Syracuse University Press, Syracuse.

Fischer, C. S., Baldassare, M., and Ofshe, R. J. 1975. Crowding studies and urban life: A critical review. J. Am. Inst. Planners 41:406–418.

Freedman, J. L., Klevansky, S., and Ehrlich, P. R. 1971. The effect of crowding on human task performance. J. Appl. Soc. Psychol. 1:7–25.

Friedman, J. L. 1975. Teacher awareness of hearing disorders. In R. H. A. Haslam and P. J. Valletutti (eds.), Medical Problems in the Classroom, pp. 33–50. University Park Press, Baltimore.

Glass, D. C., and Singer, J. E. 1972. Urban Stress: Experiments on Noise and Social Stressors. Academic Press, Inc., New York.

Griffitt, W., and Veitch, R. 1971. Hot and crowded: Influences of population density and temperature on interpersonal affective behavior. J. Pers. Soc. Psychol: 17:92–98.

Harlow, H., and Harlow, M. 1969. The young monkeys. In Readings in Psychology Today, pp. 146–153. CRM Books, Del Mar, Cal.

Heimstra, N. W., and McFarling, L. H. 1974. Environmental Psychology. Brooks/Cole Publishing Co., Monterey, Cal.

Innes, R. B. 1973. Environmental forces in open and closed classroom settings. J. Exper. Educ. 41:38–42.

Ittelson, W. H., Rivlin, L. G., Proshansky, H. M., and Winkel, G. H. 1974. An Introduction to Environmental Psychology. Holt, Rinehart & Winston, Inc., New York.

Karmel, L. J. 1965. Effects of windowless classroom environments on high school students. Percept. Mot. Skills 20:277–278.

Koneya, M. 1976. Location and interaction in row-and-column seating arrangements. Environ. Behav. 8:265–282.

Mason, W. A. 1960. The effect of social restriction on the behavior of rhesus monkeys: I. Free social behavior. J. Comp. Physiol. Psychol. 53:582–589.

Milgram, S. 1970. The experience of living in cities. Science 167:1461–1468.

Mitchell, W. J. (ed.). 1972. Environmental Design: Research and Practice. University of California, Los Angeles.

Ott, J. M. 1976. Influence of fluorescent lights on hyperactivity and learning disabilities. J. Learn. Disabil. 9:417–422.

Painter, M. 1976. Fluorescent lights and hyperactivity in children: An experiment. Academic Ther. 12:181–184.

Patterson, R. (ed.). 1972. Allergic Disease: Diagnosis and Management. J. B. Lippincott Co., Philadelphia.

Pelone, A. J. 1962. The adjustment of the partially seeing child in the regular classroom. In J. F. Magary and J. R. Eichorn (eds.), The Exceptional Child: A Book of Readings, pp. 270–279. Holt, Rinehart & Winston, Inc., New York.

Russo, N. F. 1967. Connotation of seating arrangements. Cornell J. Soc. Relat. 2:37–44.

Salt, S., and Karmel, R. J. 1967. The windowless school. Clearing House 42:176–178.

Schorr, A. L. 1963. Slums and Social Insecurity. U.S. Government Printing Office, Washington, D.C.

Shapiro, S. 1975. Some classroom ABC's: Research takes a closer look. Elem. School J. 75:436–441.

Smith, R. M., Neisworth, J. T., and Green, J. G. 1978. Evaluating Educational Environments. Charles E. Merrill Publishing Co., Columbus, Oh.

Sommer, R. 1969. Personal Space. Prentice-Hall, Inc., Englewood Cliffs, N.J.

Srole, L., Langer, T. S., Michael, S. T., Opler, M. K., and Rennie, T. A. C. 1961. Mental Health in the Metropolis. Vol. I. McGraw-Hill Book Co., New York.

Stern, G. 1970. People in Context: Measuring Person-Environment Congruence in Education and Industry. John Wiley & Sons, Inc., New York.

Stokols, D. 1976. The experience of crowding in primary and secondary environments. Environ. Behav. 8:49–86.

Valett, R. E. 1978. Developing Cognitive Abilities: Teaching Children to Think. C. V. Mosby Co., St. Louis.

Module 4

The teacher will demonstrate knowledge of perceptual, motor, language, cognitive, and social developmental milestones.

PRETEST

Part A

Answer *True* or *False*. In either case, give a justification for your answer.

1. The teacher's essential diagnostic task is to analyze the pupil's level of skill functioning, regardless of the pupil's chronological age.
2. One of the important tasks for any teacher is to analyze pupil behavior in order to assign a diagnostic label to the pupil.
3. A teacher may best understand a pupil by comparing that pupil to peers.
4. Once a pupil is able to count by rote from 1 to 10 and demonstrates an understanding of one-to-one correspondence, the next logical step, from a developmental perspective, is to teach the pupil how to count from 1 to 10 with meaning.
5. Knowing a pupil's chronological age is not necessary in selecting appropriate methods and materials for instruction.

Part B

The following groups of developmental milestones are or are not in correct order of occurrence. If incorrect, rearrange them and write the letters of the correct arrangement. If correct, write the word CORRECT in the space provided.

1. _____
   a. Visually matches identical objects
   b. Recalls previously experienced pictures and symbols
   c. Follows objects with coordinated eye movements
2. _____
   a. Turns eyes and head in the direction of noise
   b. Listens to the sound of own voice
   c. Discriminates between and among speech sounds
3. _____
   a. Sits without support
   b. Holds head erect when held in sitting position
   c. Lifts head when shoulder is supported
4. _____
   a. Cruises from object to object
   b. Able to walk up and down the stairs unaided
   c. Is able to go downstairs on hands and knees, creeping slowly in backward position

5. _____
   a. Is able to ride a tricycle
   b. Is able to jump rope
   c. Is able to roller skate
6. _____
   a. Grasps object with palm
   b. Picks up small toys and objects
   c. Transfers objects from hand to hand
7. _____
   a. Is able to turn pages of a book, but does so several pages at a
      time
   b. Is able to turn pages of a book, one page at a time
   c. Grasps a string held in front of him/her
8. _____
   a. Is able to cut with a pair of scissors
   b. Is able to turn doorknobs
   c. Is able to build a tower consisting of two cubes or blocks
9. _____
   a. Copies a triangle
   b. Copies a circle
   c. Copies a square
10. _____
   a. Imitates horizontal and vertical lines
   b. Prints first name from memory
   c. Reproduces individual capital letters from memory

Part C

Fill in an appropriate developmental milestone wherever one has been
omitted. Choose any milestone that reasonably can be inserted.

1. Language Development
   a. Turns eyes and head in the direction of noise
   b. _____
   c. Turns head and shoulders in the direction of someone vocaliz-
      ing or speaking
2. Language Development
   a. _____
   b. Vocalizes in self-initiated sound play
   c. Initiates vocal play with toys
3. Language Development
   a. Says a first word with meaning
   b. Responds to names of family members, common everyday
      objects, toys, and pets
   c. _____

4. Language Development
   a. Asks questions beginning with what, where, or who
   b. _____
   c. Asks the "how" and "why" questions
5. Language Development
   a. Uses regular plural nouns
   b. _____
   c. Uses third person singular correctly
6. Cognitive Development
   a. Names pictures of familiar objects
   b. _____
   c. Shows major parts of body
7. Cognitive Development
   a. Describes action pictures
   b. Is able to put together simple puzzles (5–7 pieces)
   c. _____
8. Cognitive Development
   a. Is able to supply his/her address on request
   b. _____
   c. Is able to indicate right and left part of body
9. Social Development
   a. Begins to play with other children
   b. _____
   c. Plays simple group games
10. Social Development
   a. Shows concern and sympathy for playmates
   b. Responds to rules and practices sportsmanship
   c. _____

INTRODUCTION AND OVERVIEW

The developmental milestones that follow have been organized categorically, i.e., by area of behavior (perceptual, motor, language, cognitive, and social) in their approximate order of development. The ordering, as provided on pages 67–79, has been compiled from a variety of sources (see Suggested Readings). A knowledge of developmental milestones is a vital competency because it influences the sequencing of instructional programs and is closely related to the task analysis process (see Module 9).

Although it is the usual practice to identify developmental patterns by assigning a time or time span designation within which that skill is expected to develop under normal conditions, no chronologically normative ages are designated for the skills listed below. This omission is deliberate to emphasize that the teacher's essential diagnostic task is to analyze the pupil's level of skill functioning across a broad range of competencies, *regardless of the pupil's chronological age.* A teacher must examine, study, and refer to normative developmental data in order to appreciate the significance of pupil behavior. The significance of pupil behavior for educational purposes, however, is not to label that behavior but rather to describe that behavior and to match that pupil performance with developmental patterns and expectations.

The central diagnostic skill is to discover what competencies a pupil already has mastered so that the teacher can proceed to prepare instructional programs designed to assist the pupil in acquiring new skills. The selection of new skills to be programmed for is the underlying reason why the teacher must diagnose and prescribe from within a developmental perspective. A teacher needs to find those points along the various developmental sequences that represent the pupil's highest level of skill development. The essential diagnostic skill then is to match the pupil's specific performance competencies with developmental patterns without comparing that pupil to anyone else and without assigning mental ages or achievement quotients.

It is the professional function of the teacher to provide a pupil with those specially selected learning experiences that will assist him/her in achieving some next developmentally higher level skill. For example, a given pupil is able to count from 1 to 10 by rote only and has demonstrated through various class activities that he/she, at the same time, understands one-to-one correspondence. From a developmental perspective, the next logical step and the one most likely to be successfully learned is the development of counting from 1 to 10 with meaning.

In examining some language developmental milestones, a better appreciation of their relationship to educational programming decisions

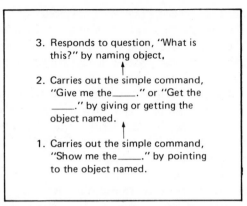

Figure 1. Developmental dependence in skill progression. (Note: Precursor skills are charted from the bottom up to the higher level skills.)

can be realized. In some cases, steps that follow a skill are developmentally dependent upon that skill (see Figure 1).

If pupil A only possesses skill 1 (as shown in Figure 1), you would first program for skill 2 and then proceed to skill 3. If pupil B possesses skills 1 and 2, you would then program for skill 3. If pupil C possesses all three skills, you would then program for a next higher step or for a later developmental milestone that is developing independently of these three skills. This alternate programming possibility may be seen in Figure 2.

If pupil D possesses skill 1, you might program for skill 2, 3, or 1' (see Figure 2) depending upon his/her level of mastery of these other skills as well as other factors, including adequacy of the student's speech, hearing, and vision.

Thus, once a teacher ascertains a performance level of a student, the instructor may program for a next skill in the hierarchy that is develop-

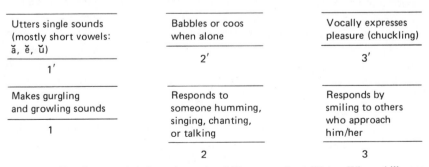

Figure 2. Developmental independence in skill progression. (Note: When skills are developing simultaneously, but are developing independently of each other, they are charted horizontally.)

mentally dependent upon the previous (mastered) one. When the next higher steps are developing independently of each other, yet at approximately the same developmental time, the teacher may program for some other developmentally higher level skill based upon a judgment of what skills are likely to be more readily acquired by an individual pupil and/or what skills are more critical to the acquisition of later key competencies. A knowledge of chronological age correlates of developmental milestones is likely to corrupt the teacher's basic diagnostic/prescriptive task: to diagnose a pupil's level of functioning independently of any other pupil in the universe of pupils and regardless of that pupil's chronological age.

If classroom teachers were responsible for diagnosis and testing procedures designed to discover etiólogy, to categorize, to label, and to establish a treatment prognosis, they *then* would need to know developmental age norms because these comparisons might then be necessary in order to identify pathological states requiring various medical and paramedical interventions. In developing individual educational objectives (IEOs), however, comparison to chronological or mental age peers is a waste of time.

Knowing the pupil's chronological age is important when establishing priorities among IEOs and when selecting appropriate methods and materials of instruction. In specific cases, a teacher might reorder objectives and even reject others because of the pupil's age. For example, the reading texts and other books selected for a 16-year-old beginning reader must be different from those selected for a six-year-old beginning reader. An 18-year-old's inability, after many years of skilled instruction, to master the skill of telling time should convince a teacher to give up on that particular objective because there is too little school time left; the remaining years should be devoted to skills that are both easier to acquire and more important to life functioning. A teacher must be zealous in the pursuit of efficiency of instruction because of this critical time factor.

Because of the variations in the findings of the several investigators and because an analysis of various tests suggests different sequencing patterns to developmental milestones, judgments had to be made as to hierarchical order. No time order is presented herein because of:

1.   Differences occuring in authoritative sources
2.   The existence of simultaneously and independently developing skills
3.   The listing of skills by time periods rather than specific months

All three factors interfere with a true ordering of skill development. The order presented here approximates the listings as constructed by various authorities and test makers.

If you feel that there is a pupil in your class with obvious and marked deviation from normal developmental expectations, and if he/she has not been seen for an extensive diagnosis based upon the medical or psychological model, refer that pupil for medical, paramedical, and/or psychological evaluation and/or treatment (see Module 6).

Visual Perception

Individual:

1. Fixates on rudimentary basis and tracks reflexively for brief periods
2. Is able to accommodate with greater flexibility, coordinates head and eye movements
3. Sees and differentiates objects
4. Follows objects with coordinated eye movements
5. Usually matches identical objects
6. Perceives and separates objects in foreground from background
7. Recalls objects removed or changed in environment
8. Follows pictures and symbols with coordinated eye movements
9. Visually matches symbols, designs, numerals, letters, and words
10. Perceives and separates objects in foreground and background of pictures
11. Perceives and separates words from the background
12. Recalls previously experienced pictures and symbols, including words and phrases
13. Is able to draw designs and symbols and produce letters, numerals, and words from memory (revisualization)
14. Is able to carry out a motor plan involving visual monitoring of fine motor skills
15. Is able to recreate designs and assemble three-dimensional materials, including puzzles and the construction of arts, crafts, and shop projects
16. Is able to draw complete pictures and to move about freely in his/her environment and during various leisure time and sports activities

Auditory Perception

Individual:

1. Responds to sound (e.g., noise of rattle or other toy noisemaker)
2. Responds to someone humming, singing, chanting, or talking
3. Turns eyes and head in the direction of noise
4. Turns eyes and head in the direction of someone vocalizing or speaking

5. Vocalizes in response to the vocalization of others
6. Responds differentially to friendly and angry talking
7. Listens to the sound of own voice
8. Differentiates between and among gross sounds
9. Discriminates between and among speech sounds
10. Recalls sounds of words and phrases
11. Comprehends individual words and simple commands
12. Comprehends more complex commands and directions
13. Recalls auditory information (e.g., plots of television shows, what he/she heard yesterday, a story read by a teacher or parent)
14. Recalls in correct sequence auditory information (e.g., carrying out previously given directions with only a minimal lapse of time)
15. Recalls in correct sequence auditory information where there has been a substantial lapse of time between stimulus and expected response
16. Recalls in correct sequence auditory information when there has been marked auditory interference (i.e., competing and intervening auditory stimuli)

Gross Motor Development

Individual:

1. Lifts head when shoulder is supported
2. Moves head from side to side
3. Makes crawling movements when in prone position
4. Lifts and turns head when in prone position
5. Holds head erect when held in sitting position, steadying head when necessary
6. Rolls over
7. Lifts foot when held in standing position
8. Pulls himself/herself to a sitting position
9. Sits without support
10. Extends legs while in sitting position
11. Supports himself/herself on one arm while in sitting position
12. Stands, holding on, when placed in a standing position
13. Pulls self to standing position
14. Stands with or without support
15. Walks while being held
16. Attains sitting position unaided
17. Crawls rapidly on all fours
18. Cruises from object to object (cruising is the action of moving from object to object by holding on to each object encountered for support)

19. Walks unaided (individual is able to arise from a supine position to a standing position and walk independently)
20. Is able to walk sideways and backwards
21. Returns from standing to sitting position
22. Kneels unaided
23. Is able to stoop to pick up objects from floor
24. Stands on one foot with or without support
25. Is able to pick up objects from floor without stooping and without losing balance
26. Is able to go downstairs on hands and knees, creeping slowly in backward position
27. Is able to push and pull toys and other objects around the floor
28. Is able to walk unaided while carrying toys and other light, manageable objects in his/her hands
29. Is able to walk downstairs with assistance
30. Is able to get on and off a regular size chair unaided
31. Is able to walk up and down the stairs unaided (walking rhythm generally becomes stabilized)
32. Jumps in place crudely with a two-feet take-off
33. Is able to pedal a tricycle
34. Is able to throw a small ball 4 to 5 feet
35. Is able to balance on one foot for at least 5 seconds
36. Is able to walk a line, heel to toe
37. Is able to hop from two to three steps on preferred foot
38. Is able to jump off bottom step of a staircase
39. Is able to throw a ball about 10 feet
40. Is able to climb stairs alternating feet
41. Is able to run with good form and with leg-arm coordination
42. Is able to catch a bouncing ball
43. Is able to stand on one foot for 5 to 10 seconds (usually preferred foot)
44. Is able to walk balance beam for short distances
45. Is able to jump with skill
46. Is able to climb ladders
47. Is able to skip on alternate feet
48. Is able to jump rope
49. Is able to broad jump from 2 to 3 feet
50. Is able to hop 2 to 3 yards on each foot separately
51. Is able to dance
52. Is able to ride a tricycle with facility
53. Is able to roller skate
54. Is able to hop and jump into small squares with accuracy
55. Is able to play a large variety of games involving diverse gross motor activities

56. Improves in gross motor skills depending upon physical health, amount of practice, motivation, and natural talent

Fine Motor Development (General)

Individual:

1. Touches objects
2. Retains small toys, objects, and playthings when placed in his/her hand
3. Holds hands together
4. Reaches for objects
5. Watches movement of own hands
6. Alternates glance from object to hand
7. Grasps small toys, objects, and playthings held at hand
8. Reaches for objects
9. Corrals objects/swipes at objects
10. Grasps objects with palm
11. Grasps objects with fingers
12. Grasps objects with fingers and examines them
13. Exploits objects, i.e., bangs, shakes, hits
14. Releases small toys, objects, and playthings
15. Picks up small toys and objects
16. Picks up and lets go of objects, i.e., drops and throws
17. Passes objects, materials, and playthings
18. Rakes in and attains very small objects
19. Transfers objects from hand to hand
20. Lifts cup with handle
21. Grasps a string held in front of him/her
22. Pulls out pegs and removes objects from forms
23. Becomes skilled in pincer grasp in picking up small objects
24. Is able to imitate simple grasping, releasing, removing, and other similar motor behaviors
25. Is able to hold crayon
26. Holds and marks with a pencil
27. Is able to recover small toys and objects placed under a cup
28. Is able to build a tower of two cubes or blocks
29. Is able to pick up and hold two small objects in one hand
30. Is able to turn pages of a book, but does so several pages at a time
31. Is able to pick up and throw small rubber ball
32. Is able to build a tower of three to six blocks or cubes
33. Is able to turn pages of a book one page at a time
34. Indicates well-defined hand preference
35. Is able to turn doorknobs

36. Is able to place objects into their appropriate forms
37. Is able to fill and dump pails with sand
38. Is able to manipulate clay
39. Is able to make mud and sand pies
40. Is able to cut with a pair of scissors
41. Is able to hammer nails and pegs
42. Is able to hold crayons and pencils with fingers
43. Is able to string beads
44. Is able to build a bridge with cubes or blocks
45. Is able to build a tower with eight or more blocks
46. Is able to open and close snaps
47. Is able to open and close zippers
48. Is able to button and unbutton clothing
49. Is able to draw simple sketches
50. Is able to tie shoes

Fine Motor Development (Pre-writing)

Individual:

1. Holds crayon
2. Holds and marks with a pencil
3. Indicates well-defined hand preference
4. Uses crayons and pencils to scribble
5. Imitates horizontal and vertical lines
6. Imitates circular scribbling or writing movements
7. Uses fingers for finger painting and for tracing
8. Holds crayon and pencil with fingers
9. Copies a circle
10. Imitates cross
11. Copies capital letters consisting of vertical and horizontal lines
12. Copies cross
13. Draws simple sketches (man, house)
14. Reproduces (from memory) individual capital letters consisting of vertical and horizontal lines
15. Prints capital letters of first name
16. Copies a square
17. Copies a triangle
18. Copies a rectangle
19. Reproduces first name
20. Copies numerals 1 through 5
21. Copies capital and small letters consisting of straight lines, curved lines, circles, and semicircles
22. Draws complete sketch of a man

23. Copies a diamond
24. Copies numerals 6 through 10
25. Reproduces numerals 0 through 9
26. Reproduces the capital manuscript letters
27. Reproduces the small manuscript letters
28. Reproduces complete name in manuscript letters
29. Reproduces various geometric shapes
30. Writes in cursive style

Language Development

Individual:

1. Vocalizes reflexively with differentiated crying emerging gradually
2. Responds to sound (e.g., noise of rattle or other toy noisemaker)
3. Makes gurgling and growling sounds
4. Responds to someone humming, singing, chanting, or talking
5. Utters single vowel sounds (mostly short vowels: ă, ĕ, ŭ)
6. Responds by smiling at others who approach him/her
7. Babbles or coos when alone
8. Vocally expresses pleasure (chuckling)
9. Responds vocally to others who approach him/her
10. Turns eyes and head in the direction of noise
11. Turns eyes and head in the direction of someone vocalizing or speaking
12. Turns head and shoulders in the direction of noise
13. Turns head and shoulders in the direction of someone vocalizing or speaking
14. Babbles or vocalizes two (duplicated) syllables
15. Vocalizes in response to the vocalization of others
16. Babbles or vocalizes two or more syllables
17. Vocalizes in self-initiated sound play
18. Vocalizes displeasure when favored object is withdrawn
19. Responds differentially to friendly and angry talking
20. Initiates vocal play with toys
21. Babbles or coos to music
22. Listens to the sound of his/her own voice
23. Articulates several well-defined syllables
24. Locates precisely the source of sound
25. Initiates vocal play with people
26. Vocalizes to own reflection in mirror
27. Responds to single words, e.g., looks at the light

28. Vocalizes pleasure or satisfaction upon obtaining desired or favored object
29. Vocalizes "dada" and/or "mama"
30. Imitates speech sounds
31. Stops an activity when scolded ("No-No")
32. Responds to gestures, including bye-bye
33. Imitates vocal noises, e.g., clicking of the tongue, clearing of throat, and coughing
34. Responds to own name
35. Vocalizes when shown or when playing with eating utensils
36. Imitates syllables, such as "ma-ma," "pa-pa," and "da-da"
37. Says a first word with meaning
38. Responds to common action verbs
39. Responds enthusiastically to simple songs and rhymes
40. Says three to five words with meaning
41. Jabbers with vocal expression and inflection
42. Indicates wants by pointing and other body language
43. Responds to names of family members, common everyday objects, toys (dolly), and pets (doggie) by pointing and other body language
44. Says the names of favored objects
45. Carries out simple command, "Show me the _____."
46. Carries out the simple commands, "Give me the _____" and "Get the _____" by giving or getting the object named
47. Says five to eight words with meaning
48. Points to nose, eyes, hair, and mouth on request
49. Says eight to ten words with meaning
50. Responds to question "What is this?" by naming object
51. Says "Hello," "Goodbye," "Thank you," "Please," and other simple language courtesies
52. Combines two words (usually noun/verb combinations)
53. Carries out two-step commands or directions
54. Indicates wants and thoughts by naming object desired
55. Indicates wants and thoughts by naming and gesturing
56. Says 20 words with meaning
57. Attempts to sing along with simple songs and tunes
58. Finds pictures in a book
59. Refers to self by name
60. Uses pivot words such as *a* kitty, *my* car, and want *that*
61. Adds subject to predicate
62. Echoes words and phrases of others
63. Names pictures of common objects

64. Asks for food and water when desired
65. Speaks in three- and four-word sentences
66. Uses first pronouns: I, me, and you (not necessarily correctly)
67. Says 50 to 75 words with meaning
68. Responds correctly to function questions, e.g., "What do you see with?"
69. Carries out commands containing common prepositions
70. Listens attentively to simple stories
71. Responds correctly to commands involving concept of "one" when there is more than one, i.e., "Give me one!"
72. Says his/her full name when asked
73. Uses present progressive form (-ing) of verbs
74. Uses regular plural nouns
75. Uses past tense of regular verbs
76. Uses nouns in the possessive case
77. Uses third person singular verbs
78. Says 200 or more recognizable words with meaning; comprehends 400 or more words
79. Says several nursery rhymes or simple TV commercials
80. Utters negative statements
81. Identifies actions depicted in pictures
82. Uses demonstrative pronouns: this and that
83. Talks about himself/herself and to himself/herself
84. Shifts between "me" and "I" in talking about self
85. Transforms kernel sentences (subject + verb + direct object) into questions
86. Asks unsolicited questions
87. Responds correctly to questions, "Are you a girl? boy?"
88. Speaks in sentences up to six words in length
89. Names the primary colors
90. Indicates toilet needs
91. Says approximately 1,000 words with meaning
92. Gains mastery over vocal rate and volume
93. Identifies time of day (i.e., day or night) in pictures as well as in actuality
94. Is able to repeat three digits
95. Asks questions beginning with what, where, and who
96. Compares objects by size (long-short)
97. Verbalizes opposite analogies
98. Speaks of object by category (animals, toys, food)
99. Is able to repeat six-word sentences
100. Is able to produce correctly all English vowels

101. Produces intelligibly the consonants: /p/, /b/, /m/, /w/, and /h/
102. Says 1,500 words with meaning; comprehends 1,500 or more words
103. Names own scribbling and drawings
104. Speaks in compound and complex sentences
105. Talks to self in long monologues mostly involved with the present and including fantasy
106. Relates experiences and describes activities
107. Carries out multiple step commands or directions
108. Asks the "How" and "Why" questions
109. Speaks of objects and persons not in immediate environment
110. Counts up to three objects
111. Is able to select two and three items from a larger group of the same items (concepts of "two" and "three")
112. Begins to appreciate that common words have multiple meanings
113. Articulates intelligibly the consonants: /t/, /d/, /n/, /k/, /g/, /ng/, and /y/
114. Corrects errors in grammar spontaneously
115. Is able to define simple words
116. Identifies home address in response to question
117. Says his/her age and month and date of birthday in response to question
118. Speaks in a well-modulated voice with appropriate pitch, resonance, quality, and inflection patterns
119. Speaks about past and present events and links them
120. Says approximately 2,000 words with meaning; comprehends 3,000 or more words
121. Responds correctly to, "Show me your right _____!"
122. Becomes less egocentric in his/her speech and more involved with others in carrying on simple conversations
123. Is able to recount the plots of stories, television programs, and movies
124. Is able to describe pictures in detail, using a variety of sentences
125. Articulates intelligibly the consonants: /f/, /v/, /s/, and /z/ (Note: The /s/ and /z/ are lost later because of the loss of the upper incisors but return when the upper teeth appear at approximately eight years of age)
126. Uses all the basic types of structures of sentences
127. Asks meanings of abstract words and unfamiliar or idiomatic expressions
128. Is able to carry out directional commands, e.g., "Put your left hand on your right shoulder."

129. Uses idiomatic, colloquial, and figurative expressions in one-to-one and/or group conversations
130. Speaks in all the patterns of acceptable adult speech, adding vocabulary as he/she matures so that he/she is speaking with fluency, accuracy, sophistication, and flexibility in a voice that reflects size, age, and sex

Cognitive Development

Individual:

1. Responds to sound (e.g., noise of rattle or other toy noisemaker)
2. Responds to sudden voices
3. Reaches for familiar persons
4. Reacts excitedly to the sight of a favored toy
5. Grasps toys when presented
6. Responds differentially to strangers
7. Turns to look for dropped objects
8. Shakes head when moving object stops
9. Plays peek-a-boo and claps hands on imitation
10. Claps hands on request
11. Rings bell deliberately
12. Responds to first name
13. Waves bye-bye appropriately
14. Stops an activity when told, "No-No!"
15. Looks at pictures in book
16. Squeezes noisemakers to make squeak
17. Carries out intentional behaviors (places adults's hand on desired toy)
18. Looks in appropriate place for toys that have rolled out of sight
19. Searches out and/or carries favored objects
20. Says the name of familiar objects
21. Imitates putting objects in container
22. Carries out simple commands
23. Invents new means of solving simple sensorimotor problems
24. Points to one or more body parts
25. Retrieves or attains toys using a stick
26. Discovers new means of solving cognitive motor problems with active experimentation
27. Follows simple commands
28. Points to three body parts: hair, eyes, and nose
29. Identifies pictures in response to simple commands
30. Attempts to sing to music

31. Points to body parts of doll or mannequin
32. Carries out two-part commands
33. Names pictures of familiar objects
34. Responds to own picture by naming it
35. Matches familiar objects
36. Carries out three-part commands
37. Joins in simple songs and nursery rhymes
38. Shows major parts of body including basic wearing apparel
39. Sings words and phrases of simple tunes and TV commercials
40. Points to objects to indicate use
41. Is able to repeat two digits
42. Participates in storytelling by supplying words and phrases
43. Names six or more common, everyday objects
44. Is able to point to less familiar parts of face like cheek, teeth, eyebrow
45. Responds correctly to questions, "Are you a boy? girl?"
46. Matches primary colors
47. Names primary colors
48. Identifies tongue, neck, knee, arm, by pointing
49. Describes action pictures
50. Identifies pictures by naming approximately 10 common objects in pictures
51. Is able to recall a pictured object from memory
52. Is able to count two blocks, cubes, beads, etc.
53. Is able to put together simple puzzles (five to seven pieces)
54. Is able to differentiate between past and present events
55. Responds appropriately to commands involving comprehension of prepositions
56. Matches pictures of similar objects
57. Is able to answer function questions: "What do we do with scissors?"
58. Is able to count up to two when shown sketches of familiar shapes
59. Is able to respond verbally to simple analogies
60. Identifies by naming approximately 15 to 17 common objects in pictures
61. Tells a story by reading pictures in a sequence
62. Is able to assemble a seven-piece puzzle in approximately 2½ minutes
63. Is able to name materials from which basic or common objects are made
64. Identifies day and night in pictures and in actuality
65. Is able to identify pictorial likenesses and differences
66. Is able to count up to four objects and name the amount counted

67. Is able to count up to three sketches of geometric shapes such as squares, circles, rectangles
68. Is able to make opposite analogies
69. Is able to identify past, present, and future events and activities
70. Is able to define simple words
71. Is able to supply his/her address upon request
72. Is able to answer action questions, "What (*action verb*)?"
73. Is able to act out stories in creative dramatic activities
74. Is able to tell age and birth date upon request
75. Is able to form rectangle from two triangular cards
76. Is able to identify coins: penny, nickel, and dime
77. Is able to indicate left and right part of body
78. Is able to tell differences and similarities in approximately 10 pictures
79. Is able to count up to six objects when asked the "How many" question
80. Is able to compare two objects or things by size: "Which is bigger?"
81. Is able to count up to nine and tell what number comes after each number in the series up to nine
82. Is able to use numbers up to 10 in functional counting

Social Development
Individual:

1. Smiles spontaneously
2. Responds to someone humming, singing, chanting, or talking
3. Responds by smiling at people who approach him/her
4. Discriminates strangers from significant family members
5. Vocally expresses pleasure
6. Vocalizes in response to the vocalization of others
7. Vocalizes in self-initiated sound plan
8. Initiates vocal play with toys
9. Initiates vocal play with people
10. Stops an activity when told "No-No"
11. Responds to gestures, including bye-bye
12. Plays peek-a-boo and claps hands
13. Reaches for familiar persons
14. Imitates adult motor patterns
15. Says a first word with meaning
16. Begins to play with other children
17. Picks up and puts away toys
18. Responds to own name
19. Helps with simple household activities

20. Plays alone, contentedly, if adult or adults are nearby
21. Inititates own play activities
22. Participates in water and sandbox play
23. Helps in cleaning up and putting things away
24. Plays simple group games
25. Engages in make-believe play reflecting happenings in home and seen on television
26. Joins other children in play
27. Listens enthusiastically to stories
28. Requests favorite rhymes, stories, books
29. Engages in active play with toys in floor activities alone, in parallel play, or with others
30. Begins to take turn
31. Begins to share toys
32. Engages in imaginative or creative play
33. Plays cooperatively with peers
34. Enjoys pretending games in adult clothes and in specially created costumes, designed from objects and materials found around house
35. Participates in competitive games
36. Exhibits concern and sympathy for playmates at times; criticizes, bosses, and shows aggression at other times
37. Responds to rules and practices sportsmanship
38. Begins to choose desired playmate
39. Plays simple card and other table games
40. Participates successfully in small groups
41. Plans and builds constructively
42. Sets up schedule of activities and conforms to time restraints
43. Interacts with adults and responds positively to their directions and ideas
44. Participates as a member of a family

ACTIVITIES AND EXPERIENCES

1. Arrange a visit(s) to a program in which a physical therapist is working with a physically handicapped pupil functioning in the preambulation stage of development. Observe a session(s), and then describe the program of therapy being followed. Discuss the pupil's present developmental level and the planned progression of therapy.
2. Arrange a visit a program in which an occupational therapist is working with a physically handicapped pupil who is evidencing problems with fine motor development because of neurological impairment, orthopaedic disability, or delayed development. Observe a session(s), and then describe the program of therapy

being followed. Discuss the pupil's present developmental level and the planned progression of therapy.

3. Arrange to visit a program in which a speech and language therapist is working with a pupil who is evidencing problems in language development. Observe a session(s), and then describe the program of therapy being followed. Discuss the pupil's present developmental level and the planned progression of therapy.
4. Observe a young child over a period of time (minimum of 3 months). Keep a record of significant developmental changes.
5. Observe groups of children at play; discuss the various levels and kinds of social interactions observed.
6. Obtain a copy of the Stanford-Binet Intelligence Scale. Discuss cognitive, motor, social, and language development milestones implied from this test of general intellectual functioning.
7. Discuss the ways in which normal developmental sequences might be distorted or changed for a pupil who is:
    a. blind
    b. deaf
8. Observe a pupil in your class over a period of time. Chart that pupil's developmental changes as they occur.
9. Discuss the developmental interrelatedness that exists between and among the various categorical areas of human behavior discussed in this module.
10. Write a brief essay that supports the position that competent teachers should have a knowledge of developmental milestones. In your essay, cite sources for obtaining developmental data.

CONCLUDING STATEMENT

While it is not expected that teachers will memorize lists of developmental milestones, they nevertheless must maintain a developmental perspective in analyzing student performance and in planning instructional sequences. Teachers should have books and articles from authoritative sources in their professional libraries to which they can refer in order to review developmental sequences whenever necessary. Teachers should remember that they should describe a pupil's behavior as normal even when the behavior demonstrated is one expected of someone chronologically younger unless there is an underlying physiological pathology. Teachers must view each pupil as a distinct individual who is proceeding developmentally at his/her own rate. The term *abnormal* should be reserved for those behaviors that would be considered pathological whenever they occur in any individual, regardless of chronological age or physical status.

POSTTEST

At this point retake the Pretest.

SUGGESTED READINGS

Anastasi, A. 1968. Psychological Testing. 3rd. Ed. Macmillan Publishing Co., Inc., New York.

Anderson S., and Messick, S. 1974. Social competency in young children. Develop. Psychol. 10:282–293.

Bayley, N. 1969. Bayley Scales of Infant Development. The Psychological Corporation, New York.

Bender, M., and Valletutti, P. J. 1976. Teaching the Moderately and Severely Handicapped. Vol. I. University Park Press, Baltimore.

Bender, M., and Valletutti, P. J. 1976. Teaching the Moderately and Severely Handicapped. Vol. II. University Park Press, Baltimore.

Cattell, P. 1950. Measurement of Intelligence of Infants and Young Children. The Psychological Corporation, New York.

Cratty, B. J. 1970. Perceptual and Motor Development in Infants and Children. Macmillan Publishing Co., Inc., New York.

Doll, E. A. 1965. Vineland Social Maturity Scale. American Guidance Service, Circle Pines, Minn.

Doll, E. A. 1966. Preschool Attainment Record. American Guidance Service, Circle Pines, Minn.

Ferguson, C. A., and Slobin, D. I. (eds.). 1973. Studies of Child Language Development. Holt, Rinehart & Winston, Inc., New York.

Ferinden, W., and Jacobson, S. 1969. Educational Interpretation of the Wechsler Intelligence Scale for Children. Remediation Associates, Inc., Linden, N.J.

Frankenburg, W. K., and Dodds, J. B. 1969. Denver Developmental Screening Test. University of Colorado Medical Center, Denver.

Gagne, R. M. 1968. Contributions of learning to human development. Psychol. Rev. 75:177–191.

Gagne, R. M. 1970. The Conditions of Learning. Holt, Rinehart & Winston, Inc., New York.

Gesell, A. L. 1940. The First Five Years of Life. Harper & Row Publishers, New York.

Gesell, A., and Amatruda, C. 1967. Developmental Diagnosis. 2nd Ed. Harper & Row Publishers, New York.

Gronlund, N. E. 1971. Measurement and Evaluation in Teaching. 2nd Ed. Macmillan Publishing Co., Inc., New York.

Inhelder, B., and Piaget, J. 1958. The Growth of Logical Thinking from Childhood to Adolescence. Basic Books, Inc., New York.

Johnson, D. J., and Myklebust, H. 1967. Learning Disabilities: Educational Principles and Practices. Grune & Stratton, New York.

Kirk, S., McCarthy, J., and Kirk, W. 1968. Examiner's Manual. Illinois Test of Psycholinguistic Abilities. University of Illinois Press, Urbana.

Menysk, P. 1971. The Acquisition of Language: The Study of Developmental Psycholinguistics. Harper & Row Publishers, New York.

Sanford, A. R. (undated). Learning Accomplishment Profile, Chapel Hill Training-Outreach Project. Kaplan School Supply Corporation, Winston-Salem, N.C.

Stallings, L. 1973. Motor Skills Development and Learning. W. C. Brown, Dubuque, Iowa.

Terango, L. 1977. Early Recognition of Speech, Hearing and Language Disorders in Children Under Six Years of Age. Interstate Printers & Publishers, Inc., Danville, Ill.

Thorndike, R. L., and Hagen, E. 1969. Measurement and Evaluation in Psychology and Education. 3rd Ed. John Wiley & Sons, Inc., New York.

Travis, L. E. (ed.). 1972. Handbook of Speech Pathology and Audiology. Appleton-Century-Crofts, New York.

Valett, R. E. 1974. The Remediation of Learning Disabilities. Fearon Publishers, Belmont, Cal.

Valett, R. E. 1978. Developing Cognitive Abilities: Teaching Children to Think. The C. V. Mosby Co., St. Louis.

Module 5

The teacher will demonstrate knowledge of the possible effects of sensory, neurological, physical, and mental disabilities/dysfunctions on pupil behavior and learning. The teacher will list those behaviors that suggest the possible presence of medical problems in pupils.

PRETEST

1. Why is it necessary for teachers to be aware of the possible existence of medical problems in their students? In your answer, list the several ways in which this diagnostic/prescriptive skill influences or is prerequisite to making judicious decisions.
2. Define the term *residual diathesis* (the imponderable X factor).
3. List those behavioral clues that suggest the possible presence of a hearing loss in a pupil. For each behavior selected, identify an equally feasible alternate explanation, i.e., other than hearing loss.
4. List those behavioral clues that suggest the possible presence of a visual loss in a student.
5. Describe the procedures that a teacher should follow during a student's grand mal seizure.
6. Describe the behavior of a pupil manifesting a petit mal seizure. Include in your discussion a way to differentiate petit mal seizures from daydreaming.
7. List the associated dysfunctions that frequently occur in pupils afflicted with cerebral palsy. In your answer, do not differentiate among the various types of cerebral palsy.
8. List several names that have been used to label individuals with minimal cerebral dysfunction.
9. List those behaviors that have become associated with the syndrome known as minimal cerebral dysfunction.
10. List the common signs that indicate an orthopaedic problem.
11. List the classic symptoms of diabetes.
12. List the symptoms generally associated with the presence of an abnormally low blood sugar level.
13. In a brief essay, describe the psychological/environmental impact on pupils whose height and weight deviate markedly from that of their peers.
14. Cite specific examples of life-threatening and fatal chronic diseases. Discuss the special problems encountered by teachers in working with such pupils.
15. List some of the more severe emotional problems that occur in pupils.
16. List as many different alternate feasible explanations you can think of that could possibly justify labeling a pupil "hyperactive." Be sure to include explanations that are less plausible or subtle but nevertheless have validity.

INTRODUCTION AND OVERVIEW

Because of changes in educational philosophy, judicial decisions, and legislative action, e.g., PL 94-142, special pupils are being placed in increasing numbers in the mainstream of education. Public education is being provided to all children and youth, regardless of the severity and multiplicity of handicapping conditions and despite the delaying tactics of some educators. Since most handicapped individuals, especially those with more severe disabilities, are multiply impaired, it will become increasingly necessary for *all* teachers, regular class as well as special, to develop a heightened sophistication relevant to the possible effects of medical disabilities on pupils. Increased diagnostic awareness of medical problems will be necessary as public education accepts its responsibility to educate all of its youth *and* as teachers engage in the critical process of identifying IEOs (Individual Educational Objectives) for each of their students. In addition, as teachers instruct more widely heterogeneous classes and serve on interdisciplinary teams, they must be familiar with the role, scope, function, and terminology of a variety of professionals who provide service to handicapped persons.

Teachers must eventually realize that a heightened awareness of medical problems, as they may exist in their pupils, is an essential diagnostic/prescriptive skill since their proficiency is prerequisite to making judicious decisions about:

1. The need for medical and paramedical diagnosis and/or treatment (see Module 6)
2. Appropriate referral sources
3. Logical individual educational objectives
4. Effective and efficient learning activities and experiences
5. Suitable classroom organization practices and procedures
6. Perceptive behavioral management strategies and techniques
7. Facilitative methods, materials, and specialized equipment
8. Skillful and productive teacher-parent interactions

Certainly it is not contemplated that teachers will become competent in medical diagnoses. What is necessary is an increased sensitivity to those patterns or constellations of behaviors that suggest the presence of a medical problem(s), especially when the problem can be ameliorated or reversed and when that problem may adversely affect pupil behavior and learning. The prolonged contact with pupils provides teachers with a valuable opportunity to contribute to the prevention of primary and secondary disabilities by helping pupils obtain critical medical and other noneducational therapeutic services. It is axiomatic that the earlier the identification of disability, the greater the likelihood that it will be reversed or its debilitating effects minimized.

Sensory Impairments

Among the most significant physiological reasons that could account for a pupil's underachievement and/or deviant behavior are impairments in sensory acuity. Since vision and hearing are the primary sensory modalities through which learning occurs, pupils with more than minimal deficits in these areas may encounter difficulties in acquiring knowledge and skills in a broad range of instructional domains. Pupils with auditory acuity deficits will probably encounter problems in language, cognitive, and social skill development; pupils with visual impairments are predisposed to develop problems in sensorimotor, social, and preacademic/academic areas, particularly those areas that require intact visual acuity, processing, and memory.

Hearing Loss   When one considers the possible effects of a hearing loss on pupil behavior and learning, it is best to view the loss from a functional perspective, i.e., the relationship between severity and type of loss and their relative impact on an individual. Severity of hearing loss is measured, typically, using class categorization.

Class 1 or mild hearing loss refers to a loss ranging between 21 and 40 dB. (A decibel, dB, is the unit of measure indicating the relative measure of sound intensity.) A pupil with a mild hearing loss experiences little difficulty in a typical classroom setting, although he/she may have problems in hearing distant or faint speech. In addition, he/she may demonstrate some minor articulation problems.

Class 2 or moderate bilateral loss falls between 41 and 55 dB and, invariably, impairs a student's ability to follow conversations at a distance of more than 3 to 6 feet. The student's speech usually is characterized by misarticulations, especially in the articulation of the high frequency consonant sounds that are acoustically similar, e.g., /s/, /f/, and the voiceless /th/.

Class 3 or moderately severe bilateral loss (56–70 dB) generally makes it impossible for pupils thus affected to function in group situations since they are unable to follow conversational speech unless it is very close or unusually loud. Speech and voice production and the development of language skills are usually impaired.

Class 4 or severe bilateral loss (71–90 dB) makes it impossible for an individual to follow conversations. Although single words may be heard at a distance of about one foot, several loud environmental sounds may also be heard. Individuals with such losses, even when a hearing aid or aids prove beneficial, often (in the absence of special education and speech, hearing, and language therapy) speak unintelligibly because of their faulty articulation and abnormal voice production. Oral language comprehension usually is markedly impaired, as is expression.

Class 5 or bilaterally profound hearing loss (greater than 90 dB) results in the pupil's functioning as an educationally deaf student. Although the pupil may react to very intense sounds on occasion, he/she is profoundly handicapped in the ability to communicate orally and in the development of cognitive and affective skills.

While there are five classes of hearing loss, as well as several different types (i.e., conductive, sensorineural, mixed, and central auditory problems), and a variety of causes, it is not necessary that teachers differentiate these several aspects. Diagnostic precision *is* required in such professions as audiology, otology, and otolaryngology, the practitioners of which understand the importance of time of loss, duration of loss, and the sound frequencies involved. While they are concerned with exact measurements and their interpretations, the perceptive teacher will be sensitive to the existence of the so-called residual diathesis or the imponderable X factor, which explains variations in performance between and among pupils with approximately similar conditions, knowledge, and attributes. The unknown factor, undoubtedly, includes such intrapsychic variables as interest, motivation, accommodation, and adaptability.

The behaviors that should alert a teacher to the possibility of a hearing loss are listed below. In reviewing this list, it should be remembered that each behavior identified only assumes importance if it occurs in concert with others and with a degree of consistency. Diagnostic awareness involves sophisticated risktaking, i.e., a delicate balance between aggressive sleuthing and humility. Teachers must not be afraid to make errors in their diagnostic hypothesizing as long as they realize fully that they are dealing merely with hypotheses. With increased awareness of behavioral clues to medical problems, there will be a tendency initially to over-refer pupils for suspected medical problems. Considering the devastating impact an undetected pathology can have on an individual, over-referral is preferable to under-referral. It is better to refer many who, when tested, are found to be functioning within normal limits than to miss one pupil who needs help.

As you examine the list, it should prove valuable to suggest alternate feasible explanations (AFEs), other than hearing loss, that explain the behavior stipulated. Through this process, it should become clear that matching a particular behavior with a specific condition may *just* be reckless hypothesizing. For each behavior listed, one or more AFEs is offered. A number of these AFEs appear obvious and logical while others seem remote and implausible. Both types of AFEs have been included because teachers will discover that that which appears to be most plausible sometimes provides a spurious lead, while, on occasion, the more subtle or implausible explanation is the true one.

Behavioral Clues Suggesting Hearing Loss

1. The pupil responds better when closer to the sound source.
   AFE (Alternate Feasible Explanation): The pupil has attention problems and is less distracted when nearer the sound source.
2. The pupil's ability to respond increases markedly when there are only slight decreases in distance from speaker.
   AFE: The pupil attends better when closer to the speaker and benefits from nonverbal clues such as body language.
3. The pupil responds to sound but is unable to follow simple commands or answer simple questions.
   AFE: The pupil has difficulty in language comprehension although he/she hears the sounds.
   AFE: The pupil has difficulty in remembering the words he/she has just heard.
4. The pupil may distort or omit sounds, especially consonants. This may be particularly true for final sounds and word endings.
   AFE: The pupil speaks that way because his/her parents and peers speak that way.
5. The pupil's voice quality, pitch, resonance patterns, and volume may be poor. (Problems in speech and voice production are highly symptomatic of hearing impairment.)
   AFE: There is something organically wrong with the pupil's vocal mechanism.
   AFE: The pupil is speaking at too low a pitch for his/her vocal apparatus, resulting in a hoarse voice with low volume and poor resonance because he/she wants to sound older and tougher to survive in the family and/or neighborhood.
6. The pupil may stare closely at the speaker's face in order to benefit more fully from visual clues to supplement defective hearing.
   AFE: The pupil is having problems with auditory processing, e.g., auditory discrimination, and is seeking visual clues to what is being said.
7. The pupil may suffer a lag in speech and language development despite a higher level of general overall intellectual functioning.
   AFE: The pupil has a problem with speech production, i.e., an expressive aphasia in which, despite satisfactory auditory skills, he/she is unable to carry out the motor plan necessary to speak with facility.
8. The pupil may present behavioral problems from frustration and confusion due to an inability to comprehend the auditory cues and general behavior of others. He/she may be inattentive, hyperactive, uncontrollable, and even destructive.

AFEs: The pupil may be hungry, tired, or suffering from physical abuse.

9. The pupil may fail to respond or responds inappropriately to oral directions or questions.

    AFE: The teacher speaks too softly. (Note: Teachers tend to believe that the cause of the problem lies within the pupil rather than within their own behavior *or* because of the classroom or school environment.)

    AFE: The pupil does not know the answer.

10. In response to oral questions, the pupil uses expletives such as "Huh?" or "What?"

    AFE: The pupil has problems processing speech when it is spoken at too fast a rate and says "Huh?" while he/she is still processing the information.

11. The pupil may complain about an inability to hear. (Pupils frequently self-diagnose, so teachers should be especially alert to self-diagnostic statements.)

    AFE: The pupil is confusing poor ability to discriminate or comprehend with the inability to hear.

    AFE: The pupil is seeking attention.

12. The pupil may tilt his/her head to one side to hear better with the better ear.

    AFE: The pupil is tilting his/her head to one side because of a visual defect.

    AFE: A physical anomaly of the neck vertebrae exists.

In addition to the above actions that suggest the possibility of a hearing impairment, behaviors may occur that suggest the presence of active pathology involving the ear. Such behaviors include:

1. The pupil may pull on or rub an earlobe, rub the ear itself or behind the ear, and/or place an index finger in and scratch the opening of the ear.

    AFE (Alternate Feasible Explanation): The pupil has an allergy that causes an itching in the ear canal.

2. The pupil has an obvious discharge from the ear.

    AFE: This occurrence is such a hard sign of active pathology that no AFE is necessary.

3. The pupil complains of earaches or frequent ringing in his/her ear. Again, teachers should not disregard a pupil's self-evaluation.

    AFEs: The pupil is seeking the attention of the teacher *or* is trying to avoid a specific assignment.

Furthermore, whenever a pupil has been absent because of a disease process characterized by a high fever, the teacher should be alert to the possibility that the high fever disease process might have caused damage to the highly fragile peripheral auditory nerve endings. An audiometric test should be scheduled whenever a pupil returns to school after having been ill with a febrile disease.

Visual Impairments It should be recognized that early diagnosis and treatment of visual problems, in a majority of cases, might have prevented permanent disabilities. Thus, it is essential that teachers be sensitive to possible visual defects not only because of their possible deleterious effects on pupil learning and behavior but because the teachers can assist pupils in obtaining needed diagnosis and/or treatment from an ophthalmologist.

Some of the pupil behaviors that suggest the presence of ocular pathology include the following:

1. Rubbing his/her eyes frequently
2. Squinting
3. Closing one eye and tilting the head to one side
4. Assuming unusual reading and writing positions when working with books or at chalkboards
5. Sitting too close to a television set or movie screen
6. Performing academically at an inadequate level despite level of general intellectual functioning
7. Complaining of blurred vision
8. Complaining of double vision
9. Complaining of ocular pain and/or headache
10. Pupil's eyes seem to be "crossed," i.e., misalignment of the eyes, for example, one eye deviates toward the nose
11. Rapidly moving eyes especially in the horizontal plane
12. Complaining of ocular discomfort when exposed to bright lights
13. Complaining that he/she cannot see at night or in dim light
14. Experiencing difficulty catching a ball or reaching for objects
15. Exhibiting a lack of physical coordination with mobility problems
16. Complaining of a dark or black spot in the center of his/her eye(s)
17. Inability to see small letters and requiring large print books and/or magnifying equipment
18. Is handicapped in athletics and other physical activities

Neurological Disorders

Epilepsy Epilepsy is one of the most misunderstood of all handicapping conditions. The myths surrounding epilepsy abound, associating epilepsy with various forms of degeneracy and perverted practices of the parents or the pupil. These negative myths have resulted in active discrimination against persons with epilepsy. This discrimination is evidenced in prejudicial laws and employment policies and in various forms of bigotry, including physical and psychological abuse, ranging from ridicule to ostracism.

There are four principal types of epilepsy that occur in children.

Grand Mal or Major Motor Seizures The child with this most common form of epilepsy, at times, can anticipate a seizure because of an aura or other prodromal sign, e.g., flashing lights, a characteristic odor, fatigue, and confusion. Usually the seizure begins with a sudden loss of consciousness followed by rhythmic, synchronous movements of both the face and rigid extremities. The child may stay in this stage for minutes, or even hours, before he/she relaxes and begins to move spontaneously. Usually, the child is tired and prefers to sleep after the seizure is over.

Because of its dramatic nature and potentially dangerous effects, a grand mal seizure requires the judicious intervention of the teacher. During the seizure, the pupil should be removed from dangerous areas, e.g., a woodworking or metal shop. Hard-surfaced furniture should be removed to prevent damage to extremities striking against them. The pupil should be placed in a position where he/she is lying on his/her side with any confining clothing loosened. The pupil's mouth and nose should be uncovered, and, if possible, food and gum removed from the mouth. If movements are vigorous, the pupil should be restrained gently and comforted. A padded object, such as a stick, prepared in advance should be gently inserted between the teeth to prevent a pupil from biting his/her tongue during a seizure. A comfortable, private place should be provided in which the pupil may rest after the seizure is over. When a pupil fails to come out of the seizure, emergency medical help should be obtained. Strategies for obtaining specialized medical help should be established beforehand.

Petit Mal Seizures This type of epilepsy manifests itself by brief episodes of staring. The pupil appears to lose control momentarily or drifts away. If speaking, speech will be interrupted, staring into space will occur, and eyelids will flutter. After a brief moment, the vacuous look will disappear and the conversation will be resumed where previously left off. These seizures may occur so frequently that attention to tasks is impossible and school performance disintegrates. Although it is somewhat difficult to differentiate petit mal seizures form daydreaming, lapses in behavior during active learning as opposed to passive learning may indicate seizure activity.

Psychomotor or Temporal Lobe Epilepsy These seizures are difficult to identify without instrumentation because their bizarre nature resembles the behavior sometimes witnessed in pupils with psychiatric disorders. The multiplicity of ways in which these seizures manifest themselves further complicates differential diagnosis, i.e., the process through which a diagnosis is made among several conditions that closely resemble each other.

The symptoms of temporal lobe epilepsy include the following:

1. Hallucinatory behavior
2. Complaints of abdominal discomfort
3. Complaints of headaches
4. Unusual movements of the tongue and lips
5. Repetitive, ritualistic motor movements
6. Learning disorders
7. Shortened attention span
8. Bizarre behavior—the pupil behaves as though frightened (he/she might run after and hold on to a teacher or classmate as though panic-stricken)
9. Physical signs appear: pallor or flushing, salivation, perspiration, and rapid pulse rate
10. Temper tantrums and other acting-out behaviors

Minor Motor Seizures   Symptoms of minor motor seizures include:

1. Brief lapses of consciousness
2. Loss of body tone
3. Falling

Teachers, in establishing individual educational objectives (IEOs) for pupils afflicted with epilepsy, should keep in mind that these pupils should be encouraged to lead as normal a life as possible. Pupils with epilepsy need to understand and appreciate the reasons for long-term medication. Pupils who manifest seizures should be allowed to engage in all activities, except swimming, unattended. Timeout techniques, in which the pupil is left unattended in an area set off from the rest of the class, should be discouraged. The teacher of a class in which there is a pupil with epilepsy should add a unit of experience on epilepsy and other developmental disabilities so that the stigma of being handicapped may be lessened and then, it is hoped, eradicated. Occasionally, the teacher may become aware of a specific stimulus that triggers seizures; the teacher should use such insights in program planning and in helping the pupil avoid adversive stimuli.

Cerebral Palsy   Cerebral palsy may be defined as a developmental disability in which the individual has difficulty in the motor control of certain muscle groups accompanied by associated problems in intellectual, sensory, perceptual, speech, and behavioral functioning and development. Cerebral palsy is a multidimensional syndrome reflecting underlying brain damage.

The various types of cerebral palsy have been classified as follows: spasticity, athetosis, ataxia, tremor, atonia, rigidity, and mixed types.

Spasticity   The symptoms of spasticity include:

1. Increase in muscle tone
2. High incidence of seizures
3. High incidence of sensory impairment, including diminished ability to recognize an object by touch and a reduced awareness of pain and light touch
4. Loss of vision including visual field defects, i.e., part of the 360° sphere of vision is impaired
5. Weakness or paralysis of one or more extremities
6. A high incidence of mental retardation
7. A high incidence of perceptual and other learning disabilities

Athetosis   The symptoms of athetosis include:

1. Slow, involuntary, writhing movements that increase upon intention, i.e., whenever the pupil attempts to perform some purposeful activity, such as speaking, the involuntary movements increase (this factor has major implications for the establishment of IEOs since the teacher typically expects pupils to perform specific motor tasks, such as writing, speaking, and playing)
2. High incidence of sensorineural high frequency hearing loss
3. High incidence of speech disorders
4. High incidence of seizure disorders but lower in frequency than in spasticity
5. High incidence of dental abnormalities
6. High incidence of mental retardation but higher intelligence than in other types of cerebral palsy
7. High incidence of feeding problems, particularly chewing and swallowing, because of the repetitive tongue thrust and excessive stiffening of the body in an extended position during attempts to eat or speak

Ataxia   The symptoms of ataxia include:

1. Disturbance of balance sense
2. Loss of kinesthesia, i.e., loss of sense of awareness of position in space
3. High incidence of mental retardation
4. High incidence of visual deficits

Tremor   The essential symptom of tremor is regular and rhythmical involuntary shaking movements.

Atonia   The essential symptom of atonia, an extremely rare form of cerebral palsy, is the lack of muscle tone or flaccidity.

Rigidity   The main symptoms of this type of cerebral palsy are rigidity of the musculature and a high incidence of mental retardation.

The effect of all types of cerebral palsy on behavior and learning is directly related to the existing motor impairment, its type, severity, parts affected, and to the presence of associated dysfunctions. While the pupil's motor impairment may require special devices, materials, facilities, and the services of a wide range of therapists and various medical specialists, the establishment of individual educational objectives cannot proceed with any wisdom unless attention is paid to the multiple handicaps usually associated with this organic syndrome. For example, the level of cognitive functioning will help determine both educational goal selection and program planning. Since a significant number of pupils have perceptual and other learning discrepancies, these additional deficits must be considered in any program plan. Along with the motor, perceptual, and cognitive correlates of brain damage, frequently the pupil manifests behavior often associated with cerebral dysfunction, e.g., hyperactivity, perseveration, impulsivity, and distractibility. When these behavioral deficits occur, the teacher must incorporate appropriate and relevant goals in an individually designed curriculum hierarchy. The existence of sensory impairments in vision and/or hearing must be considered in a total program of education and rehabilitation as must the fact of emotional disturbance; many cerebral palsied pupils, especially those who are brighter, suffer from frustration, social isolation, bitterness, depression, and hostility if and when they come to realize their relative helplessness, hopelessness, and deviance from others. The presence of seizure activity further complicates the problem of educational goal identification, program planning, and implementation. The presence of communication deficits not only influences educational programming and management but also hampers effective educational diagnosis.

Minimal Cerebral Dysfunction   Perhaps no other category of handicapping conditions has provoked as much controversy or been responsible for as much confusion as has the syndrome of minimal cerebral dysfunction. The vagueness surrounding this condition is perhaps best demonstrated by the profusion of alternate labels, definitions, and symptom enumerations which, in effect, renders minimal cerebral dysfunction a non-entity categorization. Because of the lack of symptom homogeneity, a long list of identifying labels has emerged. Out of the confusion has arisen a multitude of remedial and therapeutic interventions from a variety of professionals and from those whose professionalism is easily challenged. Unfortunately, in the absence of clarity, many parents have been victimized by cultists and opportunists who have taken advantage of this enigmatic condition. As one *views* the list of symptoms that has been subsumed under the diverse rubrics (Strauss syndrome, hyperkinetic syndrome, minimally brain damaged, psychoneurological learning disability, specific learning disabilities), *looks* at the subjectivity of these symptoms (e.g., hyperactivity and short attention span), *examines* the presence in the syndrome of two diametrically opposed behaviors (i.e., hyperactivity and hypoactivity), and *questions* the inclusion of practices that are, at times, nonpathological because of normal or slight lags in development (e.g., letter reversals, short attention span, and minor fine motor problems), it becomes abundantly clear that minimal cerebral dysfunction (MCD) as a separate and distinct syndrome has fostered much magical thinking and rewarded program and material designers who have exploited desperate parents and their children.

The many symptoms that are included in the MCD syndrome follow:

1. Short attention span or distractibility
2. Perseveration (an inability to shift attention and to persist in a particular thought or action)
3. Hyperactivity (hyperkinesis) (drivenness)
4. Hypoactivity
5. Poor impulse control (impulsivity)
6. Low frustration tolerance
7. Emotional lability
8. Clumsiness, awkwardness, incoordination (fine and gross motor)
9. Reading problems (dyslexia)
10. Writing problems (agraphia)
11. Oral language problems (the aphasias)
12. Arithmetic problem (acalculia)
13. Social imperception
14. Poor response to reward and punishment
15. Antisocial behavior
16. Incompetent learning through pictures
17. Perceptual problems (e.g., figure-ground confusion, letter and word reversals, poor auditory and visual discrimination, etc.)
18. Memory deficits (i.e., poor auditory and visual memory)
19. Body image difficulties
20. Spatial orientation inadequacy
21. Confusion in laterality or lack of cerebral dominance
22. Problems with left-right orientation
23. Paradoxical response to stimulant drugs such as Ritalin and

Dexedrine, i.e., stimulants decrease activity and increase attention in individuals with MCD, while in others, these drugs would have the opposite effects

From a perusal of the above list of symptoms, a teacher must realize that heightened awareness to the presence of this syndrome requires a degree of sophistication, insight, and understanding of behavioral dynamics that is awesome. Since any pupil labeled as having this broadly heterogeneous syndrome may have various combinations of the symptoms noted, the possible effects on pupil behavior and learning are virtually limitless.

Other Physical Disabilities

Orthopaedic Problems Orthopaedic problems refer to injuries, deformities, and diseases of the musculoskeletal and neuromuscular systems resulting in impairments in the functioning of the muscles, bones, and joints. Common signs that indicate an orthopaedic problem include:

1. Pain in the spine, the extremities, and/or the hips
2. A limp, with or without pain
3. Deformity
4. Restriction of movement
5. Peculiarities in gait
6. Swelling, buckling, and locking of joints

There are countless orthopaedic problems that affect the entire musculoskeletal and neuromuscular systems. Teachers are not expected to know the medical names of these conditions, but they should be responsive to those signs that indicate the possible presence of an orthopaedic condition and should be cognizant of its possible impact on pupil behavior and learning. For example, orthopaedic deformities of the back may make sitting in the classroom uncomfortable; injuries to the upper extremities may interfere with and limit activities such as cutting, writing, drawing, and other fine motor skills. Abnormalities of the hip and lower extremities are frequently more obvious because of the presence of a limp, with or without pain, during ambulation and other gross motor activities in the classroom, gymnasium, and school play areas. Many pupils with orthopaedic problems will be out of school for long periods of time after surgery or even when nonwalking casts are applied. In many cases, pupils will require physical therapy, splinting, bracing, and other prostheses and orthoses. (Prostheses replace missing limbs and limb segments; orthoses are devices fitted on patients with disabling conditions of the spine and limbs.)

Many pupils with orthopaedic problems require daily medication, and those with pain may become hostile, irritable, uncooperative, bitter, manipulative, and demanding.

Endocrine Disorders

Diabetes Diabetes is the most common endocrinological disorder of childhoood. The classic symptoms of this disorder are:

1. Excessive urination (polyuria)
2. Excessive thirst (polydipsia)
3. Excessive appetite and hunger (polyphagia)
4. Dry skin
5. Sweet or fruity odor to the breath
6. Weight loss

The management of diabetes involves balancing the intake of insulin with a controlled and balance diet and the adjustment of these two management components according to the amount and time of exercise and to the presence of illness. Exercise lessens the need for insulin and illness increases the need.

Hypoglycemia Hypoglycemia refers to an abnormally low blood sugar level which, although it may be caused by various factors, typically is manifested by one or more of the following:

1. Restlessness and irritability
2. Sweating
3. Pallor
4. Throbbing headache
5. Sudden changes in behavior
6. Excessive appetite and hunger (polyphagia)
7. Twitching in the arms and legs
8. Convulsions
9. Coma

In both diabetes (hyperglycemia) and hypoglycemia, the teacher should respond to the pupils as they would to pupils without these conditions. The teacher should participate with significant family members, the physician, and the school nurse in order to help these youngsters manage their behavior, including the use of medication, the intake of food, and the amount and timing of exercise to prevent convulsions, coma, or shock. As is true of any chronic disease or condition, a further emphasis must be on the prevention of secondary effects that interfere with good mental health.

Disorders of Growth In our society, shortness, expecially among males, is viewed in extremely negative terms. Frequently, extremely short pupils are ridiculed unmercifully by their peers and penalized throughout their lives as they compete for jobs, mates, and status. For the short pupil there may also be practical problems in carrying out functional tasks: reaching standing telephones, drinking from a water fountain, and putting school supplies back on shelves. Scapegoating, ridicule, ostracism, and environmental barriers often combine to cause emotional problems, including depression, anger, and withdrawal.

Tallness, on the other hand, in our society is generally rewarded, especially when it occurs in males. Through the years (although styles recently have changed), females who have been abnormally tall have suffered serious secondary effects. Tall females often find it difficult to obtain mates and are viewed as aggressive and competitive by those chauvinistic males who prefer females to be shorter and therefore weaker. Sometimes the rapidly growing female pupil or her family become so alarmed that they seek hormonal therapy: large dosages of estrogen. While a reduction in height may occur, the physical dangers are so great (e.g., cancer) that this mode of treatment generally is discouraged by most physicians.

In cases of disturbances in growth patterns, the role of the teacher as counselor, human development specialist, and mental health worker becomes paramount. As with other handicapping conditions (socially determined), the humanistic teacher strives to provide lessons designed to help normal peers accept the individual differences of their peers who deviate significantly, in any way, from them.

Hyperthyroidism   The overproduction of thyroxin may cause a wide variety of symptoms, including:

1. Protruding eyes
2. Sweating
3. Restlessness, nervousness, and irritability
4. Weakness
5. Insomnia
6. Excessive hunger and unexpected weight loss
7. Emotional lability
8. Deterioration of school performance and achievement

Obesity   While the cause of obesity appears related to faulty eating behaviors and patterns of exercise, genetic factors apparently play a significant role. Obesity is considered to be a serious nutritional, behavioral, emotional, and metabolic disorder. The teacher must bear in mind, however, that regardless of etiology, the obese pupil usually suffers similar indignities as does the short pupil. The fat child invariably is subjected to merciless ridicule by peers and others; self-hatred, bitterness, anger, and hostility often result, although these feelings may be masked by the jolly fat person and the clown syndromes. Because of the adverse impact on physical and mental health, the teacher must be sensitive to the problems facing the obese pupil. By judiciously selecting healthy snacks and party foods, he/she helps not only the obese but all members of the class. The teacher must also plan lessons on proper nutrition and incorporate physical fitness activities in the daily routine. More important, he/she must become an advocate for removing all junk food and drink dispensers from school cafeterias.

Life-Threatening and Fatal Chronic Diseases

In establishing IEOs for pupils with fatal illnesses, a teacher has two major concerns: providing an educational program for these pupils because school is the normal work of chidhood and young adulthood, and dealing with the emotional responses of these pupils to their illnesses. Anxiety, regression, loss of appetite, apathy, restlessness, guilt, depression, anger, bitterness, and acting-out behavior may be characteristic. A marked preoccupation with death and destruction may permeate their expressive verbal and nonverbal behaviors. Teachers working with pupils who are facing death or who suspect that they are dying must deal first with their own attitudes and feelings toward death and the dying, second with those of their pupils, and third with those of parent, siblings, and other family members. Parents may pass through several stages of adaptive mechanisms in coping with the impending death of their child. It is not clear, however, whether there is a predictable pattern to those stages or that all of the stages are passed through regardless of sequence.

Common life-threatening diseases include:

Cystic Fibrosis As cystic fibrosis progresses, physical activities must be severely limited because of shortness of breath. Hospitalization, physical therapy, and postural drainage are frequently necessary.

Congenital Heart Disease Before correction, congenital heart disease is characterized by shortness of breath, limited exercise tolerance, and possible bluish appearance of the skin. The pupil with heart problems that persist (despite partial surgical correction) should be encouraged to participate in all activities but not to the point of excessive fatigue. When there is complete correction, however, they should be encouraged to participate in all activities. Both children and adults who have had heart conditions often become cardiac cripples, afraid to participate fully in normal and enriching life experiences.

Kidney Failure When the kidneys are damaged by infections and other disease processes, including congenital malformations that are progressive, they may become nonfunctioning. The failure to rid the body of waste products results in a variety of symptoms, including swelling of the ankles, impaired growth, fatigue, susceptibility to infections, and hypertension (high blood pressure). Confusion, coma, and death characterize the final stages of kidney (renal) failure. Dialysis and transplantation remain the only hope for individuals with progressive degeneration of the kidneys, although these procedures may only delay the final stages of the disease process.

Leukemia   Leukemia is a malignancy of the bone marrow. Symptomatology of developing leukemia include excessive fatigue, weight loss, joint pains, fever, pallor, and excessive bruising. These symptoms are also common to other diseases including mononucleosis.

Tumors   Tumors result from the excessive growth of cells that may occur in any organ or bodily system. Malignant tumors are those with such a degree of uncontrolled cell growth that death is likely. Methods of medical management include medication (chemotherapy), radiation, and surgery. Teachers must be sensitive to the fears and anxieties of pupils who have benign or malignant tumors, in an active state or in remission, and whether the pupils are in a public school or a hospital classroom.

Juvenile Muscular Dystrophy   The juvenile form of muscular dystrophy leads to death generally by the late teens. Because of the progressive deterioration in motoric performance in previously healthy young children (usually young boys), the anticipation of death and the progressive disintegration of the pupil dramatically affects pupil personality and teacher-pupil interaction. A teacher must be aware that the prognosis of an early death has great impact on the establishment of individual educational objectives and plans, especially since educators typically function from within a long-term frame of reference. How does a teacher deal with the anger expressed by a dying pupil, anger expressed against him/her? How does a teacher handle the pupil's responses to a missing classmate who has died over the weekend? How does a teacher prepare a pupil for the goal of an independent adulthood when there is increasing physical dependency and no adulthood to be expected? These are, indeed, difficult questions for a teacher to deal with.

Hemophilia   Despite recent advances in the management of pupils with hemophilia (classic hemophilia occurs only in males), a threat to life still exists depending upon the severity of the condition, the availability and cost of antihemophilic factor (AHF), and the boy's interests and risk-taking behaviors. Like many other handicapping conditions, teachers (and parents) must avoid interactions that encourage excessive dependency and that foster pupil tyranny and manipulation.

Sickle Cell Anemia   Sickle cell anemia is an ethnic disease, occurring most frequently in Black Americans, that may cause death in childhood. Symptoms of excessive fatigue, fever, abdominal discomfort, and bone pain may not only require hospitalization, but when they do occur, they may affect pupil behavior and learning. Most pupils suffering from sickle cell anemia, when not in the acute stage, usually can function in most school activities, with the exception of physical activities, which may be too exhausting.

Other Chronic Diseases

Kidney Infection   Students with kidney infections may run a fever, urinate frequently, and complain of back pain or burning when voiding. Frequent trips to the bathroom have many AFEs, including getting away from a boring classroom, going out for a smoke, meeting a friend from another classroom, anxiety, and, possibly, diabetes.

Allergies   Allergies refer to an excessive and abnormal response to foreign substances. Allergic conditions include allergic rhinitis, which may cause pupils to miss school, to be extremely uncomfortable and irritable from its symptoms, or to be drowsy or confused in response to antihistamines. Asthma is a chronic disorder characterized by labored breathing that may occur in response to various allergens, colds, and emotional stress. Because severe wheezing can be a traumatic experience, pupils may develop excessive dependency on parents, thus adding a further responsibility to the teacher, who should assist the pupil toward independence and minimize school-based stress factors that may precipitate asthmatic attacks.

Eczema   Eczema is characterized by thickened, reddened, itchy areas usually occurring in the creases of the elbows, at the back of the knees, and on the neck. Skin blemishes may be a source of acute embarrassment to a pupil, especially when the pupil's classmates are repelled by the sores. Any form of skin blemish, especially those that occur around the face, and facial disfigurements of any kind may be especially repugnant to classmates, and thus cause serious emotional and social problems for pupils so afflicted.

Results of Accidents

Burns   An individual who survives serious burns from fire, hot water, or steam frequently is left with scars, limb contractures, and disfigured appearances. These conditions may lead to serious emotional problems, including emotional regression, nightmares, and withdrawal. When the pupil's sibling(s) has died from the fire, the pupil frequently may require psychotherapeutic intervention to deal with the resulting guilt for having been spared.

Limb Deficiences   While many limb anomalies are congenital in origin, many result from vehicular accidents: bicycle, cars, and tractors. The prosthesis applied to replace a missing limb must achieve a balance between functional use and cosmetic appearance. Pupils will react differently at various stages of their lives to the use and type of prosthesis e.g., teenagers tend to be more concerned with cosmetics than with function.

Brain Damage   Head injuries result from trauma: falls, diving and car accidents, and gunshot wounds; oxygen deprivation from carbon monoxide poisoning and near drownings; ingestion of poisons (e.g., lead and cleaning fluids); and ingestion of medicines in abnormal quantities. Brain damage may result in sensory impairments; perceptual, memory, and learning deficits; mental retardation; cerebral palsy; and epilepsy.

Birth Defects

There are so many birth defects that it is impossible to describe them in sufficient detail without interfering with the balance of this book. It should be remembered, however, that an awareness of the presence of a specific condition will invariably have implications for the establishing IEOs and IEPs (individualized educational programs). For example, a teacher who has a pupil with spina bifida will find it necessary to modify the teaching objectives and to change the methods and materials selected because of the effects of paraplegia, possible paralysis of the bladder and/or sphincter muscles, and the loss of sensory function.

In other cases, carefully controlled diets, special drug regimens, and specialized therapeutic interventions will be necessary. Whenever a pupil is enrolled in a specific class, the teacher must conduct the necessary research to determine the idiosyncratic impact of that condition on pupil behavior and learning.

Emotional Problems

Many of the behaviors identified below may be normal when viewed from a developmental perspective. For example, temper tantrums may be within normal limits for a preschooler but not for a 16-year-old. Other behaviors, when they occur singly and do not persist over time, may be explained as transient and do not indicate serious problems, e.g., anxiety and oversensitivity that are situation specific and will diminish with time. However, there are certain behaviors that tend to indicate serious psychological/psychiatric problems, especially when they persist.

The more severe indicators of emotional problems occurring in pupils include, but are not limited to:

1. Excessive lethargy or its opposite, hyperactivity
2. Noncommunicative behavior, such as elective mutism
3. Frequent use of the toilet for evacuation
4. Tics and ritualistic behaviors
5. Extreme withdrawal, apathy, depression, and grief
6. Self-destructive behavior

7. Sexual exhibitionism, sexual assaults, and sexual aberrations
8. Extreme somatic complaints in the absence of physical causes
9. Recurrent hypochondriasis
10. Stealing
11. Pathological lying
12. Cruelty to animals
13. Cruelty to the defenseless and weak (the young, the elderly, and the handicapped)
14. Firesetting
15. School phobia and truancy

ACTIVITIES AND EXPERIENCES

1. For each of the behaviors identified as indicating possible emotional problems, suggest alternate feasible explanations.
2. A pupil in a hypothetical classroom is diagnosed as being "hyperactive." List at least 10 alternate reasons for this type of behavior.
3. Review several articles found in medical journals that discuss diseases of children and youth. For each of the diseases discussed, describe the implications for the establishment of individual educational objectives.
4. Visit a special school for the visually impaired. Describe the modifications in programming, methods, materials, and equipment. Make sure you describe program objectives and their priorities that deviate significantly from those of other school populations.
5. Visit a special school for hearing-impaired pupils. Describe the modifications in programming, methods, materials, and equipment. Make sure you describe program objectives and their priorities that deviate significantly from those of other school populations.
6. Visit a special school for the physically impaired. Describe the modifications in programming, methods, materials, and equipment. Make sure you describe program objectives and their priorities that deviate significantly from those of other school populations.
7. Visit a special school for the neurologically impaired. Describe the modifications in programming, methods, materials, and equipment. Make sure you describe program objectives and their priorities that deviate significantly from those of other school populations.
8. Visit a special school for the emotionally disturbed. Describe the modifications in programming, methods, materials, and equipment. Make sure you describe program objectives and their priorities that deviate significantly from those of other school populations.
9. List the behaviors that suggest that a pupil may be autistic. Discuss the possible effects of autism on pupil behavior and learning. Describe the impact on establishing educational objectives.

10. Select a pupil with a medical problem. The pupil may be in your present class, in a previous class, or in a class in which you are student teaching or involved in some other field experience. Describe how the medical condition influences his/her behavior. Discuss how his/her condition affects the selection of educational objectives.

11. Write a position paper on why knowledge of the possible effects of sensory, neurological, physical, and mental disabilities/dysfunctions on pupil behavior and learning is prerequisite to the establishment of suitable, relevant, and appropriate individual educational objectives.

12. Discuss and describe the problems that could arise from inferring that a pupil in your class possesses a medical problem based upon your classroom observation of his/her behaviors. Be sure to include in your discussion the need for diagnostic humility, the importance of noting patterns or constellations of behavior over time, and the requirement of making judgments from a developmental perspective.

CONCLUDING STATEMENT

In arriving at IEOs, the teacher must, in carrying out various diagnostic procedures, pay special attention to the existence of untoward medical problems that will influence curriculum priorities, methodological approaches, classroom organization and behavioral management procedures, and the selection and preparation of instructional materials.

Teachers must continue to add to their knowledge regarding the impact that medical problems have on pupil behavior and learning. As supreme generalists they must, nevertheless, develop a sensitivity to or heightened awareness of those factors affecting pupil performance, factors that may indicate the existence of physiological, psychological, and sociological problems that would require the interventions of other professionals who provide services to humans in need.

POSTTEST

At this point retake the Pretest.

SUGGESTED READINGS

Anthony, E. (ed.). 1975. Exploration in Child Psychiatry. Plenum Press, New York.

Bakwin, H., and Bakwin, R. M. 1972. Behavior Disorders in Children. 4th Ed. W. B. Saunders Co., Philadelphia.

Berkler, M. S., Bible, G. H., Boles, S. M., Deitz, E. D., and Repp, A. C. 1978. Current Trends for the Developmentally Disabled. University Park Press, Baltimore.

Bigge, J. L., and O'Donnell, P. A. 1976. Teaching Individuals with Physical and Multiple Disabilities. Charles E. Merrill Publishing Co., Columbus, Oh.

Bleck, E. E., and Nagel, D. A. (eds.). 1975. Physically Handicapped Children—A Medical Atlas for Teachers. Grune & Stratton, New York.

Cruickshank, W. M. (ed.). 1971. Psychology of Exceptional Children and Youth. 3rd Ed. Prentice-Hall, Inc., Englewood Cliffs, N.J.

Cruickshank, W. M., and Johnson, G. O. (eds.). 1967. Education of Exceptional Children and Youth. Prentice-Hall, Inc., Englewood Cliffs, N.J.

Davis, H., and Silverman, S. R. 1970. Hearing and Deafness. Holt, Rinehart & Winston, Inc., New York.

Debuskey, M. 1970. The Chronically Ill Child and His Family. Charles C Thomas Publisher, Springfield, Ill.

Denhoff, E., and Robinault, I. P. 1960. Cerebral Palsy and Related Disorders. McGraw-Hill Book Co., New York.

Doster, M. E. 1975. School vision screening. Sight-Saving Rev. 45:168–170.

Downey, J. A., and Low, N. 1974. The Child with a Disabling Illness: Principles of Rehabilitation. W. B. Saunders Co., Philadelphia.

Dunn, L. M. (ed.). 1963. Exceptional Children in the Schools. Holt, Rinehart & Winston, Inc., New York.

Gardner, L. E. (ed.). 1969. Endocrine and Genetic Diseases of Childhood. W. B. Saunders Co., Philadelphia.

Garner, A. M., and Thompson, C. W. 1974. Factors in the management of juvenile diabetes. Pediatr. Psychol. 2:6–7.

Gearheart, B. R., and Weishahn, M. W. 1976. The Handicapped Child in the Regular Classroom. C. V. Mosby Co., St. Louis.

Gerwin, K. S., and Glorig, A. 1974. Detection of Hearing Loss and Ear Disease in Children. Charles C Thomas Publisher, Springfield, Ill.

Goldenson, R. M., Dunham, J. R., and Dunham, C. S., (eds.). 1978. Disability and Rehabilitation Handbook. McGraw-Hill Book Co., New York.

Guyton, A. 1977. Basic Human Physiology: Normal Functions and Mechanisms of Disease. 2nd Ed. W. B. Saunders Co., Philadelphia.

Hammill, D. D., and Bartel, N. R. 1971. Educational Perspectives in Learning Disabilities. John Wiley & Sons, Inc., New York.

Haslam, R. H. A., and Valletutti, P. J. (eds.). 1975. Medical Problems in the Classroom: The Teacher's Role in Diagnosis and Management. University Park Press, Baltimore.

Johnson, D. J., and Myklebust, H. R. 1967. Learning Disabilities: Educational Principles and Practices. Grune & Stratton, New York.

Johnson, W., and Moellers, D. (eds.). 1967. Speech Handicapped School Children. 3rd Ed. Harper & Row Publishers, New York.

Kirk, S. A. 1972. Educating Exceptional Children. 2nd Ed. Houghton Mifflin Co., Boston.

Kirk, S. A., and Lord, F. E. (eds.). 1974. Exceptional Children: Educational Resources and Perspectives. Houghton Mifflin Co., Boston.

Krajicek, M. J., and Tearney, A. I. (eds.). 1977. Detection of Developmental Problems in Children. University Park Press, Baltimore.

Kubler-Ross, E. 1969. On Death and Dying. Macmillan Publishing Co., Inc., New York.

Laron, Z. (ed.). 1975. Diabetes in Juveniles: Medical and Rehabilitation Aspects. S. Karger, Basel.

Lerner, J. W. 1971. Children with Learning Disabilities: Theories, Diagnosis and Teaching Strategies. Houghton Mifflin Co., Boston.

Livingston, S. 1972. Comprehensive Management of Epilepsy in Infancy, Childhood and Adolescence. Charles C Thomas Publisher, Springfield, Ill.

Lloyd, L. L. (ed.). 1976. Communication Assessment and Intervention Strategies. University Park Press, Baltimore.

Love, H. D., and Walthall, J. E. 1977. A Handbook of Medical, Educational, and Psychological Information for Teachers of Physically Handicapped Children. Charles C Thomas Publisher, Springfield, Ill.

Magrab, P. R. (ed.). 1978. Psychological Management of Pediatric Problems. Vol. I. University Park Press, Baltimore.

Magrab, P. R. (ed.). 1978. Psychological Management of Pediatric Problems. Vol. II. University Park Press, Baltimore.

Meier, J. H. 1976. Developmental and Learning Disabilities. University Park Press, Baltimore.

Meyen, E. L. 1978. Exceptional Children and Youth: An Introduction. Love Publishing Co., Denver.

Patterson, R. (ed.). 1972. Allergic Disease: Diagnosis and Management. J. B. Lippincott Co., Philadelphia.

Reynolds, M. C., and Birch, J. W. 1977. Teaching Exceptional Children in All America's Schools. Council for Exceptional Children, Reston, Va.

Robinson, N. M., and Robinson, H. E. 1976. The Mentally Retarded Child. 2nd Ed. McGraw-Hill Book Co., New York.

Schrag, P., and Divoky, D. 1975. The Myth of the Hyperactive Child. Random House, Inc., New York.

Scott, E. P., Jan, J. E., and Freeman, R. D. 1977. Can't Your Child See? University Park Press, Baltimore.

Smith, R. M., and Neisworth, J. T. 1975. The Exceptional Child: A Functional Approach. McGraw-Hill Book Co., New York.

Spinetta, J. J., Rigler, D., and Karon, M. 1973. Anxiety in the dying child. Pediatrics 52:841–845.

Stanbury, J., Wyngaarden, J., and Fredrickson, D. (eds.). 1972. The Metabolic Basis of Inherited Disease. McGraw-Hill Book Co., New York.

Tachdjian, M. O. 1972. Pediatric Orthopedics. W. B. Saunders Co., Philadelphia.

Travis, L. E. (ed.). 1971. Handbook of Speech Pathology and Audiology. Appleton-Century-Crofts, New York.

Vaugh, V., and McKay, R. J. (eds.). 1975. Nelson Textbook of Pediatrics. W. B. Saunders Co., Philadelphia.

Wender, P. H. 1971. Minimal Brain Dysfunction in Children. John Wiley & Sons, Inc., New York.

Wender, P. H. 1975. The minimal brain dysfunction syndrome. Ann. Rev. Med. 26:45–62.

Wilkins, L., Blizzard, R. M., and Migeon, C. J. 1965. The Diagnosis and Treatment of Endocrine Disorders in Childhood and Adolescence. 3rd Ed. Charles C Thomas Publisher, Springfield, Ill.

Module 6

The teacher will recommend for diagnosis and/or treatment those pupils suspected of having medical or paramedical problems. The teacher will follow an appropriate referral process and will carry out those recommendations that have implications for classroom organization, instruction, pupil management, and continuing evaluation. Whenever feasible, the teacher also will carry out those suggestions that will assist in meeting therapeutic goals, reporting relevant classroom behaviors to those professionals providing various therapeutic interventions.

PRETEST

Part A

Answer *True* or *False*.

1. Teachers are likely to overlook pathological states as the cause of behavioral and learning disabilities, and, instead, search for reasons in the cognitive, motivational, and affective systems or the sociocultural history of pupils.
2. Teachers interact with children and youth on a sustained basis more often than any other professional group and, perhaps, even more so than parents.
3. Teachers have an exceptional opportunity to make perceptive judgments vis-à-vis the existence of physical and mental conditions that interfere with learning.
4. The earlier the detection of a medical problem, the more likely its effects may be diminished, the pathology reversed, and the secondary symptoms, usually of a psychological nature, minimized.
5. Differentiating behaviors of pupils that represent normal development and those that signal a possible abnormality requires the same degree of skill in evaluating the preschooler as it does in evaluating other pupils.
6. Before proceeding with carrying out any educational program, teachers must be alert to the possibility that a physiological or psychological factor may be interfering with the attainment of a prescribed educational objective.
7. The role of teachers as diagnosticians, programmers, classroom organizers, and behavior managers will increase in difficulty and importance as handicapped pupils are integrated into regular classrooms.
8. Teachers often must initiate the referral process in order to obtain medical and/or paramedical services for pupils suspected of having problems.
9. When the school system employs specialized personnel, the referral process usually starts with the classroom teacher carrying out screening tests.
10. When diagnostic and treatment services are required that are not provided within the school system, the referral process is, at times, ambiguous.
11. Teachers often must decide whether to recommend referrals through direct communication with parents or through an intermediary such as a principal.

12. Parents may resist advice relevant to medical or paramedical refer-
    ral because of financial reasons, fear, guilt, or disinterest.
13. Teachers do not need to establish follow-up procedures in which the
    professionals or agencies consulted would inform the teachers of
    their findings that would require modifications in classroom
    practices.
14. Teachers should cooperate with paramedical and medical personnel
    by incorporating their therapeutic goals into their educational goals,
    regardless of instructional priorities for the pupil involved or the
    class as a whole.
15. The best type of documentation for referral purposes is the anec-
    dotal report, in which the teacher describes in detailed, behavioral
    terms those pupil behaviors that indicate the possible presence of a
    pathological state.
16. Teachers should interpret pupil behaviors and suggest the diagnosis,
    including diagnostic label and possible etiology.
17. Some large medical centers provide a variety of special clinics and
    itinerant clinical services.
18. State, county, and city departments of health provide diagnostic,
    but not treatment, services on either a regular or itinerant basis.
19. A parent group, such as a chapter of the Association for Retarded
    Citizens, provides diagnostic and treatment programs for a wide
    range of disability groups.
20. Teachers, if they are to serve as effective referral agents, must know
    the health services available in their communities.
21. Teachers, in cooperation with other pertinent professionals, must
    set up mechanisms through which they can provide feedback on the
    pupil's response to the therapeutic regimen.
22. The problem of selecting an appropriate professional to whom to
    refer a pupil with a suspected problem is sometimes compounded by
    the ambiguity of professional boundaries.

Part B

1. Write a referral request to a school principal, nurse, psychologist, or
   a specially established team. Include in your request sufficient data
   to support the referral. Whenever possible, use an actual pupil.
2. For your home, college, or teaching community, give the names,
   addresses, and phone numbers of *major* public and private agencies
   that provide diagnostic and treatment services to children and youth
   with medical and paramedical problems. For each agency identified,
   furnish the following information:
   a. Type of clients served
   b. Referral procedures

    c. Fee structures
    d. Nature of services
    e. Approximate waiting times
    f. Accreditation status
    g. Revenue sources

3. Define the following medical specialties:
    a. Dermatology
    b. Endocrinology
    c. Internal medicine
    d. Neurology
    e. Ophthalmology
    f. Orthopaedics
    g. Otolaryngology
    h. Pediatrics
    i. Psychiatry
    j. Urology

4. Define the following therapies:
    a. Art
    b. Dance
    c. Music
    d. Occupational
    e. Physical
    f. Speech and language

5. Define the professional concern of the following professionals:
    a. Nutritionists
    b. Orthotists
    c. Prosthetists
    d. Rehabilitation counselors
    e. Social workers
    f. Therapuetic recreation specialists

INTRODUCTION AND OVERVIEW

Teachers, in their daily observations and in more structured evaluations, must be sensitive to the possibility that discrepancies in the school performance of pupils may result from underlying physical or mental pathologies. Typically, teachers are assigned pupils who are free of disabling conditions; therefore, they are likely to overlook pathological states as the cause of behavioral and learning disabilities and, instead, search for reasons in the cognitive, motivational, and affective systems or the sociocultural history of pupils. Teachers, unlike other adults in pupils' lives, have unparalleled opportunities to observe the behavior of children and youth over an extended period of time. They interact with children and youth on a sustained basis more often than any other professional group, and, perhaps, even more so than parents, especially after the early years of life. Many parents, in their efforts to attain higher standards of living or in their search for self-enhancement and fulfillment, often spend little time with their children, who, in turn, spend more and more time in peer interactions and in front of television, away from parental influence or surveillance. Thus teachers, on the basis of their prolonged contact with pupils in a variety of activities, are exceptionally situated to observe student behavior and to make perceptive judgments vis-à-vis the existence of physical and mental conditions that interfere with learning, overall development, or that even may be life-threatening.

With an acute awareness of the impact that physical and mental disorders have on pupil growth and development, teachers can play a quintessential role in facilitating the delivery of medical and paramedical services to those pupils suspected of requiring such human services. Evaluation for referral purposes assumes special importance when one considers the truism that the earlier the detection of a medical problem, the more likely its effects may be diminished, the pathology reversed, and the secondary symptoms, usually of a psychological nature, minimized. The early identification of pathological states invariably leads to early intervention and an increased probability of arresting or curing the condition. Moreover, early detection and intervention of untoward physical and mental problems will reduce the aversive effects of these conditions on learning.

As increased emphasis is placed on the early childhood education of handicapped and nonhandicapped children, the task of identifying behaviors of pupils that suggest atypical mental and physical states assumes greater importance and complexity. This task is more difficult during the early, critical years of development. During this period and later, teachers must differentiate between those behaviors that represent normal patterns of development and those that signal a possible abnormality. In order to make such discriminations skillfully, teachers must not only be proficient in observing behavior but also in recognizing patterns or constellations of behaviors that, when considered in their totality, point with logical directness to specific pathological states.

The importance of this proficiency is best seen, perhaps, in its impact on instruction. Teachers must be cautious before implementing an educational program. They must be alert to the possibility that an unknown physiological or psychological factor may be interfering with the attainment of a prescribed educational objective. Teachers cannot simply identify the point from which instruction must proceed without questioning whether a medical or paramedical problem exists or whether a student is developmentally ready for the next step in an instructional sequence. Furthermore, the role of teachers as diagnosticians will continue to increase in both difficulty and importance as handicapped pupils are integrated into regular classrooms and as growing numbers of moderately to profoundly handicapped pupils are educated in local public schools.

The role of teachers cannot be restricted merely to identifying behaviors that typify pathology. In addition, teachers must assist in obtaining needed medical and paramedical services. In fact, teachers often must initiate the referral process, especially when the services required are not provided within the school. In those instances when the school employs specialized personnel, such as psychologists, speech and language pathologists, social workers, occupational therapists, and nurses, the referral process is usually established and simple. Typically, these professionals request referrals from teachers and supply them with appropriate referral forms.

On the other hand, when diagnostic and treatment services are required that are not provided within the school system, the referral process is usually more ambiguous. To serve as effective referral agents to outside agencies and professionals, teachers must become familiar with whatever referral system exists within the school or total school system. Frequently, however, structured referral procedures have not been developed by either the central or local school administration, and decisions must be made and processes initiated by teachers on an ad hoc basis. Teachers often must decide whether to proceed through direct communication with parents or through an intermediary, such as the school principal, nurse, pupil personnel worker, or an especially established interdisciplinary team concerned with placement, programming, and referral decisions.

At times teachers may decide that parents should be approached directly. This would be appropriate whenever special rapport with the parents has been established; suggested consultations would be less likely viewed as interference or threats. It should be recognized that parents may resist advice relevant to medical or paramedical diagnosis and/or treatment. This reluctance may be due to several reasons: financial resources, fear, guilt, or disinterest. Whenever parents fail to heed referral recommendations, teachers must seek alternate approaches and strategies; when parents follow through on referral suggestions, teachers must establish follow-up procedures through which they, the teachers, may be informed of pertinent findings that will require modifications in classroom organization, instruction, and behavior management practices. Teachers must also encourage parents to communicate to consulting personnel that they, the teachers, are willing to incorporate therapeutic goals into their educational program if they do not interfere with previously established instructional priorities for the pupil involved or the class as a whole.

At other times, teachers may decide or be expected to recommend the referral through an intermediary within the school. In a small school the most logical intermediary is likely to be the school principal; in larger schools, it may be a specially established team, the nurse, or school psychologist. Regardless of the intermediary agent selected or required, teachers, before initiating the referral process, should compile sufficient relevant data that would support the referral. The best type of documentation is the anecdotal report, in which teachers describe, in sufficient detail and in behavioral terms, those behaviors of the referred pupil that indicate the possible presence of a pathological state. Included in these reports should be the conditions under which suspected behaviors occurred, the frequency and duration of these behaviors, and their consistency over a period of time. Pertinent factors that may bear a relationship to the behaviors should be reported, e.g., the pupil began to behave in ways that suggested the presence of a hearing loss. Before this, the pupil had been ill with a contagious disease, characterized by a high fever of several days duration. Furthermore, teachers should be careful to avoid interpreting the behaviors described since medical and paramedical diagnoses are not within their professional province. Indeed, teachers, as careful observers, provide a significant professional service: reporting, with as much precision as possible, those events that point to the possible existence of a debilitating mental or physical problem, without engaging in interpretations or in establishing etiology.

On still other occasions, the referral process may require that a referral be made to an outside agency rather than a specific individual. When this is the case, teachers must be aware of those community agencies that provide medical and paramedical diagnostic and/or treatment services. Familiarity with hospital-related programs and those offered by public and private agencies is necessary. Many general hospitals offer a variety of special clinics as part of their comprehensive medical programming. Some of the largest medical centers provide itinerant services. State, county, and city departments of health often provide diagnostic and treatment services on a regular, and even on an itinerant, basis so that all areas of the community, no matter how remote, may receive needed medical or paramedical services. Mobile units in specially constructed and equipped vans often carry professional services to relatively inaccessible areas of a community. Private organizations, usually established by parent groups, provide diagnostic and treatment programs for individuals with special medical problems, e.g., Association for Retarded Citizens and the United Cerebral Palsy Association. Specialized hospitals, such as children's hospitals and university-affiliated facilities, also provide special diagnostic clinics and treatment facilities. Teachers, as effective referral agents, must not only know the health services available in their communities, but the type of clients these agencies serve, referral requirements, fee structures, nature of services provided, and approximate waiting time for appointments and treatments.

Whatever referral procedures are followed and whether individual professionals or agencies are consulted, teachers should ensure that provisions are made to have the results of professional consultations communicated quickly and directly to them, except when it would constitute an invasion of privacy. The lines of communication must be established between teachers and other human service professionals. Teachers, in cooperation with other key professionals, must set up mechanisms through which they can provide feedback to these other professionals regarding the results of their therapeutic interventions on the learning and behavior of pupils. In order to accomplish this important goal, teachers must know the professional scope of such medical specialties as dermatology, endocrinology, internal medicine, neurology, ophthalmology, orthopaedics, otolaryngology, pediatrics, physical medicine and rehabilitation, and psychiatry. They must also be familiar with the nature and scope of the various paramedical professions that serve people in need so that they may more fully appreciate potential contributions of these professions to their pupils and so that they can make judicious referral decisions. The problem of selecting an appropriate professional to whom to refer a pupil with a suspected problem is sometimes compounded by the ambiguity of professional boundaries. Nevertheless, educators should know the nature, scope, and limitations of such professional disciplines as art, dance, music, occupational, physical, and speech and language therapies. They should be familiar with the goals, purposes, and functions of dentists, nurses, nutritionists, orthotists, prosthetists, psychologists, rehabilitation counselors, social workers, and therapeutic recreation specialists.

Finally, it should be noted that for handicapped pupils, educators are expected to incorporate treatment interventions from other professions into the larger educational plan. In addition to preparing individual educational objectives and individual education programs, teachers are expected to:

1. Identify the most efficacious times for remediation
2. Provide needed information to referral sources
3. Interpret information and recommendations from referral agents
4. Infer programmatic implications
5. Implement suggestions from referral sources
6. Evaluate the effects of specialized treatments
7. Provide feedback to other professionals so that appropriate modifications may take place when necessary

ACTIVITIES AND EXPERIENCES

1. If you are currently teaching or student teaching, identify the specialists working within your school system. For each profession represented, describe that discipline's goals, purposes, and functions and discuss the existing referral procedures. If you are not currently teaching, select a school in your home or college community, and carry out the assignment. When available, obtain copies of referral forms.
2. Describe in a brief essay why the role of teachers as diagnosticians will increase in both difficulty and importance as handicapped pupils are integrated into regular classrooms and as growing number of moderately to profoundly handicapped pupils are educated in local public schools.
3. Describe those conditions under which you as a teacher would approach a parent or parents directly to recommend a pupil's referral for diagnosis and/or treatment. Cite specific types of pupil behaviors and problems in your response.
4. Write a referral request to a school nurse, a principal, a school psychologist, or a specially established team. Include in your request sufficient relevant data to support the referral. Whenever possible, use an actual pupil. Do not use the pupil's name, however, to ensure that pupil's privacy. After writing a referral request that reports objectively on relevant student behaviors, compose a referral request that is subjective and interpretative. Discuss why the latter referral is unacceptable.
5. For your home, college, or teaching community, give the names, addresses, and phone numbers of public and private agencies that provide diagnostic and treatment services to children and youth with medical and paramedical problems. For each agency identified, furnish the following information:

    a.   Type of clients served
    b.   Referral procedures required
    c.   Fee structures
    d.   Nature of services provided
    e.   Approximate waiting time for appointments
    f.   Approximate waiting time for treatments
    g.   Accreditation status
    h.   Revenue sources
    If the agency has multiple units or various clinics, respond to items
    a–f for each subunit or clinical program.
6. Discuss the ways in which teachers can ensure that results of
    professional consultations pertinent to classroom practices are com-
    municated quickly to them.
7. Describe briefly the professional nature and scope of the following
    medical specialties:
    a.   Dermatology
    b.   Endocrinology
    c.   Internal medicine
    d.   Neurology
    e.   Ophthalmology
    f.   Orthopaedics
    g.   Otolaryngology
    h.   Pediatrics
    i.   Psychiatry
    j.   Urology
8. Describe briefly the nature, scope, and limitations of the following
    professional disciplines:
    a.   Art therapy
    b.   Dance therapy
    c.   Music therapy
    d.   Occupational therapy
    e.   Physical therapy
    f.   Speech and language therapy
9. Describe briefly the goals, purposes, and functions of the following
    professionals:
    a.   Dentists
    b.   Nurses
    c.   Nutritionists
    d.   Orthotists
    e.   Prosthetists
    f.   Psychologists
    g.   Rehabilitation counselors
    h.   Social workers
    i.   Therapeutic recreation specialists

10. Select at least five of the medical and paramedical specialties identified in Activities 7–9 and describe those behaviors of pupils that would lead you to refer them to each of the specialists selected.
11. Create a follow-up form that you would recommend for use by other professionals that would assist you in carrying out their recommendations.
12. Discuss and describe what other professionals should *not* do in making recommendations to teachers regarding classroom practices.
13. Discuss in an essay of no more than three double-spaced typewritten pages, the role that teachers should play in the total referral process from initial referral through follow-up.

CONCLUDING STATEMENT

As the role of classroom teachers expands, so, too, will their professional competencies have to undergo concomitant growth. Key among these extended functions of teachers is the role of referral agent. Teachers no longer can function from the myopic perspective that views health care as a separate and alien process. They are now performing the roles of referral agent, facilitator of therapeutic goals, and supplier of critical feedback information that illuminate and clarify the efficacy of a specific therapeutic regimen. The individualization of instruction, then, requires an extension of roles into areas not normally considered germane to teacher preparation or teacher performance. This module assumes that teachers will continue to play a critical part in preventive health and in facilitating health care, especially as handicapped pupils are integrated into society and the educational mainstream.

POSTTEST

At this point retake the Pretest.

SUGGESTED READINGS

Allen, K. E., Holm, V. A., and Schiefelbusch, R. L. (eds.). 1978. Early Intervention—A Team Approach. University Park Press, Baltimore.
Alvin, J. 1975. Music Therapy. Hutchinson & Co. (Publishers), London.
Arievi, S. (ed.). 1975. American Handbook of Psychiatry. Basic Books, Inc., New York.
Bolton, B., and Jaques, M. E. (ed.). 1978. Rehabilitation Counseling: Theory and Practice. University Park Press, Baltimore.
Cooke, R. (ed.). 1968. The Biological Basis of Pediatric Practice. McGraw-Hill Book Co., New York.

Downey, J. A., and Low, N. 1974. The Child with a Disabling Illness: Principles of Rehabilitation. W. B. Saunders Co., Philadelphia.

Freedman, A. M., and Kaplan, H. I. (eds.). 1967. Comprehensive Textbook of Psychiatry. The Williams & Wilkens Co., Baltimore.

Gardner, L. I. 1969. Endocrine and Genetic Diseases of Childhood. W. B. Saunders Co., Philadelphia.

Goodhart, R. S., and Shils, M. E. 1974. Modern Nutrition in Health and Disease. Lea & Febiger, Philadelphia.

Hamburg, J. (ed.). 1973. Review of Allied Health I. The University of Kentucky Press, Lexington.

Haslam, R. H. A., and Valletutti, P. J. 1975. Medical Problems in the Classroom. University Park Press, Baltimore.

Jaques, M. E. 1970. Rehabilitation Counseling: Scope and Services. Houghton Mifflin Co., Boston.

Johnston, R. B., and Magrab, P. R. (eds.). 1976. Developmental Disorders: Assessment, Treatment, Education. University Park Press, Baltimore.

Kanner, L. 1972. Child Psychiatry. 4th Ed. Charles C Thomas Publisher, Springfield, Ill.

Lerner, J. W. 1971. Children with Learning Disabilities: Theories, Diagnosis, and Teaching Strategies. Houghton Mifflin Co., Boston.

Masserman, J. H. (ed.). 1974. Current Psychiatric Therapies. Vol. 14. Grune & Stratton, New York.

Michel, D. E. 1976. Music Therapy. Charles C Thomas Publisher, Springfield, Ill.

Naumburg, M. 1966. Dynamically Oriented Art Therapy: Its Principles and Practice. Grune & Stratton, New York.

Nowak, A. J. (ed.). 1976. Dentistry for the Handicapped Patient. C. V. Mosby Co., St. Louis.

Pearson, P. H., and Williams, C. E. 1972. Physical Therapy Services in the Developmental Disabilities. Charles C Thomas Publisher, Springfield, Ill.

Peter, L. J. 1972. Individual Instruction. McGraw-Hill Book Co., New York.

Reil, J. P., and Roy, C., Sr. 1974. Conceptual Models for Nursing Practice. Appleton-Century-Crofts, New York.

Rusk, H. A. 1971. Rehabilitation Medicine. 3rd Ed. C. V. Mosby Co., St. Louis.

Shivers, J. S., and Fait, H. F. 1975. Therapeutic and Adapted Recreation Services. Lea & Febiger, Philadelphia.

Stubbins, J. (ed.). 1977. Social and Psychological Aspects of Disability: A Handbook for Practicioners. University Park Press, Baltimore.

Tachdjian, M. O. 1972. Pediatric Orthopedics. W. B. Saunders Co., Philadelphia.

Travis, L. E. (ed.). 1971. Handbook of Speech Pathology and Audiology. Appleton-Century-Crofts, New York.

Ulman, E., and Dachinger, P. 1975. (eds.). Art Therapy in Theory and Practice. Schocken Books, New York.

Valletutti, P. J., and Christoplos, F. (eds.). 1977. Interdisciplinary Approaches to Human Services. University Park Press, Baltimore.

Valletutti, P. J., and Christoplos, F. (eds.). 1979. Preventing Physical and Mental Disabilities: Multidisciplinary Approaches. University Park Press, Baltimore.

Wehman, P. (ed.). 1978. Recreation Programming for Developmentally Disabled Persons. University Park Press, Baltimore.

Weiner, I. (ed.). 1976. Clinical Methods in Psychology. John Wiley & Sons, Inc., New York.

West, R., and Ansberry, M. 1968. The Rehabilitation of Speech. Harper & Row Publishers, New York.

Wiederholt, J. L., Hammill, D. D., and Brown, V. 1978. The Resource Teacher. Allyn & Bacon, Boston.

Willard, H. S., and Spackman, C. S. (eds.). 1971. Occupational Therapy. 4th Ed. J. B. Lippincott Co., Philadelphia.

Wilson, A. B., Jr. (ed.). 1973. Orthotics and Prosthetics. American Orthotic and Prosthetic Association, Washington, D.C.

Module 7

The teacher will identify individual educational objectives for each pupil based upon an analysis of that pupil's knowledge, skills, concepts, interests, and needs. Toward this end, the teacher will engage in several informal assessment procedures, including:

A. The development and administration of test inventories
B. The observation and documentation of pupil behaviors as they occur during teaching/learning experiences
C. The sampling and analysis of pupil behavior and work products
D. The interviewing of the pupil and the pupil's parents

PRETEST

Part A   Test Inventories

Construct a test inventory that attempts to assess a pupil's skill in the comprehension and use of noun plurality.

Part B   Observation and Documentation of Pupil Behaviors

1. Make a series of videotapes of your class. If you are not currently teaching or student teaching, ask your college instructor to make a series of videotapes of a class in progress. These tapes will be seen by fellow students and you. After the viewing, submit an observational report to your instructor for evaluation purposes. Compare your report with those of several of your peers. If you are currently teaching, ask a colleague to review your report. If you are student teaching, ask your college supervisor and/or cooperating teacher to review your report.
2. Select a curriculum area and compose a checklist for diagnostic purposes. Ask a colleague or your college instructor to evaluate its usefulness.

Part C   Sampling Behaviors

Examine the following written language sample and answer the following five questions:

Spring

Spring is the most beatifulest of seasons. The flowers are very pretty. And so are the trees. Wood you like to come for a walk with me to the park. Look at the too lovely swan swimming in the lake. Smell the pretty flowers. They are red, pink, blue, yellow, and purple. Pick some flowers for mother and take it home an suprize her.

Spring is allso special becaus summers just around the corner an el can goto Ocean City to swim and may be el can fish for Blue fish. See you in Setpember, Ha! Ha!

Splash!

1. What skills, knowledge, and concepts has the pupil demonstrated in this sample?
2. What problems has the pupil demonstrated?
3. What patterns, if any, exist among these problems?
4. What further diagnostic information do you need before making educational programming decisions?
5. Based upon *this* sample, what teaching objectives would you recommend for this pupil?

Part D   Interviewing and Interacting With the Pupil and the Pupil's Parents

Make several videotapes of meetings with parents of a pupil in your class. If you are not teaching or student teaching, try to arrange a conference or hold a mock conference. Ask your college instructor, a supervisor, or a peer to evaluate your performance, especially as it relates to the gathering of relevant diagnostic information.

SECTION A   TEST INVENTORIES

INTRODUCTION AND OVERVIEW

A key problem in evaluating behavior is ascertaining whether that behavior is representative of the individual's typical and natural performance. Although while waiting for a behavior to occur in a natural setting and under real conditions may provide the evaluator with a sample of behavior that is most representative, such an approach is essentially inefficient unless it is supplemented with more structured observations. The use of inventory tests provides more structured means by which a pupil's knowledge and skills may be determined.

Although constructing a test inventory can be a time-consuming endeavor, it can, nevertheless, be beneficial. Certainly such an exercise helps teachers in self-evaluation relevant to their own knowledge and skills pertinent to a specific, circumscribed area of behavior. When constructing a test inventory, teachers are compelled to organize knowledge and skills into levels of difficulty, to analyze the relationships existing between stimulus presentation and mode of response, and to explore in detail the nature of the specific subject or content area. The construction of any test inventory involves a blend of research and thought that will assist in defining not only the diagnostic task but the nature of instructional activities.

The starting point in the development of a test inventory involves deciding upon a specified aspect of human behavior that is deemed important in the hierarchy of educational skills and/or knowledge. It must be emphasized, at this point, that a *comprehensive* test inventory should not be developed with a specific grade or age level in mind. Rather, it should be constructed to assess a wide range of skills/knowledge levels so that one can evaluate those pupils with minimal knowledge or skills as well as those with advanced performance levels. For example, a teacher may be interested in discovering the skills pupils may possess relevant to noun plurality. In constructing such an inventory whose purpose would be to assess a pupil's competencies relating to the comprehension and use of noun plurals, the teacher must first determine the various ways in which knowledge and skills vis-à-vis noun plurality manifest themselves, i.e.:

1. In oral comprehension
2. In oral expression
3. In written language comprehension
4. In written language expression

Second, the teacher then must chart the various ways or forms in which nouns form plurals, i.e.:

1. By adding *s*
2. By adding *es*, when the noun ends in an *s*, *ch*, *sh*, *x*, or *z*
3. By dropping *y* after a consonant and adding *ies*
4. By changing the *f* or *fe* to *ves*
5. By remaining the same, e.g., deer, sheep, and moose
6. By changing the *us* to *i* (stimulus)
7. By changing the *on* to *a* (criterion)
8. By changing the *um* to *a* (stadium)
9. By changing in unpredictable or irregular ways (child and mouse)
10. By adding an apostrophe and an *s*, e.g., IQ's and 7's

Third, the teacher must then develop test items of various levels of difficulty that attempt to measure a broad range of pupil abilities, i.e., from those with minimal skills through those who have advanced abilities. Levels of subtest or item difficulty are best attained by analyzing both complexity level of the item and stimulus-response modality levels. For example, the *oral* comprehension of nouns formed by simply adding an /s/ sound to the singular form is, undoubtedly, the simplest task related to noun plurality since it is the most commonly used plural form and involves oral language comprehension—the language skill fundamental to all others. The next more difficult levels must then be worked out on the basis of research, experience, and logic. For each level of competency tested, there should be at least several (three or more) items to minimize the effect of guessing and chance factors. A teacher-made inventory of noun plurality skills follows with test directions furnished. The various subtests are presented by adjudged level of difficulty.

NOUN PLURALITY INVENTORY

Subtest I (Oral Comprehension)

A. Directions: Show the pupil a set of 11 picture cards (1 sample and 10 inventory items). On each card there are two pictures; one of the pictures shows one of an object, e.g., "cat"; the other picture shows two or more of the same object, i.e., "cats." All cards should have pictures of familiar objects, and all should form their plurality by the addition of the /s/ or /z/ phoneme (sound). Begin the test by showing the pupil card 1, a sample item. (Note: Each subtest should have a sample or demonstration item to make sure the pupil understands the nature of the test.) When showing the pupil each card say, "Show me the (cat)." "Now, show me the (cats)." Vary the order, sometimes saying the plural form first.

B. Directions: Use the same type of materials and directions as in Subtest IA; however, this time use pictures that depict plurals formed by adding the schwa plus /z/ phonemes to nouns that end with the consonants *s, ch, sh, x,* or *z.*

C. Directions: Use the same type of materials and directions as in Subtest IA; however, this time use pictures that depict plurals formed by changing the *f* or *fe* to *ves.* Since there are but a few common examples of this noun plurality pattern, only use three cards, e.g., leaf—leaves, knife—knives, and loaf—loaves.

D. Directions: Use the same type of materials and directions as in Subtest IA; however, this time use pictures that depict more commonly used plurals that are formed in irregular patterns, e.g., mouse—mice, tooth—teeth, goose—geese, and child—children.

Subtest II (Oral Expression)

A. Directions: Use the materials employed in Subtest IA. This time, however, say, "I see one _____. Here, I see three _____." Say these sentence patterns while pointing to the pictures on each card indicating in some way that the pupil is expected to fill in the missing word.

B–D. Directions: Use the materials employed in Subtest IB–D and follow the directions described in Subtest IIA above.

E. Directions: Show the pupil a set of three to five pictures that depict plurals that are the same as the singular form, e.g., deer, fish, and sheep. Say, "I see one _____. Here, I see two _____." Say these sentence patterns while pointing to the pictures on each card, indicating in some way that the pupil is expected to say the missing word.

Subtest III (Oral Expression)

A. Directions: Explain to the pupil that you are going to say one of two sentence patterns, i.e., "There is one _____." or "There are two or more _____." Indicate in some way that, if you supply one pattern, he/she must say the other, e.g., Examiner: "There is one stimulus." Pupil: "There are two or more stimuli." (Note: For this subtest use all those difficult plurals, i.e., "us—i," "on—a," and "um—a," that come from Greek and Latin roots.)

Subtest IV (Written Comprehension)

A–E. Directions: Use the same materials as in Subtest IIA–E. This time, however, ask the pupil to look at each picture and the accompanying written word pairs. Next have the pupil select the one word in each pair that describes the picture shown.

F. Directions: Use the same words as in Subtest III. This time rather than asking the pupil to say the correct word, ask him/her to point to the word that correctly completes the sentences you say. Vary the order of the presentation so that the pupil may not guess the correct answer from your presentation pattern. If the pupil has not performed with any degree of success on Subtest III, skip this item.

G. Show the pupil a set of three to five pictures that depict plurals formed by changing the *y* following a consonant to *ies.* Ask the pupil to point to the word that describes the picture, i.e., party—parties, puppy—puppies, and lady—ladies.

Subtest V (Written Expression)

A.   Directions: Repeat Subtest IVA–G. This time, however, ask the pupil to write down his/her answer from memory.

B.   Directions: Dictate a list of numbers and abbreviations in both their singular and plural forms. Ask the pupil to write his/her answer. You are interested only in the use of the correct pluralities, not in the correct formation of the dictated numbers or letters.

In administering the test inventory, there are several cautions to be observed:

1.   Make sure that the pupil does not perform unsatisfactorily on a test item because of a deficiency in a precursor skill and/or a necessary sensorimotor function. For example, failure on Subtest I may not reflect a problem with auditory comprehension but may represent a problem in hearing acuity, auditory discrimination, and/or auditory memory.

2.   Be certain that the pupil does not perform unsatisfactorily on a subtest involving pictures because of problems associated with the interpretation of graphic representations. For this type of pupil, it will be necessary to use real objects.

3.   Make sure that the pupil does not perform unsatisfactorily because of a speech defect rather than because of an inability to express noun plurality.

Teachers should always be cautious in assuming that a pupil has failed a test item because he/she lacks the skill being tested. Frequently the failure results from another variable. When a pupil succeeds on a test item and chance factors can be eliminated, the fact of passing is noteworthy. Failure rarely is as illuminating.

Along with the inventory, construct a Noun Plurality Inventory Scoring Sheet upon which the pupil's responses can be recorded while the test is being administered. The responses can later be analyzed so that decisions can be made relevant to specific instructional experiences. For each pupil, decisions will have to be made regarding the teaching of a particular skill or competency, i.e., should a particular problem that has been discovered be ignored or remediated in light of other and, perhaps, more pressing needs?

The information obtained from the inventory should be supplemented with less structured observations. Information on noun plurality can be obtained from listening to the everyday speech of pupils and from examining their written work. Along with the Noun Plurality Inventory Scoring Sheet there should be a blank section to be used for recording data from other diagnostic sources, including skills demonstrated as well as problems encountered with noun plurality. Specific examples of each should be recorded according to the various plurality patterns.

ACTIVITIES AND EXPERIENCES

1. Construct an inventory test for at least one of the following areas:
    a. Arithmetic computation: Addition of whole numbers
    b. Arithmetic computation: Addition of fractions
    c. Arithmetic computation: Subtraction of whole numbers
    d. Arithmetic computation: Subtraction of fractions
    e. Arithmetic computation: Multiplication of whole numbers
    f. Arithmetic computation: Multiplication of fractions
    g. Arithmetic computation: Division of whole numbers
    h. Arithmetic computation: Division of fractions
    i. Arithmetic computation: Decimals
    j. Arithmetic computation: Percentages
2. Construct an inventory test for at least one of the following areas:
    a. Noun-verb agreement
    b. Verb forms
    c. Adjective usage
    d. Adverbs
    e. Punctuation: Commas
    f. Punctuation: Colons and semicolons
    g. Capitalization
    h. Syllabication
    i. Phonics
    j. Suffixes
    k. Prefixes
3. Construct an inventory list for at least one of the following areas:
    a. Swimming skills
    b. Basketball skills
    c. Tennis skills
    d. Bowling skills
4. Select an area or areas of the curriculum other than those identified in Activities 1–3, and construct inventory(ies) for each area selected.
5. Select five of the inventories constructed in response to Activities 1–4 and use them to test four or five pupils. Report on your results.

A sample of a student-made inventory follows:

SUBTRACTION INVENTORY[1]

Inventory Objective

Determination of student's strengths and weaknesses in basic subtraction skills.

Strategy

Exercise A tests ability to read numbers and subtraction examples correctly. Exercise B tests recognition of the subtraction sign and awareness of proper order of terms. Exercises C and D test student's ability to count and subtract with blocks. Section E tests oral comprehension and auditory processing, F tests written comprehension and G tests oral comprehension, written comprehension, and written expression. Section H tests written comprehension and expression of some of the more difficult forms of subtraction examples. This inventory in its entirety is appropriate for testing only one student at a time; however, certain sections, such as B, G, and H, can be easily adapted to group testing.

Instructions

Exercises A, C, E, and G are presented orally, one example at a time, and B, D, F, and H are presented in written form. Allow a maximum of 30 seconds per example in A through F.

Materials

20 blocks are needed for sections C and D.

A. Ask the student to read the following 5 examples:

9	17	21	59	725
-2	-4	-20	-38	-691

B. Ask the student to circle the correct example:
   1. 7 minus 6 $7+6$ 7×6 $6-7$ $6+7$ $7-6$
   2. 24 minus 20 $24\div20$ $24-20$ $20-24$ $24+20$ $20\div24$
   3. 1 minus 0 $1+0$ $0-1$ $1-0$ $1\div0$ 1×0
   4. 182 minus 128 $128-182$ $182+128$ $128+182$ $182-128$ $182\div128$
   5. 938 minus 570 $938\div570$ $570-938$ $938-570$ $570\div938$ $938+570$

C. Read the following, waiting for the student to perform each step:
   1. Show me 10 blocks. Take 5 of them away. How many are left?
   2. Show me 7 blocks. Take 8 of them away. How many are left?
   3. Show me 14 blocks. Take 9 of them away. How many are left?
   4. Show me 20 blocks. Take 20 of them away. How many are left?
   5. Show me 9 blocks. Take 0 of them away. How many are left?

D. Instruct the student to solve these written examples using blocks:

9	12	15	13	4
-8	-4	-1	-0	-5

---

[1] Developed by Harvey L. Hoffman, graduate student, Coppin State College and reproduced with his permission.

E. Present the following examples orally, and ask the student to answer orally. Use each phrase twice: "take away," "minus," "less," "subtract _____ from _____," and "What is the difference between _____ and _____?"

9	13	17	20	23	0	5	19	68	78
−5	−6	−1	−0	+13	−0	−7	−10	−68	−52

F. Present the following written examples. Ask the student to read each example and answer orally.

8	10	13	17	21	30	$.43	$2.39	12	91
−3	−2	+5	−9	−0	−32	−.22	−1.08	−19	−91

G. Present the following examples orally, as done in section E. Ask the student to write each example and solve it. Allow up to 1 minute per example in G and H.

98	165	$5.36	52	93	$.80	692	534	$5.90	700
−72	+30	4.22	−28	−47	−.72	−375	−247	−8.27	−289

H. Instruct the student to solve and check each example, showing all computations:

1. 197 − 68
2. 925 minus 807
3. 500 take away 294
4. $9.00 − $1.11
5. Subtract $1.05 from $4.72
6. From 931 take 487
7. What is the difference between 301 and 299?
8. Find the difference between $7.80 and $7.08
9. 29 − 35
10. 615 less 316

CONCLUDING STATEMENT

As inventories are developed, they should be saved for use with future pupils. Readily available teacher-made inventories can save substantial time in the years ahead and can contribute immeasurably to skill in measuring both pupil status and pupil progress. It should also be noted that while skill inventories may be found in textbooks and other books concerned with skill development, frequently these texts do not meet the specific needs of a particular group of pupils. These tests, however, can serve as the basis for developing your own inventories. Inventories should be modified as problems are encountered in their administration and as the teacher acquires greater knowledge in the area being tested.

SECTION B   OBSERVATION AND DOCUMENTATION OF PUPIL BEHAVIOR

INTRODUCTION AND OVERVIEW

As teachers react on a daily basis throughout the months of school, they are constantly exposed to varying kinds of behavior exhibited by their pupils. Since school takes place in a group setting, teachers have access to much information that could be used diagnostically to aid in teaching their pupils. The flood of data cannot but be confusing and overwhelming unless strategies have been established for observing and recording both *representative* and *emerging* behavior.

A key to the sophisticated observation of pupils is an appreciation for what is representative behavior. Representative implies that the behavior is typical of the individual's present performance level. It is representative only if it occurs with a degree of regularity and in differing situations. Teachers, therefore, must begin their observations by engaging in a cognitive/creative game somewhat akin to the creative process of an artist. In effect, observant teachers commence their task by attempting to portray in words the behavioral essence of the pupil under study. Teachers must ask the question, "What is the unique constellation of skills and needs characteristic of _____?" Everyday teachers should record those behaviors that appear to be important in developing a pupil profile. At first, such behaviors should be recorded only if they appear to be characteristic or representative.

Once representative behaviors have been identified and added to the composite picture, emerging behaviors can more easily be appreciated and understood within a holistic framework. The observation task then becomes, "What is new about _____?" Every day teachers should add more details, both representative and emerging, to the portrait, details that help make the pupil more visible and more compellingly alive.

The sketch of the pupil may be viewed as a self-portrait inspired by the pupil but executed by the teacher. Throughout, teachers must be impartial observers who record what occurs, shunning interpretation and cause and effect peregrinations. Perhaps the best approach to executing the sketch is for teachers to accept the challenge of discovering what each pupil is really like, free from their own biases and preconceptions.

The Diagnostic Checklist

The development of a diagnostic checklist offers a means of systematically recording and analyzing behavior by a rater. The value of any checklist is its use in identifying what the pupil does in an actual situation rather than what he/she can do as assessed in an artificial testing situation. The diagnostic checklist should parallel the curriculum so that the pupil will be monitored in terms of the goals specified there. Before carrying out an instructional program, a checklist may be used to determine what skills a pupil possesses relevant to a specific unit of experience as well as what skills are yet to be mastered.

While the need for checklists is generally accepted, the specific form and structure have not received any degree of unanimity. Bender and Valletutti[2] developed a checklist based on the premise that an individual teacher should establish a required performance level (RPL) as part of each of the objectives in the curriculum. While this performance level may be identified in general terms, a variant mastery level for a specific student could be accepted because of his unique profile of abilities and disabilities and because of diverse environmental standards. For example, styles of dress, patterns of grooming, choices of food, and language usage all reflect sociocultural values. For each specific task, the assigned RPL represents the criterion performance level that a teacher regards as generally acceptable at that time. An instructional objective may be stated as follows: The student turns his eyes and head in the direction of sound 80 percent of the time *or* four out of five times. In this case, the required performance level (RPL) has been set at 80 percent.

It is not enough, however, to assign a required performance level without indicating at the same time the minimum number of observations that must be made before a rater feels relatively certain that the behavior observed is not an accidental occurrence or partial mastery but a behavior that is well established within the student's repertoire of behaviors. Teachers, therefore, need to identify the recommended number of observations (RO) of behavior that will satisfy them that a student truly possesses the behavior in question. In individual cases, a teacher may require a different number of observations for a specific student and/or a specific behavior. Once a teacher has established an RO (recommended observations) for a behavior, then the strategy for evaluating the student's performance level (SPL) has been identified as well. Once the SPL has been determined for a specific task, this score may then be compared to the RPL to determine whether the student has sufficient mastery of the skill or requires further evaluation and/or a program of instruction.

For instance, in the behavioral objective cited above: The student turns his eyes and head in the direction of sound 80 percent of the time or four out of five times, the required performance level (RPL) is 80 percent and the recommended number of observations (RO) is five. A teacher then can use this information to measure initial student competencies and to evaluate the success of an instructional program.

The formula to be used to determine whether the student is perform-

---

[2] The remainder of this section is reprinted from *Teaching the Moderately and Severely Handicapped*: Curriculum, Objectives, Strategies, and Activities. Vol. 1. Behavior, Self-Care, and Motor Skills (Bender and Valletutti, 1976, pp. 23–30, used with permission of authors and publisher).

ing at an acceptable level is as follows:

SPL (student performance level)

$$= \frac{\text{ssp (successful student performance)}}{\text{RO (recommended observations)}} \times 100 = \_\_\_\_ \%$$

OR

$$\text{SPL} = \frac{\text{ssp}}{\text{RO}} \times 100 = \_\_\_\_ \%$$

The SPL is expressed in terms of a percentage which then can be compared with the percentage assigned as the RPL.

Suppose Student A, on five different observations, successfully turns his eyes and head in the direction of sound two out of five times, His SPL is computed in the following manner:

$$\text{SPL} = \frac{2}{5} \times 100 = 40\%$$

Because the RPL for this task had been previously established at the 80 percent level, the student has failed to meet criterion and requires further evaluation and/or instruction.

Suppose Student B successfully turns his eyes and head in the direction of sound five out of five times. His SPL is computed as follows:

$$\text{SPL} = \frac{5}{5} \times 100 = 100\%$$

Because the RPL is 80 percent, Student B exceeds criterion and requires no further diagnostic exploration and/or programming for that task.

Consider Student C, who successfully turns his eyes and head in the direction of sound four out of five times. His SPL is:

$$\text{SPL} = \frac{4}{5} \times 100 = 80\%$$

Because the RPL is 80 percent, Student C meets the criterion measure and requires no programming and/or further exploration for that specific skill.

By utilizing the formula to compute the SPL and then comparing it to the RPL specified for the task, teachers are able to determine whether or not a student requires educational programming for the task.

The information obtained from using a diagnostic checklist must be supplemented with additional information before a teacher begins an instructional program. If a student accomplishes an educational task, only periodic rechecking is necessary. If the student fails to meet the evaluative criterion, however, it is not sufficient to know that he has failed. A teacher must discover what skills or competencies the student possesses that are prerequisite to the achievement of the objective. For example, awareness of the existence of sound is a precursor of speech and language development. A student who does not respond to sound obviously will obtain a low SPL on a task involving the auditory discrimination of sounds. Programming designed to develop auditory discrimination of sounds will be largely unproductive unless the teacher views the failure to meet this objective from a developmental or task analysis perspective, i.e., if the student fails to obtain a satisfactory SPL score, the teacher must determine what prerequisite skills are absent before initiating programs of remediation or skill development. The use of the diagnostic checklist must be supplemented with descriptions of a student's performance written in anecdotal form, an analysis of the teaching materials used, and the stimuli employed.

Before proceeding with any educational program, teachers should be alert to the possibility that underlying physiological and/or psychological reasons may exist that can interfere with achievement of an educational task. A teacher must be aware of those behaviors which suggest that a student requires medical and/or paramedical intervention if he is to achieve mastery. For example, a student may not be able to acquire toileting skills because he is physiologically incapable of attaining control over his bladder and/or sphincter muscles. Teachers, therefore, must not only determine whether there is a behavioral deficit but also must question whether there are any medical reasons that have caused or contributed to the deficit in learning. The search for cause is particularly appropriate when the precipitating condition is still physiologically and/or environmentally operating and thus accessible to treatment.

In order to clarify the structure, form, and function of a diagnostic checklist, the following sample section is presented.

Sample Diagnostic Checklist

_____ Student
_____ Rater

Legend

    RPL = required performance level (%)
    RO   = recommended observations
    ssp = successful student performance
    SPL = student performance level (%)

$$SPL = \frac{ssp}{RO} \times 100 = \underline{\quad}\%$$

Self-Care Skills

II. Cleaning and Grooming

A.   The student controls drooling when physically able to do so.

	Observations		
	Dates	Yes	No
___ Functions independently at RPL	1.		
	2.		
___ Does not function independently at RPL	3.		
	4.		
	5.		

$$\text{SPL} = \underline{\quad}\%$$
$$\text{RPL} = 100\%$$
$$\text{RO} = 5$$

B.   The student adjusts the water temperature in the sink for washing his hands and face.

	Observations		
	Dates	Yes	No
___ Functions independently at RPL	1.		
	2.		
___ Does not function independently at RPL	3.		
	4.		
	5.		

$$\text{SPL} = \underline{\quad}\%$$
$$\text{RPL} = 100\%$$
$$\text{RO} = 5$$

C.   The student washes his hands and face.

	Observations		
	Dates	Yes	No
___ Functions independently at RPL	1.		
	2.		
___ Does not function independently at RPL	3.		
	4.		

$$\text{SPL} = \underline{\quad}\%$$
$$\text{RPL} = 100\%$$
$$\text{RO} = 4$$

D.   The student dries his hands and face after washing.

Observations

	Dates	Yes	No
____ Functions independently at RPL	1.		
	2.		
____ Does not function independently at RPL	3.		
	4.		

SPL = ____ %
RPL = 75%
RO   =   4

E.   The student washes his underarms and uses a deodorant.

Observations

	Dates	Yes	No
____ Functions independently at RPL	1.		
	2.		
____ Does not function independently at RPL	3.		
	4.		

SPL = ____ %
RPL = 100%
RO   =   4

F.   The student brushes his teeth and rinses his mouth.

Observations

	Dates	Yes	No
____ Functions independently at RPL	1.		
	2.		
____ Does not function independently at RPL	3.		
	4.		
	5.		

SPL = ____ %
RPL = 100%
RO   =   5

G. The student cleans and cares for his nails.

Observations

Dates	Yes	No

____ Functions independently at RPL

____ Does not function independently at RPL

1.
2.
3.
4.

SPL = ____%
RPL = 75%
RO   = 4

H. The student wipes and blows his nose.

Observations

Dates	Yes	No

____ Functions independently at RPL

____ Does not function independently at RPL

1.
2.
3.
4.
5.

SPL = ____%
RPL = 100%
RO   = 5

I. The student takes a sponge bath.

Observations

Dates	Yes	No

____ Functions independently at RPL

____ Does not function independently at RPL

1.
2.
3.
4.

SPL = ____%
RPL = 100%
RO   = 4

J. The student bathes in a tub.

Observations

Dates	Yes	No

____ Functions independently at RPL

____ Does not function independently at RPL

1.
2.
3.
4.

SPL = ____%
RPL = 100%
RO   = 4

K. The student takes a shower.

Observations

Dates	Yes	No
1.		
2.		
3.		
4.		

___ Functions independently at RPL

___ Does not function independently at RPL

SPL = ___%
RPL = 100%
RO   = 4

L. The student washes and dries his/her hair.

Observations

Dates	Yes	No
1.		
2.		
3.		
4.		

___ Functions independently at RPL

___ Does not function independently at RPL

SPL = ___%
RPL = 100%
RO   = 4

M. The student combs, sets, and/or styles his/her hair.

Observations

Dates	Yes	No
1.		
2.		
3.		
4.		

___ Functions independently at RPL

___ Does not function independently at RPL

SPL = ___%
RPL = 75%
RO   = 4

N. The student has his/her hair cut and/or styled.

Observations

Dates	Yes	No
1.		
2.		
3.		
4.		

___ Functions independently at RPL

___ Does not function independently at RPL

SPL = ___%
RPL = 100%
RO   = 4

O.   The student shaves his face or body hair.

	Observations		
	Dates	Yes	No
____ Functions independently at RPL	1.		
	2.		
____ Does not function independently at RPL	3.		
	4.		

SPL = ____%
RPL = 100%
RO   =   4

P.   The student uses facial blemish treatments when needed.

	Observations		
	Dates	Yes	No
____ Functions independently at RPL	1.		
	2.		
____ Does not function independently at RPL	3.		
	4.		
	5.		

SPL = ____%
RPL = 100%
RO   =   5

Q.   The female student applies make-up when appropriate.

	Observations		
	Dates	Yes	No
____ Functions independently at RPL	1.		
	2.		
____ Does not function independently at RPL	3.		
	4.		

SPL = ____%
RPL = 75%
RO   =   4

R.   The student wears jewelry when appropriate (watch, rings, and neck chains).

Observations

Dates	Yes	No
1.		
2.		
3.		
4.		

____ Functions independently at RPL (1., 2.)

____ Does not function independently at RPL (3., 4.)

SPL = ____%
RPL = 75%
RO = 4

S.   The student uses and cares for eyeglasses and hearing aids.

Observations

Dates	Yes	No
1.		
2.		
3.		
4.		
5.		

____ Functions independently at RPL

____ Does not function independently at RPL

SPL = ____%
RPL = 100%
RO = 5

T.   The female student cares for herself during menstruation.

Observations

Dates	Yes	No
1.		
2.		
3.		
4.		
5.		

____ Functions independently at RPL

____ Does not function independently at RPL

SPL = ____%
RPL = 100%
RO = 5

ACTIVITIES AND EXPERIENCES

1.   Visit a classroom and select one pupil for observation. Observe him/her over a period of time. Write a sketch that describes representative and emerging behaviors. Discuss the implications for the selection of relevant educational objectives. Review with the classroom teacher.

2. Visit a second classroom. Select several pupils for observation. Observe them over a period of several weeks. Write sketches that describe each pupil in terms of representative and emerging behaviors. Discuss the implications for the selection of relevant educational objectives. Review with the classroom teacher.
3. If you are a student teacher or are currently teaching a class, prepare observation reports on each pupil in your class. Ask your college supervisor, cooperating teacher, or supervisor to review your "portraits." For each pupil, list suggested instructional objectives.
4. After one month, review the reports prepared in response to Activity 3. Revise as needed.
5. Spend a day visiting a classroom and prepare observations of pupils' behaviors. At the end of the day share your observations with the teacher.
6. Observe a pupil functioning outside the classroom setting, e.g., in the resource room, in speech therapy, in remedial reading, in occupational therapy, in art, in physical therapy, etc. Discuss your impressions with the therapist or teacher involved.
7. Select an area of the curriculum from the school system in which you are teaching, student teaching, or plan to teach. For this area prepare a diagnostic checklist.
8. Teach a series of lessons in a variety of content areas. After each lesson write a report containing relevant observations. Identify, in behavioral terms, educational objectives for each pupil in the group. In addition, suggest instructional materials, strategies, and techniques recommended for each pupil based on the observations. Prepare a written report on each pupil to be submitted to the parents and/or to an evaluation/programming team.

CONCLUDING STATEMENT

While it is no small task to observe and synthesize pupil behavior as it occurs in a group setting for a variety of conditions and subjects, it is not an insurmountable one. It requires that teachers engage in professional development activities designed to assist them in:

1. Selecting representative behaviors
2. Identifying emerging behaviors
3. Retaining and recording at a later time observations made previously
4. Avoiding interpretations of behavior
5. Reporting in an unbiased, straightforward manner the observations made

SECTION C   SAMPLING BEHAVIOR

INTRODUCTION AND OVERVIEW

A sophisticated educational evaluator or diagnostic/prescriptive teacher necessarily must be a skilled observer of pupil behavior. These behaviors that occur naturally and in direct response to instructional activities are certainly the best indicators of actual pupil knowledge, skills, and concepts. As pupils engage in a series of learning activities and as they interact with teachers and peers, they are providing teachers with an imposing array of diagnostic data. For example, a pupil who is reading aloud several paragraphs from a reader will shed light on his/her word attack skills, the use of voice to communicate meaning, and the mechanical aspects of speech production. A pupil who has written a paragraph on a specified theme will provide the teacher/evaluator with diagnostic information about spelling, word usage, and syntactical or formulation skills. The composition will provide the raw material from which teachers will be able to analyze vocabulary diversity, variety of sentence structure, specialized information acquired, and concepts understood. Responses to oral directions and questions will supply teachers with information relative to the pupil's knowledge and thought processes. Thus, teachers are constantly being supplied with diagnostic data that must be recorded and analyzed. Accomplishing this task for just one pupil is overwhelming. Since it must be carried out for a class of many students, it becomes herculean unless it is approached using a carefully worked out system for obtaining and then analyzing behavior.

Obtaining a Behavior Sample

One way of becoming a skillful, sophisticated observer is through the collection and study of samples of pupil behavior. The analysis of pupil work products is confounded, however, by the question of the reliability of data over time, i.e., are specific patterns of behavior consistent rather than random? The *continuous* analysis of behavior samples and work products minimizes errors in remedial planning resulting from insignificant or transitory behavioral discrepancies.

The method for obtaining a behavior sample is determined by the nature of the sample desired.

Oral Language   It is usually necessary to obtain a sample of a pupil's oral expressive language. Since speech is elusive, the evaluator should make a high fidelity tape or cassette recording of a representative sample of the pupil's speech. One way to obtain a good sample is to prepare a series of situational pictures of high interest to pupils and then ask them to respond to each stimulus picture by describing what they see in the picture. A 10- to 15-minute sample obtained and recorded in a quiet environment should then be analyzed for skills and problem areas. It should be recognized that this is one sample taken at one particular moment in time; therefore, one should be cautious in making diagnostic judgments and establishing educational programs based on a single sample.

The sophisticated diagnostician respects the conditional and subjunctive tenses: phrases such as, "It would appear from this sample that . . .;" "On the basis of this limited sample, one wonders whether . . .;" "It would seem from this one sample that the most critical area to concentrate on is most likely to be . . ." These equivocations are not offered to support fence straddling. Rather they are meant to emphasize the fact that judgments based on *limited* samples of behavior are, in reality, hypotheses that can only be borne out on a clinical basis, i.e., through the empiric proof that comes from future interactions. These conditional statements are also meant to spotlight the tentative nature of any diagnostic hypothesis that is likely to change as the pupil being evaluated changes.

Written Language   A written language sample is best obtained by encouraging the pupil to write about an experience. The topic, whenever possible, should be self-selected. It then is more likely to be part of the emotional and experiential life of the pupil and, thus, is more likely to be representative of the pupil's expressive language. When there is a pupil in your class with limited experiences and/or with restricted oral language skills, it may be necessary to spend abundant time providing that pupil with stimulating and enlightening experiences and/or developing oral language skills before exploring written language expression and comprehension.

Oral Reading   While there are excellent formal and informal tests of oral readings skills, teachers can easily develop their own tests. Selections from the basal readers used in the school system should be obtained. These will be more relevant to the specific educational objectives for the pupils involved. A passage from the beginning of each reader in the series should be selected. The length of each passage should be geared to the grade level of the pupil. The teacher should ask the pupil to begin reading from the selection. If there is little difficulty, then the pupil can proceed to the next higher level. Reading should be discontinued when the pupil experiences significant frustration or difficulty or when the pupil has advanced to reading a selection two years above grade level. If the pupil initially experiences great difficulty then the approach should be to proceed to levels below grade level until the pupil is reading with ease.

Reading Comprehension   Once a level of readability has been established, companion passages selected from the basal readers should be employed to assess reading comprehension. Reading comprehension should be determined by asking the pupil to read a passage silently and then to answer specially prepared questions. The pupil should be permitted to refer back to the passage in responding to the questions. Before testing, the teacher should have prepared a single-spaced, typed copy of the selections with the comprehension questions typed below leaving sufficient space to record the pupil's responses. These questions should be representative of reading comprehension and should include, depending upon grade level, the following types of questions:

1.   Defining words based on their usage in the selection
2.   Recalling key facts
3.   Drawing inferences based upon facts
4.   Articulating the main idea
5.   Drawing conclusions
6.   Recapitulating events in sequence
7.   Predicting outcomes

Social Science and Science   While social science and science concepts and information are wide-ranging and, thus, not easily subject to ready sampling, there are a number of stratagems that may be used to good effect. For example, class discussions on topics of current national and international interest may shed light on the knowledge possessed by the pupils. Such discussions will reveal knowledge possessed in the areas of geography, history, economics, sociology, anthropology, psychology, and political science. Stories appearing in the media can also stimulate provocative discussions that will illuminate the concepts, knowledge, and interests held by pupils. Stories from the basal reader and from various supplementary readings may also be used as the stimuli for diagnostic question and answer periods. For example, the story "Goldilocks and The Three Bears" can be used as the framework for questions designed to determine pupil knowledge of literature, the sciences, and the social sciences. Samples of possible diagnostic questions include:

1.   If you were lost in the woods, what might be the ways you could find your way to safety?
2.   Animals cannot really talk; however, they can communicate. What are examples of the ways animals communicate?
3.   The use of the number three is common in stories. Why is the number three so popular and what other stories employ this number in their plots?

4. Why is it scientifically impossible for the porridge to be too cold in one bowl, too hot in another, and just right in the third? Are there any circumstances, however, where this difference in temperature could occur?
5. Bears do not live on porridge. What do bears live on, i.e., what is their food supply? Where can bears be found? Where can bears be found in the United States?
6. Bears have been used by people for commercial purposes. In what ways have bears supplied jobs and goods to people?
7. Bears hibernate. What is hiberation and what other animals hibernate?
8. Discuss the ways that visitors to some national parks have to behave in order to avoid problems with bears. How many national parks and their locations can you name?
9. Why is the character of a bear in many children's stories called Bruin?
10. Trichinosis can be gotten from eating bear meat. Trichinosis usually occurs from eating what kind of meat? What other diseases can come from animals? How can those diseases be prevented?

These are just a few of the questions that can arise out of a simple story. The questions are only limited by a teacher's imagination and general knowledge. It should be noted that these questions focus not on deficits or defects but on possible areas of instructional enrichment. Teachers should be involved in diagnostic procedures not only to uncover discrepancies or deficiencies but to add to the knowledge and information base of pupils. Lastly, when pupils fail to answer the diagnostic questions, teachers should provide learning experiences to further their education in those areas where knowledge and concept formation are absent, scanty, or incomplete.

Analyzing a Behavior Sample

It is best to have a strategy established for the analysis of behavior samples. A particularly useful method of analysis has been developed by the authors and involves studying the sample or work product and responding to the following five questions:

1. What skills, knowledge, and concepts has the pupil demonstrated in this sample?
2. What problems has the pupil demonstrated in this sample?
3. What patterns, if any, exist among these problems?
4. What further diagnostic information is needed before making educational programming decisions?

5.   Based upon *this* sample what teaching objectives if any, would you recommend for this pupil?

These questions should form the basis for teacher analysis of all the work products and behavior samples collected. Particularly important are the responses to the first question. Discrepancies in performance are best understood within the framework of existing skills and knowledge. There appears to be a professional tendency on the part of teachers to see only errors. Unfortunately, this predilection seriously hampers the diagnostic process. Further, responses to the second question should attempt to identify skills or partial mastery among the problems evidenced, e.g., a pupil misspells a word but does so according to an acceptable phonetic pattern. The third question attempts to discover patterns that suggest instructional emphasis and/or point to problem consistency. The fourth question stresses the multidimensional aspects of the diagnostic process, while the final question highlights the diagnostic purpose.

The method for obtaining each sample, of course, depends upon the behavior to be evaluated. For example, analyzing oral reading skills involves recording the pupil's reading aloud of a selection and then comparing the oral reading to the original text. In carrying out an analysis of oral reading skills, it is best to have developed a notation system for recording deviations from the original text. If a triple-spaced typewritten copy of the original text is made, it will allow enough space to make notations while listening to the recording. The following notation system has proven to be helpful:

Error	Notation
1. Addition of a word	1. Place a caret at the place the student inserted a word or words. Write the word(s) above the line. You may wish to put the word(s) in quotes.
2. Addition of a sound or a word part	2. Write the additional sound or word part where the reader has added it.
3. Omission of a word	3. Draw a line through the entire word.
4. Omission of a sound or a word part	4. Draw an "X" through the omitted sound or word part.
5. Substitution of a word	5. Draw a line through the entire word *and* write the substituted word above it.
6. Substitution of a sound or a word part	6. Draw a line through the letters that correspond to a substituted word or word part *and* write the sound or part substituted.

7. Ignoring punctuation	7. Connect the two words read without a pause with curved lines above and below the line, e.g., They rode in the car. Later . . .
8. Error in pronunciation	8. Print a capital *P* above the word followed by an equal sign followed by a phonetic approximation of the mispronunciation.
9. Distortion of sound	9. Print a capital *D* above the sound.
10. Correction of a mistake	10. Draw an arrow from right to left from the point where the pupil stopped and went back to make the correction. If the pupil succeeds, write a large *C* in front of the arrow tip. If the pupil goes back to correct but fails, print *NC* in front of the arrow tip.
11. Hesitation	11. Draw a vertical line for each 15 seconds of hesitation. After three vertical lines, provide the pupil with assistance. If assistance is provided, write the word *Aid*.

After the recording has been listened to several times and the notations verified, it is then necessary to analyze the various errors in an effort to understand their nature and frequency. For example, a pupil who has substituted a real word (or words) that makes contextual sense is comprehending what is being read while experiencing problems with word attack skills. On the other hand, a pupil who has substituted a real word that makes no contextual sense but is visually similar to the actual word is evidencing problems with comprehension but demonstrating some degree of phonetic awareness. The substitution of a nonsense word indicates not only a failure of comprehension but also a failure to check the decoded word against his/her oral vocabulary (Moran, 1978). Moran (1978) describes three types of oral reading errors:

—Overreliance on or failure to use content or meaning cues: The student omits, inserts, or substitutes a word or phrase, distorting the *sense* of the passage.
—Disregard for syntactic or word-order cues: The pupil omits, inserts, or substitutes a word or alters word order, distorting the *grammar* of the passage.
—Inattention to graphic/phonic cues: The student inserts a word which has no graphic counterpart, omits a printed word, or substitutes a word which is *graphically* unrelated to the printed word (p. 48).

Disregard of syntax or word order will result in substitutions outside the appropriate word class, such as a verb for a noun. The presence of a hesitation may mean that the pupil is having difficulty with the next occurring word in the passage or with a word that is causing difficulty as the pupil reads ahead. Additions and omissions may represent oral language deficits, and they may indicate dialectual differences, e.g., the omission of the *s* in the third person singular of verbs. A tendency to ignore punctuation, generally, indicates problems with comprehension despite graphic/phonic skill. Distortion of sounds may be dialectical in origin or may reflect the existence of a speech defect. In fact, whenever mispronunciations occur in oral reading, an effort must be made to ascertain whether it is a function of the pupil's oral language or a result of reading problems. Particularly noteworthy are self-corrected errors. "A student who allows errors of word recognition which violate the sense and the grammatical integrity of sentences to stand without correction is quite different from the reader who corrects his or her own errors along the way" (Moran, 1978, p. 51).

In order to conduct a thorough and scholarly evaluation, it is necessary that teachers understand as completely as possible the dimensions of the educational task so that their responses to the five questions enumerated above are as organized and scientific as possible. For example, an oral language sample may be analyzed along two dimensions: the mechanics of oral communication and the structure of oral communication.

The mechanics of oral communication may be evaluated in terms of the following variables:

Articulation
Voice production
Fluency of speech
Pronunciation
Visual components of speech production

The structure of oral communication may be analyzed in terms of the following variables:

Word usage
Grammatical usage
Number of words
Words per minute
Number of communication units
Mean length of communication unit
Vocabulary diversity
Structural patterns
Index of subordinate clauses
Index of phrases

Index of modification
Index of multiples
Index of compound structures used as expansion strategies
Miscellaneous structural strategies

The Mechanics of Speech

Articulation   Articulation may be measured from several different approaches including: a count of the number of defective sounds, i.e., a sound misarticulated either as a single or blend in any position in a word; a phonetic environment measure that represents the proportion of misarticulations of sound blends; a type of sound error measure that represents the proportion of errors that are omissions, substitutions, and distortions; a position of consonant sounds measure that represents the proportion of misarticulations that occur in the initial, medial, and final positions; a phonetic category measure that represents the proportion of misarticulated sounds that are vowels or diphthongs, nasals, plosives, onglides, fricatives, and affricates; and a frequency of occurrence of error measure based on sound values according to their relative frequency of occurrence in American speech.

Voice Production   Disorders of phonation fall into four major divisions: disorders of pitch, intensity, quality, and rate. Typical pitch disorders are the too high or too low pitched voice, the voice characterized by stereotyped inflections, and the monotonous voice. Typical intensity disorders are the too loud or too weak voice or the lack of any voice. Hoarse, strident, husky, hypernasal, and hyponasal voices represent common problems in voice quality, while disorders of rate include excess or insufficient rapidity and irregular or monotonous rates. A voice measure should include both type and number of defective aspects of phonation.

Disfluency of Speech   The classification of disfluency has been divided into eight different categories:

1. Interjections of sounds, syllables, words, or phrases
2. Part-word repetitions
3. Word repetitions
4. Phrase repetitions
5. Revisions
6. Incomplete phrases
7. Broken words
8. Prolonged sounds

A disfluency index may be computed that represents a count of the total number of disfluencies per hundred words spoken.

Pronunciation   Acceptability of pronunciation is based upon the conversational patterns of cultivated speakers when speaking in the normal context of life. A measure of mispronunciation may be obtained by expressing it as a ratio of pronunciation errors to the total number of words. Mispronunciations may occur according to the following types of patterns (Fairbanks, 1959, pp. 110–112):

1. Substitution: Vowel of monosyllable
2. Substitution: Vowel of accented syllable
3. Substitution: Vowel of unaccented syllable
4. Substitution: Consonant
5. Omission: Syllable preceding primary accent
6. Omission: Syllable following primary accent
7. Omission: Medial consonant
8. Addition: Syllable
9. Addition: Consonant
10. Misplaced accent: Forward-moving
11. Misplaced accent: Backward-moving
12. Miscellaneous or multiple

Errors of articulation must be distinguished from errors of pronunciation. Sounds substituted or omitted in mispronunciations of particular words are made with accuracy, ease, and fluency in other contexts, while articulation errors occur with a high degree of consistency, according to position, in a variety of words.

Visual Components of Speech Production   The visual components of speech production refer to those visual aspects, such as drooling, tics, peculiarities in sound formation, and grimaces, that accompany speech production and may be disconcerting to the listener. Obtaining a recorded sample will not, of course, allow for the analysis of cosmetic problems. These problems should be noted during the taping sessions, or, when seen as a problem, the sample should be recorded on videotape.

The Structure of Oral Communication   Before an analysis of structure can be undertaken, the language sample must be segmented according to the subject's oral intonation patterns. These patterns are determined by the contours of inflection, stress, and pause in the subject's voice. Loban (1963) speaks of these units as being phonological. These units may then be further segmented into communication units that are identified by semantic meaning. According to Loban: "The communication unit has been defined . . . as a group of words which cannot be further divided without the loss of essential meaning" (p. 6). Another element may also be identified, the maze, that can be thought of as a tangle of language that does not make semantic sense and is impossible to classify phonologically or semantically. All words and phrases that represent repetitions and revisions made by the speaker should not be considered part of the communication units. In addition, words of little meaning used as launchers or as fillers should not be considered part of the communication unit. Such words and phrases as "well," "or something," "and stuff," and "you know" fall into this category.

Word Usage   A measure of incorrect word usage may be expressed as a ratio of the total number of words misused to the total number of words in the sample.

Grammatical Usage   Mistakes in grammatical usage include: 1) errors in agreement of number, gender, and tense; 2) omission of grammatical units; and 3) substitution of the wrong case, the wrong form of comparison, and the wrong part of speech. A measure of grammatical errors may be the total number of errors expressed as a ratio to the total number of words.

Number of Words   This measure may be expressed as a simple count of the number of words found in the communication units.

Words Per Minute   This measure may be expressed as the average number of words spoken per minute.

Number of Communication Units   This measure may be expressed as a simple count of the communication units in the sample.

Mean Length of Communication Unit   This measure may be expressed as the average number of words spoken per communication unit.

Vocabulary Diversity   This measure may be expressed as a type token ratio, stated as a ratio of the number of different words per hundred word segment. Each segment should be treated separately and an average taken of all the segments. A segment of less than 50 words should not be tabulated and those of 50 words or more should be prorated to represent a complete segment.

Structural Patterns   This analysis may be based on the count of nine patterns that represent the basic structures of the English sentence (Loban, 1963) plus one partial or incomplete unit. Each of the 10 patterns may be expressed as a separate ratio to the total number of communication units. A variety score may be computed also. This measure may be stated as the count of the number of different structural patterns used.

The patterns may be evaluated as follows:

1. 1 2   or   1 ②   Mary eats. (or)   Mary is home.
2. 1 2 4   Mary eats strawberries.
3. 1 ② 5   Strawberries are berries.
4. 1 2 3 4   Mary threw the dog some biscuits.
5. 1 2 4 6   They elected Mary president.
6. (1) ② 1   Here is Mary.
7. Questions   Is he here?

8.   Passive Forms   Strawberries were eaten by Mary.
9.   Requests or Commands   Go home.
10. Partials

Numerical symbols have the following meaning:

1 = subject
2 = transitive and intransitive verbs
②= linking verbs
3 = the inner complement (indirect object)
4 = the transitive verb complement (direct object)
5 = the linking verb complement (predicate nominative or predicate adjective)
6 = the outer (objective) complement (Loban, 1963, pp. 12-13).

Index of Subordinate Clauses   This measure may be expressed as a count of subordinate clauses expressed as a ratio to the number of communication units.

Index of Phrases   This measure may be expressed as a count of the prepositional and verbal phrases expressed as a ratio to the number of communication units. A type of phrase index may be computed separately for verbal and prepositional phrases.

Index of Modification   This measure may be expressed as a count of the number of single word modifiers and the number of phrases and clauses that serve as modifiers. A type of modification index may be computed for adverbial and adjectival modifiers.

Index of Multiples   This measure may be expressed as a count of the number of multiple constructions used stated as a ratio to the number of communication units. The following multiples may be considered:

1.   A subordinate clause within another subordinate clause
2.   A verbal phrase within a subordinate clause
3.   A prepositional phrase within a subordinate clause
4.   A prepositional phrase within a verbal construction

Index of Compound Structures Used as Expansion Strategies   This measure may be expressed as a count of the number of compound subjects, compound predicates, and compound objects used expressed as a ratio to the number of communication units.

Miscellaneous Structural Strategies   Included in this analysis may be a count of the number of infinitives, participles, and appositives used. Each element may be expressed as a ratio to the total number of words.

ACTIVITIES AND EXPERIENCES

1.   Obtain and analyze a sample of oral reading skill for each of three pupils.

2. Obtain and analyze a sample of reading comprehension skill for each of three pupils.
3. Obtain and analyze a sample of written language expression for each of three pupils.
4. Obtain and analyze a sample of written arithmetic skill for each of three pupils.
5. Obtain and analyze a sample of oral language skill for each of three pupils.
6. Analyze the following written language samples:

My Halloween

On Halloween I went with Kit and Lula Jackson. First we went to pick up Katie Cockren. Then we went to Mr. and Mrs. Alxaders house, and we soaped up their windows on their car. Then we went to Mr. Mrs. Frasefelt and got some candy. By the way I was half man and half women, and Kit was a headless horseman and Lula was a vamper, and Katie was ragty ann. After we went to the Frasenfelts we went to my Aunt Kitty's and got some more candy. Then We went to the Bonsels and they threw pupkens at us so we ran away. We went to Lotts'

more house 's and el got
a hermet crab from my
ant lucy. Then we all
went home. The End

Jamaica

Last summer el visited
Jamaica. el had a very
nice time. el stayed with
my aunt and uncle and
visited my other aunts and my
cousins. Were el stayed was
very beautiful. el had a
lot of company. On
Indepence weekend we went
to a vacation resort. In
the day el went to the beach
and at night el went to a
dico with my other teenage
cousins. We stayed for
two nights and three days.
The country was very
pretty, and el really enjoyed
my trip to Jamaica a lot.

7. Using topics of current interest, make up discussion questions
   designed to explore the pupils' knowledge and concepts in the social
   sciences, science, literature, and/or the arts.
8. Select a famous short story, fairy tale, or folk tale. Write discussion
   questions designed to explore the pupils' knowledge and concepts in
   the social sciences, science, literature, and/or the arts.
9. Repeat Activity 8; this time use a story from the basal reader.

CONCLUDING STATEMENT

Samples of behavior are not only to be obtained in a planned manner. Often a sample of behavior that is particularly telling occurs and should be, whenever possible, recorded and analyzed. When these behaviors are not in written form, teachers must train themselves to remember the details of the situation with as much accuracy and skill as possible so that they can be recorded and analyzed later. Developing this skill and the ability to separate insignificant occurrences from those of greater moment frequently occurs with experience.

SECTION D   INTERVIEWING AND INTERACTING WITH THE PUPIL AND THE PUPIL'S PARENTS

INTRODUCTION AND OVERVIEW

An abundance of diagnostic information may be gathered through interactions with the pupil and with his/her parents or parent surrogates. Perhaps, there is a tendency to underestimate the value of the potential contributions to be made by these individuals because of their lack of professional training and supposed lack of objectivity. People, however, can be surprisingly objective and honest when talking about themselves and their loved ones, especially when interacting with an interviewer who is skillful in eliciting valid responses. While it is not known precisely what communication strategies are most likely to encourage honest and perceptive responses, it seems probable that a teacher who values the communications of pupils and parents is more apt to obtain insightful and valuable diagnostic information. Asking parents, for example, how a pupil spends his/her leisure time, what "turns the pupil on," what hobbies are pursued, and how the pupil's interest might be sparked may furnish information invaluable for designing instructional programs. However, the individual pupil is better able to tell a teacher what his/her interests are. Why engage in indirect ways of determining pupil interests when it is much simpler to ask the pupils directly what interests them, what books they would like to read, what topics they would like to study, etc. Indeed, much valuable information may be obtained by asking pupils what problems they are having and why these problems are occurring. Pupils have been known to make such valuable remarks as, "I can't hear the difference between those two sounds," (poor auditory discrimination?) and "I can't see the blackboard from here," (poor visual acuity?). Comments such as these are forms of self-evaluation and provide invaluable diagnostic information.

The skills necessary for encouraging pupils and parents to communicate freely must be developed if teachers are to be effective in diagnosing the pupils' educational needs and in planning individualized programs of instruction. A necessary precursor to such skill development is the growth of a concomitant professional attitude that views meetings with parents not as occasions to tell them what to do but rather as opportunities to benefit from the insights and the information collected throughout the years of living with the pupil. A good approach, perhaps, would be, "How can I help you (parents) help your child grow and develop? How can all of us working together arrive at the best possible educational program for (pupil's name)?" With this attitude undergirding all teacher-parent communication, the interaction skills should emerge naturally.

A skilled interviewer not only knows what questions to be asked, but, more important, how to listen to what is being communicated. Listening objectively requires abandoning prejudices and preconceptions in a willingness to be open-minded, to be enlightened. A teacher must communicate, verbally *and* nonverbally, "I value what you tell me. I seek your wisdom. Please, help me to help your child progress in knowledge, skills, and values. How can we as a team create an educational program that is developmental, remedial, therapeutic, meaningful, and enriching?" Remarks such as the above made as early as possible in the school year should serve as a catalyst for obtaining information from parents, information that helps to flesh out a pupil "portrait" or profile that pictures his/her abilities, disabilities, needs, interests, and values. A skilled listener selects the key information from what is being said.

Whenever possible, parent-teacher conferences should be scheduled with the pupil in attendance. This approach helps establish a milieu that implies, "We are all members of the same team, working together toward a common goal, i.e., the identification of relevant educational objectives and instructional programs for (child's name)." Meetings where pupils are allowed to participate can furnish an unexcelled opportunity for parents and their children to interact in loving, constructive, and creative ways. The information culled from such interaction can be of inestimable value in both the diagnostic and prescriptive processes. Despite the benefits accruing from meetings that involve the diverse perspectives of parents, pupil, and teacher(s), there, of necessity, will be times when the pupil should not be present. These meetings, however, should be kept to a minimum and substantial justification found before their scheduling.

Channels of communication must be kept open with both parents or parent surrogates when there are two significant adults in the life of the pupil. Sexism, unfortunately, cuts both ways, and teachers tend to ignore the important role that fathers do and can play in the education of their children. Failure to tap this potentially excellent information source may interfere grievously with the teacher's pursuit of critical diagnostic/prescriptive data. Certainly, as sex roles change and as more fathers assume the care of their children, fathers should be expected to play an increasingly important part in both the diagnostic and instructional process. The father's perspective is another source through which the nature and educational needs of pupils may be illuminated. Fathers, when feasible, must be included on the pupil, parents, and teacher(s) team.

Teachers need to supplement conferences with parents and pupils with other strategies and devices for keeping communication open and dynamic. Written communications are especially valuable provided that parents do not have disabilities in reading and writing themselves. Weekly or bimonthly "newsletters" in which information is sent home to parents relevant to class happenings and plans for the future can contribute to keeping parents informed *and* involved. Individual concerns can be handled in private notes, oftentimes with lunch boxes serving as mail carrier. The time of report cards can be used as an occasion to report in concise, descriptive, and simple detail on the progress of pupils and hoped for achievements rather than as the time to report grades that, by themselves, communicate little. Succinct, direct reports can provide an unparalleled opportunity to tell of the pupil's achievements and to specify future instructional objectives.

Parents, in turn, should be encouraged to send in notes, filled in checklists, and participation charts as a way of keeping the teacher informed of recent behaviors/occurrences that shed light on a pupil's skills, interests, experiences, and needs. For example, a note that tells of a recent family outing can provide substance for a class discussion in which the pupil is more likely to be involved. A note that reports on an accomplishment can provide important diagnostic programming information, e.g., "John put on and zippered his winter jacket all by himself Saturday morning." On the other hand, the use of a diagnostic checklist offers the parent a means of systematically recording behavior that the parent is in the most advantageous position to observe. While the teacher frequently must deal with simulated activities and situations, parents more frequently are able to observe relevant behaviors as they occur in real situations. The diagnostic checklist should mirror previously identified educational objectives and should be used to determine what skills a given pupil possesses and what skills he/she has still to master. The parent must be assisted with the skills of observing and recording behavior and be provided with a checklist or lists of those behaviors that are more likely to be observed by parents. Such functional behaviors include the following:

1. a. (Student's name) brushed his/her teeth before going to bed carrying out all the skills involved.
        Dates and Times Observed   _____
        _____
        _____

    b. (Student's name) brushed his/her teeth before going to bed but did not carry out the following tasks correctly:
        1) _____
        2) _____
        3) _____
        Dates and Times Observed   _____
        _____
        _____

2. (Student's Name), when in a local restaurant, found the ladies'/mens' room without any assistance.
    Date Occurred _____
    Label/sign on the bathroom door _____

Through these various written exchanges, parents can provide a steady flow of crucial diagnostic information to teachers as they plan essential instructional programs.

The telephone should be included as a way of communicating with parents who are unable or unwilling to come to school. The telephone is particularly useful for communicating with those who evidence problems with written communication and who are reluctant to visit the school. The telephone provides a degree of personal anonymity that may be needed by parents who are concerned with their physical appearance and clothing. It is also a useful resource when working with parents who are handicapped or who lack transportation.

ACTIVITIES AND EXPERIENCES

1. Hold a conference with a school-age child or youth. Ask the pupil what he/she would like to learn, would like to discuss, what interests him/her, etc. Continue by asking the pupil to make suggestions to his/her teacher(s) relevant to a meaningful school program.
2. Arrange a meeting with parents of a school-age child or youth. Discuss the pupil with the parents, asking them to help you gain insight into the pupil's abilities and learning problems and needs. Ask them to share their perceptions of what they believe school should be.
3. Identify a pupil who is having significant problems in learning. Ask that pupil to tell you why he/she thinks the problem exists. Ask what suggestions he/she has for correcting these problems.

4. Hold a conference with parents with the pupil in attendance. You may simulate the conference if a real situation is not feasible. Videotape this team meeting and explore as a group the ways in which the team, working together, can create an effective educational program. Play back and study the tape.
5. Compose a mock newsletter to be sent home to parents. The newsletter should report on class happenings and projections for the future.
6. Write several mock notes in which you communicate matters of a private nature to parents. Include in your note requests for nonpersonal information to help you arrive at sound individualized educational objectives.
7. Design a sample checklist to be used by parents to report on pupil progress. Select items that parents are most advantageously situated to observe and report on.
8. Write a report card for each pupil in the class in which you are student teaching, or in which you are involved in a a practicum assignment. The report card should consist of no grades, merely objectives to be worked on.

CONCLUDING STATEMENT

Throughout all the various interactions between the teacher, parents, and pupil, it is the teacher's responsibility to set the stage for free, open, honest, and productive communication. The teacher must be sensitive to the emotional needs of parents, the parents' perception of the school experience, and the parents' view of the role and status of teachers. The teacher needs to help parents feel at ease in their interactions in order to prevent the stifling effects that invariably accompany formal, structured communication. Placing parents in a coequal position while retaining professional prerogatives is a precarious balancing act requiring great skill. Keeping the channels of communication open is an essential professional competency requisite to the effective instruction that encompasses the needs of the whole child.

SUMMARY

As the foregoing sections of this module are studied and implemented it is seen that although the overall goal of objective, nonjudgmental analysis and evaluation of each pupil's knowledge, skills, concepts, interests, and needs appears to be a monumental task almost defying completion, when it is approached in an orderly, step-by-step method, it can be accomplished. Careful implementation of the methods outlined in

Section D will supply much assistance as constructive interaction with both pupils and parents is directed toward the accomplishment of overall objectives.

By proceeding in a systematic manner in developing and administering test inventories, observing and documenting pupil behaviors, sampling and analyzing pupil behavior and work products, and establishing good rapport with both pupils and their parents, individual educational objectives for each pupil can be established in a realistic way. The ultimate goal of the best possible education for each individual pupil then comes into an attainable focus.

POSTTEST

At this point retake the Pretest.

LITERATURE CITED

Bender, M., and Valletutti, P. J. 1976. Teaching the Moderately and Severely Handicapped: Curriculum Objectives, Strategies, and Activities. Vol. I. Behavior, Self-Care, and Motor Skills. University Park Press, Baltimore.

Fairbanks, G. 1959. Voice and Articulation Drillbook. Harper & Row Publishers, New York.

Loban, W. D. 1963. The Language of Elementary School Children. National Council of Teachers of English, Champaign, Ill.

Moran, M. R. 1978. Assessment of the Exceptional Learner in the Regular Classroom. Love Publishing Co., Denver.

SUGGESTED READINGS

Section A   Test Inventories

Chase, C. I. 1978. Measurement for Educational Evaluation. 2nd Ed. Addison-Wesley Publishing Co., Inc., Reading, Mass.

Flynn, J. T., and Garber, H. (eds.). 1967. Readings in Educational and Psychological Measurement. Addison-Wesley Publishing Co., Reading, Mass.

Furst, E. J. 1958. Constructing Evaluation Instruments. Longmans Green & Co., New York.

Gagné, R. M. 1970. The Conditions of Learning. 2nd Ed. Holt, Rinehart & Winston, Inc., New York.

Gronlund, N. E. 1973. Preparing Criterion-Referenced Tests for Classroom Instruction. Macmillan Publishing Co., Inc., New York.

Gronlund, N. E. 1974. Individualizing Classroom Instruction. Macmillan Publishing Co., Inc., New York.

Karmel, L. J., and Karmel, M. O. 1978. Measurement and Evaluation in the Schools. 2nd Ed. Macmillan Publishing Co., Inc. New York.

Lerner, J. W. 1971. Children with Learning Disabilities: Theories, Diagnosis, and Teaching Strategies. Houghton Mifflin Co., Boston.

Marshall, J. C., and Hales, L. W. 1971. Classroom Test Construction. Addison-Wesley Publishing Co., Reading, Mass.

McCormack, J. E., Jr. 1976. The assessment tool that meets your needs: The one you construct. Teach. Except. Child. 8:106–109.

Smith, R. M. 1969. Collecting diagnostic data in the classroom. Teach. Except. Child. 1:128–133.

Smith, R. M. (ed.). 1969. Teacher Diagnosis of Educational Difficulties. Charles E. Merrill Publishing Co., Columbus, Oh.

Smith, R. M. 1974. Clinical Teaching: Methods of Instruction for the Retarded. McGraw-Hill Book Co., New York.

Stephens, T. M. 1970. Directive Teaching of Children with Learning and Behavioral Handicaps. Charles E. Merrill Publishing Co., Columbus, Oh.

Ten Brink, T. D. 1974. Evaluation: A Practical Guide for Teachers. McGraw-Hill Book Co., New York.

Thorndike, R. L. (ed.). 1971. Educational Measurement. 2nd Ed. American Council on Education, Washington, D.C.

Wallace, G., and Kauffman, J. M. 1973. Teaching Children with Learning Problems. Charles E. Merrill Publishing Co., Columbus, Oh.

Section B   Observation and Documentation

Ahmann, J. S., and Glock, M. D. 1971. Evaluating Pupil Growth. 4th Ed. Allyn & Bacon, Boston.

Almy, M. 1959. Ways of Studying Children. Teachers College Press, New York.

Boehm, A. E., and Weinberg, R. A. 1977. The Classroom Observer: A Guide for Developing Observation Skills. Teachers College Press, New York.

Brandt, R. 1972. Studying Behavior in Natural Settings. Holt, Rinehart & Winston, Inc., New York.

Brison, D. W. 1967. The school psychologist's use of direct observation. J. School Psychol. 5:109–115.

Cartwright, C. A., and Cartwright, G. P. 1974. Developing Observational Skills. McGraw-Hill Book Co., New York.

Chamberlin, R. W. 1976. The use of teacher checklists for identifying children at risk for later behavioral and emotional problems. Am. J. Dis. Child. 30:381–387.

Chase, C. I. 1978. Measurement for Educational Evaluation. 2nd Ed. Addison-Wesley Publishing Co., Reading, Mass.

Clay, M. 1975. Preventing failure. Aust. J. Rem. Educ. 7:2–7.

Cohen, D., and Stern, V. 1958. Observing and Recording the Behavior of Young Children. Teachers College Press, New York.

Donlon, E. T., and Burton, L. F. 1976. The Severely and Profoundly Handicapped: A Practical Approach to Teaching. Grune & Stratton, New York.

Forness, S. R., and Esveldt, K. C. 1975. Prediction of high-risk kindergarten children through classroom observation. J. Spec. Educ. 9:375–387.

Gellert, E. 1955. Systematic observation: A method of child study. Harvard Educ. Rev. 25:179–195.

Glynn, E. L., and McNaughton, S. S. 1975. Trust your own observations: Criterion referenced assessment of reading progress. Slow Learn. Child. 22:91–108.

Gronlund, N. E. 1976. Measurement and Evaluation in Teaching. 3rd Ed. Macmillan Publishing Co., Inc., New York.

Haring, N. G., and Schiefelbusch, R. L. (eds.). 1978. Teaching Special Children. McGraw-Hill Book Co., New York.

Hinde, R. A. (ed.). 1972. Non-verbal Communication. Cambridge University Press, London.

Hutt, S. J., and Hutt, C. 1976. Direct Observation and Measurement of Behavior. Charles C Thomas Publisher, Springfield, Ill.

Langley, B., and Dubose, R. F. 1976. Functional vision screening for severely handicapped children. New Outlook Blind 70:346–350.

Lindzey, G. (ed.). 1954. Handbook of Social Psychology. Vol. I. Addison-Wesley Publishing Co., Inc., Cambridge, Mass.

Lindzey, G., and Aronson, E. (eds.). 1970. Handbook of Social Psychology. Vol. II. Addison-Wesley Publishing Co., Inc., Reading, Mass.

Markoff, A. M. 1976. Teaching Low-Achieving Children Reading, Spelling and Handwriting. Charles C Thomas Publisher, Springfield, Ill.

McCormack, J. E., Jr. 1976. Educational Evaluation and Planning Package: A Rationale. Massachusetts Center for Program Development and Evaluation, Medford.

Moran, M. R. 1978. Assessment of the Exceptional Learner in the Regular Classroom. Love Publishing Co., Denver.

Peter, L. J. 1965. Prescriptive Teaching. McGraw-Hill Book Co., New York.

Platts, M. E. 1970. Anchor: A Handbook of Vocabulary Discovery Techniques for the Classroom Teacher. Educational Service. Stevensville, Mich.

Quanty, C. B., and Davis, A. 1974. Observing Children. Alfred Publishing Co., Sherman Oaks, Cal.

Sackett, G. P. (ed.). 1978. Observing Behavior. Vol. II. University Park Press, Baltimore.

Safer, D. J., and Allen, R. P. 1976. Hyperactive Children: Diagnosis and Management. University Park Press, Baltimore.

Simon, A., and Boyer, E. G. (eds.). 1970. Mirrors for Behavior: An Anthology of Classroom Observation Instruments. Research for Better Schools, Philadelphia.

Stanley, J. C., and Hopkins, K. D. 1972. Educational and Psychological Measurement and Evaluation. 5th Ed. Prentice-Hall, Inc., Englewood Cliffs, N.J.

Stephens, T. M. 1970. Directive Teaching of Children with Learning and Behavioral Handicaps. Charles E. Merrill Publishing Co., Columbus, Oh.

Ten Brink, T. D. 1974. Evaluation: A Practical Guide for Teachers. McGraw-Hill Book Co., New York.

Thorndike, R. L., and Hagen, E. 1969. Measurement and Evaluation in Psychology and Education. 3rd Ed. John Wiley & Sons, Inc., New York.

Travers, R. M. W. (ed.). 1973. Second Handbook on Research in Teaching. Rand McNally, Inc., Chicago.

Wemberg, R. A., and Wood, F. H. (eds.). 1975. Observation of Pupils and Teachers in Mainstream and Special Education Settings: Alternative Strategies. Leadership Training Institute/Special Education, University of Minnesota, Minneapolis.

Wemy, J., and Quay, H. 1969. Observing the classroom behavior of elementary school children. Except. Child. 35:461–470.

White, O. R., and Haring, N. G. 1976. Exceptional Teaching: A Multimedia Training Package. Charles E. Merrill Publishing Co., Columbus, Oh.
Wright, H. F. 1967. Recording and Analyzing Child Behavior. Harper & Row Publishers, New York.

Section C   Sampling and Analysis of Pupil Behavior and Work Products

Appell, L. S. 1975. Math assessment. Diagnostique 6:6–8.
Berry, M. F. 1969. Language Disorders of Children: The Basis and Diagnosis. Appleton-Century-Crofts, New York.
Bond, G. L., and Tinker, M. A. 1967. Reading Difficulties: Their Diagnosis and Correction. 2nd Ed. Appleton-Century-Crofts, New York.
Brueckner, L. J. 1955. Diagnostic Tests and Self-Helps in Arithmetic. California Testing Bureau, Los Angeles.
Carrow, E. 1972. Assessment of speech and language in children. In J. E. McLean, D. E. Yoder, and R. L. Schiefelbusch (eds.), Language Intervention with the Retarded, pp. 52–88. University Park Press, Baltimore.
Cazden, C. B. 1972. Child Language and Education. Holt, Rinehart & Winston, Inc., New York.
Chase, C. I. 1978. Measurement for Educational Evaluation. 2nd Ed. Addison-Wesley Publishing Co., Reading, Mass.
Crystal, D., Fletcher, D. and Garman, M. 1976. The Grammatical Assessment of Language Disability: A Procedure for Assessment and Remediation. Studies in Language Disability and Remediation. Vol. I. Edward Arnold (Publishers) Ltd., London.
Dale, P. S. 1972. Language Development. Dryden Press, Hinsdale, Ill.
de Hirsch, K., Jansky, J. J., and Langford, W. S. 1966. Predicting Reading Failure. Harper & Row Publishers, New York.
Ekwall, E. E. 1976. Informal reading inventories: The instructional level. Read. Teach. 29:662–665.
Faas, L. A. 1976. Learning Disabilities: A Competency Based Approach. Houghton Mifflin Co., Boston.
Ferguson, C. S., and Slobin, D. I. (eds.). 1973. Studies of Child Language Development. Holt, Rinehart & Winston, Inc., New York.
Fodor, J. J., and Katz, J. A. (eds.). 1964. The Structure of Language. Prentice-Hall, Inc., Englewood Cliffs, N.J.
Goodman, Y. M., and Burke, C. L. 1972. Reading Miscue Inventory Manual: Procedure for Diagnosis and Evaluation. Macmillan Publishing Co., Inc., New York.
Guess, D. 1969. A functional analysis of receptive language and productive speech: Aquisition of the plural morpheme. J. Appl. Behav. Anal. 2:55–64.
Guirk, R., Leech, G., Greenbaum, S., and Svartic, J. A. 1972. Grammar of Contemporary English. Seminar Press, New York.
Johnson, W., Darley, F. L., and Spriestersbach, D. C. 1963. Diagnostic Methods in Speech Pathology. Harper & Row Publishers, New York.
Kenyon, J. S., and Knott, T. A. 1949. A Pronouncing Dictionary of American English. B. and C. Merriam Co., Springfield, Mass.
Lee, L. 1970. A screening test for syntax development. J. Speech Hear. Disord. 35:103–112.

Lee, L. 1974. Developmental Sentence Analysis. Northwestern University Press, Evanston, Ill.

Lloyd, L. L. (ed.). 1976. Communication Assessment and Intervention Strategies. University Park Press, Baltimore.

Loban, W. D. 1963. The Language of Elementary School Children. National Council of Teachers of English, Champaign, Ill.

Lovitt, T. C., and Hansen, C. L. 1976. Round one-placing the child in the right reader. J. Learn. Disabil. 9:347–353.

McCracken, R. A. 1962. Standardized reading tests and informal reading inventories. Education 82:366–369.

McLean, J. E., and Snyder-McLean, L. K. 1978. A Transactional Approach to Early Language Training. Charles E. Merrill Publishing Co., Columbus, Oh.

Menyuk, P. 1969. Sentences Children Use. The M.I.T. Press, Cambridge.

Menyuk, P. 1972. The Onset of Speech. Bobbs-Merrill Co., Inc., Indianapolis.

Milisen, R. 1971. Methods of evaluation and diagnosis of speech disorders. In L. E. Travis (ed.), Handbook of Speech Pathology and Audiology. Appleton-Century-Crofts, New York.

Miller, J. 1978. Assessing children's language behavior. A developmental process approach. In R. L. Schiefelbusch (ed.), Bases of Language Intervention, pp. 269–318. University Park Press, Baltimore.

Moran, M. R. 1978. Assessment of the Exceptional Learner in the Regular Classroom. Love Publishing Co., Denver.

Morehead, D., and Morehead, A. (eds.). 1976. Directions in Normal and Deficient Child Language. University Park Press, Baltimore.

Perry, T. E. 1961. The Most Common Mistakes in English Usage. Chilton Co., Philadelphia.

Pflaum, S. 1974. The Development of Language and Reading in the Young Child. Charles E. Merrill Publishing Co., Columbus, Oh.

Rice, M. 1978. Identification of children with language disorders. In R. L. Schiefelbusch (ed.), Language Intervention Strategies, pp. 19–55. University Park Press, Baltimore.

Schubert, D. C., and Torgerson, T. L. 1968. Improving Reading through Individualized Correction. William C. Brown, Dubuque, Iowa.

Schwartz, A. H., and Daly, D. A. 1976, Some explicit guidelines for constructing and scoring elicited imitation tasks. Lang. Speech, Hear. Services Schools 7:33–40.

Slobin, D. I. (ed.). 1971. The Ontogenesis of Grammar. Academic Press, Inc., New York.

Spache, G. D. 1976. Diagnosing and Correcting Reading Disabilities. Allyn & Bacon, Boston.

Strang, R. 1968. Reading Diagnosis and Remediation. International Reading Association, Newark, Del.

Ten Brink, T. D. 1974. Evaluation: A Practical Guide for Teachers. McGraw-Hill Book Co., New York.

Weiss, C. E., and Lillywhite, H. S. 1976. Communication Disorders: A Handbook for Prevention and Early Intervention. C. V. Mosby Co., St. Louis.

Wilson, M. E. 1969. Standardized method for obtaining a spoken language sample. J. Speech Hear. Res. 12:95–102.

Wilson, R. M. 1967. Diagnostic and Remedial Reading for Classroom and Clinic. Charles E. Merrill Publishing Co., Columbus, Oh.

Section D   Pupil and Parent Interviews

Ballard, V., and Strang, R. 1964. Parent-Teacher Conferences. McGraw-Hill Book Co., New York.

Becker, W. C. 1971. Parents are Teachers. Research Press, Champaign, Ill.

Bell, V. H. 1975. An educator's approach to assessing preschool visually handicapped children. Educ. Vis. Hand. 7:84–89.

Chase, C. I. 1978. Measurement for Educational Evaluation. 2nd Ed. Addison-Wesley Publishing Co., Reading, Mass.

Dickerson, D., Spellman, C. R., Larsen, S., and Tyler, L. 1973. Let the cards do the talking—A teacher-parent communication program. Teach. Except. Child. 5:170–178.

Dreikurs, R., Grunwald, B. B., and Pepper, F. C. 1971. Maintaining Sanity in the Classroom: Illustrated Teaching Techniques. Harper & Row Publishers, New York.

Evans, J. S. 1974. A Project to Develop Curriculum for Four-Year-Old Handicapped Mexican American Children. Final Report. Appendix. Southwest Development Laboratory, Austin.

Kahl, D. H. 1973. Talking about the child's progress. Today's Educ. 62:34–35.

Kroth, R. 1978. Parents—Powerful and necessary allies. Teach. Except. Child. 10:88–90.

Lerner, J. W. 1976. Children with Learning Disabilities: Theories, Diagnosis, and Teaching Strategies. Houghton Mifflin Co., Boston.

Lowe, R. N., and Christenson, O. C. 1966. Guide to Enrollees. Community-Parent-Teacher Education Centers. University of Oregon, School of Education, Eugene.

Peter, L. J. 1975. Competencies for Teaching: Therapeutic Instruction. Wadsworth Publishing Co., Belmont, Cal.

Richards, M. J. 1975. Early Childhood Education at Home Project. Final Report. Curriculum Improvement Center, Martinsburg, W. Va.

Schaefer, E. S. 1973. A life-time, life-space perspective. Today's Educ. 62:28–31.

Ten Brink, T. D. 1974. Evaluation: A Practical Guide for Teachers. McGraw-Hill Book Co., New York.

Thorndike, R. L., and Hagen, E. 1969. Measurement and Evaluation in Psychology and Education. 3rd Ed. John Wiley & Sons, Inc., New York.

Valett, R. E. 1977. Humanizing Education: Developing the Total Person. C. V. Mosby Co., St. Louis.

Module 8

The teacher, in concert with the pupil, will establish mastery criteria for instructional tasks. The teacher will assess pupil performance relevant to the achievement of mastery and will provide experiences and techniques that will encourage pupils and assist them with self-evaluation.

PRETEST

1. Before attempting to establish a required mastery level for each of the specific objectives of the curriculum, what fundamental questions should a teacher ask himself/herself?

2. What questions should pupils be helped to incorporate into their cognitive style as an aid to self-evaluation?

3. What major accomplishments may be realized during teacher-pupil conferences designed to explain instructional objectives and to determine desired mastery levels? Why are these accomplishments significant to the teaching/learning process?

4. What would you include in a Teacher-Pupil Evaluation of Progress Contract?

5. Design a self-rating form to be used by a pupil in the elementary grades.

INTRODUCTION AND OVERVIEW

As emphasized in Module 9, it is not sufficient to identify instructional objectives in general terms. Teaching objectives must be stated in such a way that their achievement may be easily observed and readily recorded. Part of any competency-based learning experience, therefore, must be an established mastery level at the start of each learning sequence or unit. Without explicitly stated and precisely defined mastery criteria established for each pupil, the evaluation and programming of competencies are subject to differences in viewpoints and values, the exigencies of time, the emotional and authoritarian pressures of others, and the vagaries of mood. Without mastery criteria for each individual, pupil evaluation and its counterpart of teacher accountability lose their central role in diagnostic/prescriptive teaching and the goal of individualizing instruction remains elusive.

Before attempting to establish a required or hoped for performance level for each pupil for each of the specific objectives of the curriculum, a teacher must ask several fundamental questions:

1. How valued is mastery of the skill to the pupil?
2. How valued is mastery of the skill to the pupil's parents?
3. Is the mastery level of the skill consonant with the development progression of the pupil?
4. How necessary is mastery of the skill to acceptance and/or reinforcement by others, including peers and significant adults?
5. How important is mastery of the skill to the physical and mental health and safety of the pupil?
6. How critical is mastery of the skill to the daily life functioning of the pupil?
7. How significant is mastery of the skill to the future life functioning of the pupil including vocational, leisure, and recreational pursuits?
8. How essential is each subskill to the acquisition of important higher level skills?
9. How much do the local community and the greater community value mastery of the skill?

After analyzing and synthesizing the responses to the above questions, a tentative judgment should be made about the mastery level for a particular task pertinent to the specified pupil. The teacher next must hold an individual conference or conferences with the pupil to share his/her perceptions of the appropriateness and relevance of the objective and the proposed required performance level as well as to arrive at a mutually agreed upon desired performance level. During these conferences, pupils should be sensitized to the prescriptive nature of the evaluation of the progress process and the pupil's essential role in its execution. A critical part of the sensitivity development process involves helping pupils incorporate into their cognitive learning style the following self-evaluative questions:

1. What skills and knowledge do I currently possess?
2. What problems am I experiencing that are interfering with my learning progress?
3. Why am I having these problems, and what can I do to improve my performance?
4. How can I help others continuously evaluate my progress, and how can I, gradually, take an increasingly active role in evaluating my growth and development?

Two major accomplishments may be realized during these teacher-pupil interactions, namely, the pupil is given the opportunity to:

1. Become more fully acquainted with the teaching objective, especially the rationale for its inclusion in the instructional experience
2. Have an input into determining a mastery level for each task that is both realistic and motivating

Appreciating the necessity for learning a specified skill and participating in the identification of the required performance level may provide the motivation for achievement of the task at the desired mastery level.

Once a desired performance level has been mutually accepted, then, for evaluation purposes, the number of recommended teacher observations/evaluations and a pupil self-evaluation plan must also be decided upon. Procedures must be outlined and forms designed and made available to the pupil in order to maintain a record of progress. These records, depending on the nature of the task and/or the nature of the problem may be concerned with recording growth in accuracy, frequency, or speed of response. Perhaps the best method for recording behavioral change is through the use of charts. This charting procedure should be managed by the pupil whenever possible because of the therapeutic effects credited to its use. Furthermore, these charts may be used later to inform parents, school administrators, and other pertinent professionals of pupil progress.

Self-rating forms or charts, including charted task analyses (see Module 9), are essential to a total evaluation of pupil progress plan. Charts, however, must be supplemented with other materials and strategies if a comprehensive plan is to be mounted. Additional strategies include:

1. Daily conferences in which teacher and pupil share perceptions of growth experienced
2. Daily reports during which pupils tell of progress achieved

3.   Graphs of pupil progress developed by the teacher and/or pupil and
     presented to the pupil in recognition of those achievements

The key to evaluation of pupil progress is the establishment of a responsive and responsible environment where there is freedom of interchange
of evaluative detail unburdened by the necessity for grading or for reporting anything except progress.

A further element in the teacher-pupil evaluation of the pupil
progress contract must be an agreement on the number of review sessions
and later evaluations deemed necessary to assure that mastery has been
maintained over time. Such an agreement by both teacher and pupil is
necessary if they are to feel that a behavior has been mastered and that
its occurrence does not represent partial mastery or serendipitous occasion.

To review, once the behavioral objective, the required mastery level,
the recommended number of teacher observations/evaluations, the pupil
self-evaluation plan, and the number of review sessions and later evaluations have been agreed to and contracted for, both teacher and pupil
then will be able to proceed with the task of assessing pupil performance
and progress vis-à-vis the mastery of specific educational tasks. The key
to evaluating mastery of any task is the precise delineation of that task,
the identification of performance criteria including mastery over time,
and the cooperative interaction of teacher and pupil in the total evaluative process.

A sample Teacher-Pupil Evaluation of Pupil Progress Contract is
shown in Table 1.

It is clear that the pupil has a central role in the specification of
evaluation criteria and in the evaluation process. Self-evaluation
contributes significantly to motivation and to insight while simultaneously assisting the teacher in organizing and managing wide-ranging
diagnostic and programming practices for a large number of pupils.

Before the pupil begins to play a prominent role in the evaluation
process, time should be spent in providing that pupil with instructional
experiences designed to acquaint him/her with the use of self-rating
forms. During this time, the pupil should also be encouraged to generate
self-rating forms for those specific educational tasks that are to be
included in his/her educational plan. The process of creating self-rating
forms is seen as a particularly valuable technique for encouraging pupil
involvement and commitment and for fostering insight into the nature
and dimensions of educational tasks.

Samples of pupil self-rating forms are shown in Tables 2–4.

Motivating pupils to participate in self-evaluation activities is more
easily accomplished if it is part of a total evaluation process formulated,
in part, by the pupil and agreed to previously as part of a teacher-pupil

Table 1.   Teacher-Pupil Evaluation of Pupil Progress Evaluation Contract

  I. Basic Information
      Pupil's Name   _____
      Teacher's Name   _____
      Date of Agreement   _____
      Contract Number   _____
      Subject or Curriculum Area   _____

 II. Evaluation Plan
      Behavioral Objective

      Required Performance or Mastery Level _____
      Number of Teacher Observations/Evaluations _____
      Number of Other Professional Observations/Evaluations[a]
         Professional Category _____ _____
                   (Specify Title)   # of obs./eval.
         Professional Category _____ _____
                   (Specify Title)   # of obs./eval.

III. Self-Rating Charts and Forms to be Used:
      1. _____
      2. _____
      3. _____
      Recommended Number of Review Sessions
      and Later Evaluations _____
      Reinforcement Procedure When Mastery Achieved[b] _____

 IV. Signatures of Agreement
      Pupil's Signature   _____
      Teacher's Signature   _____
      Other Signature(s)   _____

  V. Signatures of Mastery
      _____ has met the terms of
         (Pupil's Name)
      Contract No. _____   Date _____
      Teacher's Signature   _____
      Pupil's Signature   _____
      Other Signature(s)   _____

[a] Other professionals such as remedial reading teachers, speech and hearing therapists, and teacher aides may be included in the observation schedule. If so, they must sign the contract as well.

[b] For example, citation to be received and displayed on bulletin board, sent home to parents, and/or put in scrapbook of pupil achievements.

Table 2.   My arithmetic accuracy chart

Pupil's Name:	Martha Schell
Teacher's Name:	Mr. Paris
Date:	November 20, 1979
Subject:	Arithmetic
Subskill:	Two Place Addition with Carrying
Purpose:	Accuracy of Computation
Duration of Lesson:	15 minutes
Total Number of Examples:	20

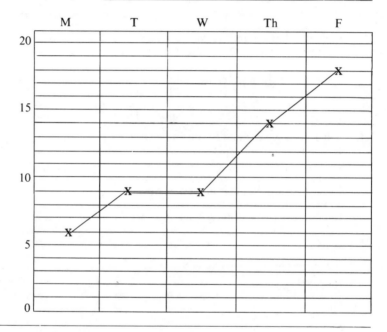

contract. Pupils are motivated to engage in self-rating exercises because they lead to a picture of their own progress. The emphasis on self and the challenge of self in relationship to task are the motivating influences that stimulate the record-keeping activities required in self-evaluation. Attractive, colorful, and imaginative charts also help to make record keeping a self-motivating endeavor for younger pupils. For advanced pupils, charts of greater sophistication may be all that is necessary.

Self-evaluation of progress toward goal is viewed as self-motivating because it does not suffer from the negative impact and connotation of grades or regularly scheduled evaluations by others. Self-evaluation involves the excitement of competition with self as opposed to the frequently destructive and debilitating effects of competition with others.

The unhealthy competition for grades and the traditional rewards associated with success have violated the educational primacy of individual progress and growth and distorted the evaluation process. Pupils all too often strive for grades not because they are testimony to achievement but because of their value to others and because of the rewards they accrue. A healthy and productive evaluation process, on the other hand, requires that the individual view problems that arise in the acquisition of a skill or knowledge as obstacles to be challenged and overcome. The constructive approach to evaluation that comes from self-evaluation is essential to the teaching/learning process and to the individualization of instruction.

Table 3. My arithmetic accuracy and speed chart

Pupil's Name:	Nicole Pinel
Teacher's Name	Ms. Stratton
Date:	Dec. 14, 1971
Subject:	Arithmetic
Subskill:	Number Facts in Subtraction
Purpose:	Speed and Accuracy
Duration of Lesson:	15 Minutes
Total Number of Examples:	20

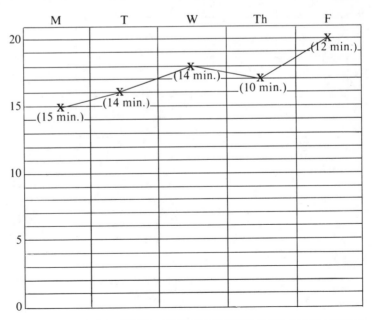

Table 4.   My spelling and progress chart (Pretest through final)

Pupil's Name:	Peter Valente
Teacher's Name:	Mrs. Hernandez
Dates:	September 23, 25, and 27
Subject:	Spelling
Purpose:	Pretest, Review, and Final Test
Duration of Test:	10 minutes
Total Number of Words:	12

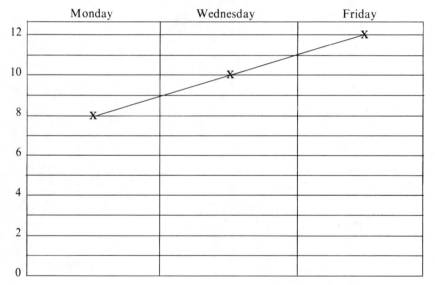

"Hop to It"   "An Elephant Never Forgets"   "Spelling Bee"

ACTIVITIES AND EXPERIENCES

1. Select a pupil in your class or in your practicum placement, or someone you are tutoring. Then select a specific curriculum objective and, in writing, respond to the nine fundamental questions outlined in the module. Next, establish a tentative mastery level for pupil and task.
2. Hold several individual conferences with the pupil identified in Activity 1. During these conferences, carry out the following tasks:
    a. Sensitize the pupil to the importance of the evaluation of progress process and to the role he/she must play in its execution
    b. Arrive at an agreed upon required performance level
    c. Determine the number of recommended teacher and other professional observations/evaluations
    d. Establish a self-evaluation plan, including the design of self-rating forms
    e. Agree on the needed number of review sessions and later evaluations
    f. Draw up a Teacher-Pupil Evaluation of Progress Contract
3. Carry out various instructional experiences while assisting the pupil in carrying out the self-rating task. Carry out the terms of the contract, indicating mastery when achieved.
4. Design self-rating forms for several different curriculum areas for pupils in the elementary grades and for older pupils.
5. Assist a pupil in designing his/her own self-rating form.

CONCLUDING STATEMENT

Finally, pupil self-evaluation of progress is considered essential because it is task oriented as opposed to grade oriented. Self-rating encourages self-reliance and responsibility for one's own growth and development. It stresses the enhancement of independence in learning and discourages competition or comparison with others. Besides these virtues, which tend to facilitate learning and adjustment, the use of pupil self-evaluation is an invaluable aid to teachers as they perform the myriad professional tasks inherent to teaching the "whole child" in all its incredible variations.

POSTTEST

At this point retake the Pretest.

SUGGESTED READINGS

Bates, S., and Bates, D. F. 1971. ". . . and a child shall lead them": Stephanie's chart story. Teach. Except. Child. 3:111–113.

Block, J. H. 1974. Schools, Society, and Mastery Learning. Holt, Rinehart & Winston, Inc., New York.

Bloom, B. S., Hastings, T. J., and Madaus, G. F. 1971. Handbook on Formative and Summative Evaluation of Student Learning. McGraw-Hill Book Co., New York.

Brandstetter, G., and Merz, C. 1978. Charting scores in precision teaching for skill acquisition. Except. Child. 45:42–48.

Broden, M., Hall, R. V., and Mitts, B. 1971. The effect of self-recording on the classroom behavior of two eighth-grade students. J. Appl. Behav. Anal. 4:191–199.

Busse, L. L., and McElroy, A. A. 1975. The blind can chart. Teach. Except. Child. 7:116–117.

Cantrell, R. P., Cantrell, M. L., Huddleston, C. M., and Woolridge, R. L. 1969. Contingency contracting with school problems. J. Appl. Behav. Anal. 2:215–220.

Cohen, M. A., and Martin, G. L. 1971. Applying precision teaching to academic assessment. Teach. Except. Child. 3:147–150.

Diggory, J. C. 1966. Self-Evaluation: Concepts and Studies. John Wiley & Sons, Inc., New York.

Dollar, B. 1972. Humanizing Classroom Discipline. Harper & Row Publishers, New York.

Duncan, A. D. 1971. The view from the inner eye: Personal management of inner and outer behaviors. Teach. Except. Child. 3:152–156.

Galloway, C., and Galloway, K. C. 1971. Parent classes in precise behavior management. Teach. Except. Child. 3:120–128.

Hall, R. V. 1971. Training teachers in classroom use of contingency management. Educ. Tech. 11:33–38.

Homme, L. E. 1969. How to Use Contingency Contracting in the Classroom. Research Press, Champaign, Ill.

Johnson, E. C. 1971. Precision teaching helps children learn. Teach. Except. Child. 3:106–110.

Johnson, S. M., and White, G. 1971. Self-observation as an agent of behavioral change. Behav. Ther. 2:488–497.

Karmel, L. J., and Karmel, M. O. 1978. Measurement and Evaluation in the Schools. 2nd Ed. Macmillan Publishing Co., Inc., New York.

Koenig, C. 1971. The behavior bank: A system for sharing precise information. Teach. Except. Child. 3:157.

Kunzelman, H. P., Cohen, M. A., Hulten, W. J., Martin, G. L., and Mingo, A. R. 1970. Precision Teaching: An Initial Training Sequence. Special Child Publications, Seattle.

Lindsley, O. R. 1971. Precision teaching in perspective: An interview with Ogden R. Lindsley. Teach. Except. Child. 3:114–119.

Meacham, M. L., and Wiesen, A. E. 1969. Changing Classroom Behavior: A Manual for Precision Teaching. International Textbook Co., Scranton, Pa.

Nelson, C. M., and Reynolds, W. T. 1971. Self-recording and control of behavior. A reply to Simkins. Behav. Ther. 2:594–597.

Popham, J. W. (ed.). 1971. Criterion-Referenced Measurements—An Introduction. Educational Technology, Englewood Cliffs, N.J.

Spates, C. R., and Kanfer, F. H. 1977. Self-monitoring, self-evaluation, and self-reinforcement in children's learning: A test of a multistage self-regulating model. Behav. Ther. 8:9–16.

Starlin, C. 1971. Peers and precision. Teach. Except. Child. 3:129–132.

White, O. R., and Haring, N. G. 1976. Exceptional Teaching: A Multimedia Training Package. Charles E. Merrill Publishing Co., Columbus, Oh.

Worrell, J., and Nelson, C. M. 1974. Managing Instructional Problems. McGraw-Hill Book Co., New York.

Module 9

The teacher will analyze educational tasks in order to establish prerequisite concepts and skills and will arrange these task elements in a sequential order for diagnostic and program sequencing purposes.

PRETEST

Part A

Which of the following objectives are stated in behavioral terms?
    The student will:

1. Write his/her signature
2. Appreciate the importance of a well-balanced diet
3. Enjoy the poem "Old Ironsides"
4. Develop an appreciation for ballet
5. Operate an electric shaver
6. Draw a sketch of a person
7. Listen to a symphony
8. Grasp the significance of the battle
9. Grasp the spoon in his/her hand
10. See the relationship between slavery and the Civil War
11. Demonstrate knowledge of the causes of the conflict
12. Acquire an understanding of the contributing conditions
13. Count from 1 to 10
14. Move the wheelchair over a threshold
15. Know how to spell
16. Recognize the parts of the body
17. Name the parts of the body
18. Understand the meaning of
19. Tolerate changes in temperature
20. Construct a bookcase

Part B

Select the phrase or clause that provides information about the conditions under which the learner is expected to perform.

1. The student, after being shown several pictures of common tools, will select . . .
2. Given a ruler, ribbon, and scissors, the pupil will measure and then cut . . . .
3. When shown a sample of a completed pattern of beads strung on a piece of yarn, the pupil will reproduce . . . .
4. The pupil will walk up the practice stairs in physical therapy, without the assistance of a cane. . . .
5. With a specially designed spoon, the pupil will eat. . . .

Part C

Complete each of the objectives in Part B by including a phrase or clause that describes the criterion of acceptable performance.

Part D

Chart the task analysis for each of the following terminal objectives.

1. When shown three common objects: a spoon, a cup, and a book, the pupil will point to each object named in response to the request, "Point to the _____." The student will do so correctly in 4 out of 5 trials.
2. When given 10 samples of actual objects, e.g., beads, the pupil will count aloud from 1–10 in response to the question, "How many beads are there?" The student will do so correctly in five out of five trials for 100% accuracy.

INTRODUCTION AND OVERVIEW

A primary responsibility of teachers is that of identifying individual educational objectives for each of their students. In addition to stating them, teachers must write them in such terms as to allow their achievement to be precisely measured. Out of the need to provide teachers with more explicit instructional goals, more clearly examined educational tasks, and more clearly defined measures for evaluating the progress of pupils and their own instructional success arose the practice of stating teaching objectives in behavioral terms (Mager, 1962; Christoplos and Valletutti, 1969; Popham and Baker, 1970; Mowrer, 1977). The writing of a behavioral objective requires that it be phrased in such terms that the achievement of that behavior may be clearly demonstrated by a pupil under previously specified conditions and at a previously identified level of competency. It has become increasingly clear that, unless a desired behavior is clearly articulated before instruction, the identification of suitable instructional methods and the selection or creation of appropriate materials are greatly diminished.

> The problem of selecting the most efficient route to your destination should not be of concern until you know what that destination is. The prescriptive teacher must first decide upon the goal or goals he intends to reach at the end of an individual instruction program. It is after objectives are established that he can intelligently select the procedures, content, and methods that are relevant to achievement of desired outcomes. It is only after the objective is described that he can know what he must teach and how he will know if he has taught it (Peter, 1972, p. 84).

Furthermore, behavioral objectives provide teachers with a critical diagnostic tool that allows them (and, of course, their pupils) to continuously evaluate pupil progress throughout the instructional sequence. Thus, the use of behavioral objectives and its accompanying task analysis approach allows the diagnostic-prescriptive process to rise above an amorphous, ambiguous, and unpredictable level since pupils are then evaluated in their relation to assigned educational objectives (Cohen, 1969; Bijou, 1970; Mann, 1971; Valletutti, 1975).

> The emphasis is on component skills and their integration into complex behaviors (skills) rather than the training of test identified 'processes' that presumably underlie (cause) skill development (Ysseldyke and Salvia, 1974, p. 181).

While most educators advocate the use of behavioral objectives, there are those who question their applicability to aesthetic, affective, and creative development. These individuals frequently cite the apparent inappropriateness of behavioral objectives in instructing and evaluating appreciation for art, music, and theatre, the enjoyment of reading, the awakening of individual interests, the understanding of the relationships between past historical events and present happenings, and the development of responsible attitudes and values. These nonbehaviorally oriented professionals, especially those from the arts and humanities, view the use of behavioral objectives, at its best, as a waste of time, and, at its most invidious, as dehumanizing and stifling since they view education as significantly more than a series of behaviors but as a gestalt in which humanism and intellectualism assume undisputed hegemony (Mowrer, 1977).

Despite philosophical disputes and the inertia of some professionals in education, most teacher educators, school administrators, and teachers have come to accept the importance of behavioral objectives in instructional planning and in the evaluation of pupils. Most educators, currently, follow the suggestions made popular by Mager (1962) that instructional objectives should specify the expected behavior of pupils, the conditions under which the performance is to occur, and the criteria for acceptable performance:

1. An instructional objective describes an intended *outcome* rather than a description or summary of content.
2. It is stated in behavioral, or performance, terms that describe what the learner will be DOING when demonstrating his achievement of the objective.
3. The statement of objectives for an entire program of instruction will consist of several specific statements.
4. The objective which is most usefully stated is one which best communicates the instructional intent of the person selecting the objective (p. 24).

3. To describe terminal behavior (what the learner will be DOING):
   a. Identify and name the overall behavior act.
   b. Define the important conditions under which the behavior is to occur (givens and/or restrictions and limitations).
   c. Define the criterion of acceptable performance (p. 53).

The writing of behavioral objectives and an analysis of the educational task should emphasize intraindividual differences in skill development, a pupil's current performance, the next skill to be mastered, and the behavioral elements of that next skill. Therefore, teachers employing a task analysis approach to educational evaluation and programming first must delineate the instructional objective, then task analyze the prerequisite behaviors necessary for the successful achievement of that objective, and last, establish instructional programs designed to facilitate the development of specific component skills and their integration into the total process. If a pupil accomplishes an educational task, i.e., achieves the behavioral objective, then he/she has mastered the task and thus, allows the teacher to proceed to another objective in that pupil's personalized list of educational objectives. If, on the other hand, a pupil fails to perform the specified task, acknowledging that pupil's failure is diagnostically insufficient; it is at that moment of failure when teachers must discover what skills the pupil possesses that are prerequisite to the achievement of the specified task and what competencies have yet to be mastered. When the performance of a pupil breaks down, it is essential that teachers pinpoint the locus of difficulty. "This means that if a task is not performed successfully, the teacher must analyze the first response requirement on which the child makes an error" (Wallace and Kauffman, 1973, p. 106). "After identifying the highest skill within the student's repertoire of behaviors relevant to a specific educational task, the teacher would then design an educational program or prescription to aid the student in bridging the gap between the achieved and the unachieved" (Valletutti, 1975, p. 4). This analysis, with its subsequent charting of the sequence of events and the prerequisite behavioral components needed to achieve a desired objective, is called a task analysis.

Steps in the Task Analysis Process

1. A task analysis is initiated with the statement of an individual educational objective written in behavioral terms. This behavioral statement then becomes the terminus for the completed task analysis and is variously known as the terminal, transitional, or enabling objective.

    a. Perhaps the major difficulty in the writing of a behavioral objective is the use of an appropriate verb. An appropriate verb is subject to few interpretations and is observable in its overt manifestations, thus allowing for measurement of the behavior. An inappropriate verb, on the other hand, is open to many interpretations and happens internally or covertly.

Inappropriate Verbs	Appropriate Verbs
to know	to write
to understand	to operate
to appreciate	to imitate
to tolerate	to follow
to enjoy	to differentiate
to demonstrate knowledge	to count
to acquire an appreciation	to draw
to see the relationship	to find
to listen	to hold
to attend	to move
to grasp (the significance)	to grasp (in hand)
to recognize	to point
to develop	to construct
to believe	to match
to have	to identify

It should be noted that many verbs that describe specific overt behaviors, actions, or performances are not clear unless completed and clarified by adverbs or adverbial phrases, e.g., the student:

1. (Only) accepts rides from relatives
2. Identifies (by naming)
3. Participates (by giving)

The verb used and its accompanying adverbial clarifiers should not describe what the teacher is going to do but rather what the pupil is expected to do, making it pupil-centered rather than teacher-oriented. Furthermore, there may be occasions when the writer of the behavioral objective may wish to include the main intent of the objective that may be covert, e.g., to recognize what a pencil is for by writing with the pencil when asked the question, "Show me what you do with this" (Mowrer, 1977). As Chase (1978, pp. 11–12) points out:

> The performance listed in our statement of objectives can be either (a) a main intent, or (b) an indicator . . . For example, we want people to communicate with each other. One aspect of this is to convey the idea of time in our expressions. When we ask a child to write past, present, and future tense of a verb, this is our basis for making an inference about the child's ability to communicate time in his or her discourse . . . it is especially important . . . that indicators . . . provide the simplest and most direct evidence of the main intent of the objective . . . To summarize . . . first, that objectives if their achievement is to be ascertained, must be stated in terms of performances. Second, we should note whether the performances listed are themselves the main intent of the objective or indicators of the main intent. And last, we should scrutinize any indicator to see if it provides the simplest, most direct line of inference to determine attainment of the objective.

    b. After selecting the appropriate verb with whatever adverbial clarifiers are needed and with direct objects specified, thus clarifying what learners are expected to exhibit or perform, teachers must further describe the terminal behavior by stating the conditions or stimuli under which the behavior is expected to occur:

After being shown shown several pictures of _____
Given a yardstick and scissors _____
When shown samples of _____
Without the assistance of a cane _____
With a specially designed spoon_____

Thus a terminal objective must include both desired pupil

behavior and specification of the conditions as, for example:

> When shown three common objects: a spoon, a cup, and a book, the pupil will point to each object named in response to the command, "Point to the _____."
>
> or
>
> The pupil will eat applesauce from a dessert saucer, using a specially bent spoon with a special handle. (Note: Pupil has psychomotor involvement due to neurological damage.)

It should be noted that the conditions should be sufficiently detailed, including the materials needed and words to be used, so that any other teacher could carry out the lesson or evaluate the pupil by merely reading the objective. Mager (1962) suggests that teachers ask themselves the following questions in evaluating the details of the terminal objectives:

1. What will the learner be provided?
2. What will the learner be denied?
3. What are the conditions under which you will expect the terminal behavior to occur?
4. Are there any skills which you are specifically NOT trying to develop? Does the objective exclude such skills? (p. 27)

c. The last step in writing a behavioral objective is specifying the criterion of acceptable performance. One way to do so is to specify a time limit:

> After being shown a completed puzzle, the four-piece puzzle will be taken apart and the pupil will be asked to reassemble it. The pupil will reassemble the puzzle correctly in less than 1 minute.

Another way of indicating mastery criterion is to indicate the minimum number of correct responses acceptable:

> Given a ruler, a slip of paper upon which three measurements are written, a pair of scissors, and a bolt of ribbon, the pupil will measure and then cut at least two out of three pieces of ribbon to the nearest $\frac{1}{16}$ of an inch.

Still another way of indicating an acceptable performance level is to indicate a percentage of the responses deemed satisfactory:

> When given a spelling list of 20 words taken from the words in his/her own word bank (index file), the pupil will attain a score of 90% or better.

Finally, another way of defining criterion is by describing a critical performance element:

> The pupil will eat applesauce from a dessert saucer using a specially bent spoon with a special handle *without spilling the applesauce or allowing it to dribble down his/her chin.*

2. Once the terminal objective of the task analysis has been stated in explicit, behavioral terms, the sequence of events and/or prerequisite skills must be identified in the order of occurrence and/or acquisition. This step is accomplished by reviewing developmental milestones (see Module 4) and by actually performing the desired objective in order to determine prerequisite skills. For example, if the behavioral or terminal objective is related to the pupils regulating or tempering the water in a one-faucet sink, the teacher would actually carry out the activity, recording the sequence of steps until the objective is attained. Whenever necessary, the task analysis should be revised to reflect the performance of pupils and insights derived from carrying out instructional sequences.

3. After the sequence of steps and/or the prerequisite behaviors are assigned an order of occurrence or acquisition, the task analysis should be charted and used for evaluation and instructional purposes.

    The charting of a task analysis involves the vertical placement of skills or events that are dependent upon earlier or precursor skills or events. Skills that occur independently are charted horizontally and are not joined by lines. At points where two or more independently developing skills come together to form a new skill, all related skills must be joined by connecting lines. The skills are placed in developmental or time sequence from bottom to top with the earliest skills placed at the bottom, with the numbering or lettering reflecting this progression.

    Examples of task analyses charts are shown in Figures 1 and 2.

ACTIVITIES AND EXPERIENCES

1. Write at least one behavioral objective for each of the following curriculum areas:
   a. Self-care skills
   b. Classroom behavior
   c. Gross motor skills
   d. Fine motor skills
   e. Communication skills: Verbal
   f. Communication skills: Nonverbal
   g. Interpersonal skills
   h. Sex education
   i. Drug education
   j. Health skills
   k. Nutrition skills
   l. Leisure time skills
   m. Consumer skills

    n. Reading
    o. Writing
    p. Arithmetic
    q. Science

2. Chart a task analysis for one behavioral objective written for each of the areas a–q in Activity 1 above.

3. After having developed and charted a variety of task analyses, use these charts to evaluate several individuals. Describe the performance of each person evaluated vis-à-vis the specific task. In your description indicate whether the person has achieved mastery. If not, pinpoint the place on the chart that represents the last area of success

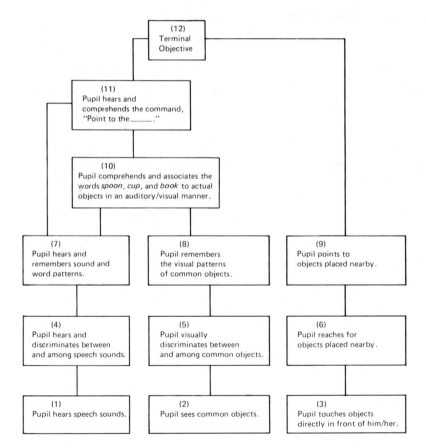

Figure 1. Task Analysis for Terminal Objective (T.O.): When shown three common objects: a spoon, a cup, and a book, the pupil will point to each object named in response to the command, "Point to the _____." The pupil will do so correctly in four out of five trials.

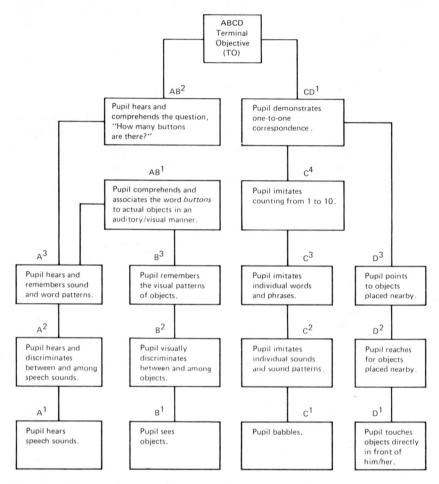

Figure 2. Task Analysis for Terminal Objective: When given ten samples of actual objects, e.g., beads, buttons, or crayons, the pupil will count aloud from 1 to 10 in response to the question, "How many _____ are there?" The pupil will do so correctly in five out of five trials for 100% accuracy.

(perhaps by checking the appropriate box). Then discuss those activities and experiences you would prescribe for the individual to assist him/her in acquiring the next skill identified in the skill sequence.

CONCLUDING STATEMENT

The emphasis in this module has been placed on stating behaviorally what pupils are expected to learn. Although objections have been raised concerning the limitations of identifying learning outcomes, their value in lesson planning, evaluation of student progress, and teaching effectiveness in developing individualized educational plans, in reporting the results of instruction to parents and other professionals, and in involving pupils in their own programs cannot be ignored. Although the emphasis has centered on identifying expected learning outcomes, of similar importance are unexpected or unanticipated ones. Certainly how more narrowly stated objectives are taught and how students are graded have a tremendous impact on broader goals of attitude and value development. Pupils will often develop interests and gain insights from learning experiences that are tangential to the defined goals. Peter (1972) refers to other adaptive behaviors acquired as concomitant development. Serendipitous and often unmeasurable outcomes of a positive nature should be encouraged while attending to the more discrete and narrowly defined goals that are behaviorally described. Johnson (1967) suggests another approach to task analysis, namely, the analysis of the method of presentation and the expected mode of response. These two dimensions can be analyzed in several ways, e.g., the perceptual channels required to receive the stimulus and to carry out the task and the level(s) of involvement, i.e., sensation, perception, memory, symbolization, and/or conceptualization required. If a pupil fails the task, then, the teacher analyzes whether failure results from either manner of presentation or expected mode of response.

It should be clear from the activities and experiences of this module that the writing of behavioral objectives and the charting of task analyses are time-consuming processes. Certainly teachers are not expected to construct a task analysis for each behavioral objective, first because of the constraints of time and second because they are, to a large extent, available in curriculum guides and in teachers' manuals. What is important is a way of thinking, i.e., that there is a continuum of achievement for each behavioral objective and that the pupil's level of performance should be considered in relationship to each continuum.

In fact, it may be valuable to identify levels of competency for each task and to characterize the pupil by level of performance. For example, when considering the task of sounding out phonograms that occur in English, the following levels of behavior may be identified and prove helpful in lieu of doing a task analysis:

Level I: The pupil is able to sound out consonant-vowel-consonant and vowel-consonant patterns.

Level II: The pupil is able to sound out consonant-vowel-consonant-silent e and vowel-consonant-silent e patterns.

Level III: The pupil is able to sound out patterns that include consonant blends.

Level IV: The pupil is able to sound out patterns that include consonant digraphs.

Level V: The pupil is able to sound out patterns that include vowel digraphs.

Level VI: The pupil is able to sound out multisyllabic words.

Until teachers are able to match individual pupils with the sequence of skills subsumed in an educational task, they will not be able to make logical decisions necessary for the development of individualized educational programs.

POSTTEST

At this point retake the Pretest.

LITERATURE CITED

Bijou, S. W. 1970. What psychology has to offer education—Now. J. Appl. Behav. Anal. 3:65–71.

Chase, C. I. 1978. Measurement for Educational Evaluation. 2nd Ed. Addison-Wesley Publishing Co., Reading, Mass.

Christoplos, F., and Valletutti, P. 1969. An undergraduate course in organization of programs for the mentally retarded. Educ. Train. Ment. Retard. 4:37–41.

Cohen, S. A. 1969. Studies in visual perception and reading in disadvantaged children. J. Learn. Disabil. 2:498–507.

Johnson, D. 1967. Educational principles for children with learning disabilities. Rehabil. Lit. 28:317–322.

Mager, R. F. 1962. Preparing Objectives for Programmed Instruction. Fearon Publishers, San Francisco.

Mann, L. 1971. Perceptual training revisited: The training of nothing at all. Rehabil. Lit. 32:322–335.

Mowrer, D. E. 1977. Methods of Modifying Speech Behaviors. Charles E. Merrill Publishing Co., Columbus, Oh.

Peter, L. J. 1972. Individual Instruction. McGraw-Hill Book Co., New York.

Popham, W. J., and Baker, E. L. 1970. Planning an Instructional Sequence. Prentice-Hall, Inc., Englewood Cliffs, N.J.

Valletutti, P. J. 1975. The teacher's role in the diagnosis and management of students with medical problems. In R. H. A. Haslam and P. J. Valletutti (eds.), Medical Problems in the Classroom, pp. 1–14. University Park Press, Baltimore.

Wallace, G., and Kauffman, J. M. 1973. Teaching Children with Learning Problems. Charles E. Merrill Publishing Co., Columbus, Oh.

Ysseldyke, J. E., and Salvia, J. 1974. Diagnostic-prescriptive teaching: Two models. Except. Child. 41:181–185.

SUGGESTED READINGS

Baker, E. L. 1966. Analysis and Sequencing of Learner Behaviors. Southwest Regional Laboratory for Educational Research and Development, Inglewood, Cal.

Bateman, B. 1967. Three approaches to diagnosis and educational planning for children with learning disabilities. Acad. Ther. Q. 2:215–222.

Becker, W. C., Engelmann, S., and Thomas, D. R. Teaching a Course in Applied Psychology. Science Research Associates, Chicago.

Bernabei, R., and Leles, S. 1970. Behavioral Objectives in Curriculum and Evaluation. Kendall Hunt, Dubuque, Iowa.

Bloom, B. S. (ed.). 1956. Taxonomy of Educational Objectives: The Classification of Educational Goals. Handbook I. Cognitive Domain. David McKay, New York.

Burns, R. W. 1967. Objectives and classroom instruction. Educ. Tech. 7:1–3.

Derer, R. B. 1978. Language assessment through specification of goals and objectives. Except. Child. 45:124–129.

Engelmann, S. 1969. Preventing Failure in the Primary Grades. Science Research Associates, Chicago.

Gagné, R. M. 1970. The Conditions of Learning. 2nd Ed. Holt, Rinehart & Winston, Inc., New York.

Gerlach, V. S., and Sullivan, H. J. 1967. Constructing Statements of Outcomes. Southwest Regional Laboratory for Educational Research and Development, Inglewood, Cal.

Glaser, R. (ed). 1965. Teaching Machines and Programmed Learning II. Data and Directions. National Education Association, Washington, D.C.

Haddan, E. E. 1970. Evolving Instruction. Macmillan Publishing Co., Inc., New York.

Hammill, D. D. 1971. Evaluating children for instructional purposes. Acad. Ther. 6:341–353.

Hasazi, S., and York, R. 1978. Eleven steps to good teaching. Teach. Except. Child. 10:63–66.

Hernandez, D. E. 1971. Writing Behavioral Objectives: A Programmed Exercise for Beginners. Barnes & Noble, Inc., New York.

Howell, K. W., Kaplan, J. S., and O'Connell, C. Y. 1978. Evaluating Exceptional Children: A Task Analysis Approach. Charles E. Merrill Publishing Co., Columbus, Oh.

Junkala, J. 1972. Task analysis and instructional alternatives. Acad. Ther. 8:33–40.

Krathwohl, D. R., Bloom, B. S., and Masia, B. B. 1964. Taxonomy of Educational Objectives: The Classification of Educational Goals. Handbook II. Affective Domain. David McKay, New York.

Kerns, A. N. 1976. H.E.L.P.: Home Educational Learning Programs. Mafex Associates, Johnstown, Pa.

Lindrall, C. M. (ed.). 1964. Defining Educational Objectives. University of Pittsburgh Press, Pittsburgh.

Mager, R. F. 1968. Developing Attitude Toward Learning. Fearon Publishers, Belmont, Cal.

Mager, R. F. 1972. Goal Analysis. Fearon Publishers, Belmont, Cal.

Mager, R. F. 1973. Measuring Instructional Intent. Fearon Publishers, Belmont, Cal.

Mager, R. F., and Beach, K. M., Jr. 1967. Developing Vocational Instruction. Fearon Publishers, Belmont, Cal.

McNeil, J. D. 1967. Concomitants of using behavioral objectives in the assessment of teacher effectiveness. J. Exper. Educ. 36:69–74.

Payne, D. A. 1968. The Specification and Measurement of Learning Outcomes. Blaisdell Publishing Co., Waltham, Mass.

Popham, J. W. 1970. The instructional objectives exchange: New support for criterion-referenced instruction. Phi Delta Kappan 52:174–175.

Resnick, L. B. 1975. Task Analysis in Instructional Design: Some Cases from Mathematics. University of Pittsburgh, Learning Research and Development Center, Pittsburgh.

Stephens, T. M. 1970. Directive Teaching of Children with Learning and Behavioral Handicaps. Charles E. Merrill Publishing Co., Inc., Columbus, Oh.

Sullivan, H. J. 1968. Improving Learner Achievement through Evaluation of Objectives. Southwest Regional Laboratory for Educational Research and Development, Inglewood, Cal.

Ten Brink, T. D. 1974. Evaluation: A Practical Guide for Teachers. McGraw-Hill Book Co., New York.

Thompson, D. G. 1978. Writing Long-Term and Short-Term Objectives. Research Press, Champaign, Ill.

Vargas, J. S. 1972. Writing Worthwhile Behavioral Objectives. Harper & Row Publishers, New York.

Module 10

The teacher will identify alternate subcategories of subject matter in each curriculum area. Based upon available subcategories, in concert with the pupil and other significant individuals, the teacher will make programming decisions appropriate and motivating to the instruction of the individual pupil.

PRETEST

1. Before determining which methods and materials are suitable for the instruction of a specified skill or concept to a particular pupil, what *two* basic subject matter-oriented tasks must a diagnostically oriented teacher engage in?

2. List at least seven different types of general activities through which fine motor skills may be practiced and developed.

3. What decisions face the classroom teacher, if, in the class, there are pupils with structural and/or neurological disorders that interfere with the development of fine motor skills?

4. Matching the materials and methods available for teaching a task is best accomplished with the help, advice, and counsel of what relevant individuals?

5. List five different types of general activities through which gross motor skills may be practiced and developed.

6. Why must special attention be paid to providing gross motor movement experiences for all pupils? What role does PL 94-142 play in this requirement?

7. Describe at least seven alternative approaches to teaching the principles of growth.

8. Describe at least five ways to generate stimulating discussions in the classroom.

9. Describe at least 12 alternative approaches to teaching the concept and application of addition.

10. Describe at least eight different functional reading subcategories available to teachers.

11. In a brief paragraph, indicate why the individualization of instruction is consonant with democratic principles.

12. Define *functionality* as the term applies to curriculum development.

13. Define the term *reinforcer* as used by behaviorists.

14. What are the two tenets that underlie all operant processes?

15. Describe shaping and backward shaping.

INTRODUCTION AND OVERVIEW

Effective and efficient diagnostic/prescriptive teachers must be, first and foremost, subject matter specialists, analyzing thoroughly each instructional area and investigating completely the underlying rationale for including each instructional experience in the curriculum. Once teachers are skilled in this basic task, then they may proceed to the analysis of which methods and materials are logical and appropriate to the instructional process for each area of the curriculum. Finally, the diagnostically oriented teacher must determine which one or more of the methods and materials suitable to the instruction of a specified skill or concept is most likely to be successful with a particular pupil. This third aspect involves the diagnosis of pupils' learning patterns in relation to the given task. The selection of appropriate methods and materials for instructional purposes depends upon the interactions existing among the nature of the educational task, the nature of the individual pupil, and the available instructional methods and materials. This module stresses the democratic approach of maximizing the choices available to pupils in each curriculum area.

Selection of Subject Matter

It seems logical that an essential first step in the selection of materials and methods suitable for the instruction of a given pupil is the identification of the nature of the subject matter to be taught. For demonstration purposes examples are offered below from just a few curricular areas: psychomotor skills (fine and gross motor), academic skills (science, arithmetic, and reading), and speech.

Psychomotor Skills

Fine Motor Skills   The development of fine motor skills may be accomplished through a variety of activities including engaging the pupil in the:

1. Playing of a musical instrument(s)
2. Production of a crafts project
3. Creation of a painting, sculpture, or other work of fine art
4. Building and/or repairing of models, toys, and projects
5. Drawing of architectural plans and designs
6. Construction and/or repair of furniture, household equipment, and furnishings
7. Design and creation of clothing
8. Preparation of foods
9. Carrying out of vocationally oriented fine motor tasks such as sorting, assembling, and packing.
10. Execution of a host of other avocational and recreational pursuits

Which of these categories are selected for instruction *should* depend on the interest and the motivation of the pupil. In every case, the selection should be relevant to a strongly motivating interest of the pupil. This motivation is more likely to be related to a product or to skills broader than the fine motor skill specifically taught. In no case, for example, should finger dexterity be taught as an isolated skill, irrelevant to other activities and without game-like qualities.

In the absence of structural anomalies of the hands and arms and in the absence of neurological impairments or deficits, fine motor skill development may be facilitated through the various fine motor tasks enumerated above. If there are pupils with structural and/or neurological disorders, then the appropriateness of each of the above subcategories must be evaluated. In addition, the assistance of an occupational therapist, physical therapist, school nurse, and/or physician may be necessary to establish and implement a therapeutic program designed to correct or to minimize the effects of the physical problem on fine motor functioning.

Once diagnostically oriented teachers have explored the various activities appropriate to the general task of fine motor skill development, they must then identify the methods and materials available for teaching the task utilizing these approaches. The final step is to match the materials and methods available to the individual pupil in order to maximize teaching/learning. This matching process is best accomplished with the help of the pupil, the pupil's parents or surrogate parents, and other teachers and school resource personnel. Asking the pupil what subcategories of a skill or curriculum area and what methods and materials he/she would prefer is invariably omitted, yet is an essential program individualization step. Asking the pupil's parents is also a critical step that is often ignored. Seeking the advice of other teachers who teach or who have taught the pupil and encouraging the counsel of teacher aides, class parents, and classroom volunteers help in making judicious programming decisions. The information thus obtained adds insights to those already acquired and helps in the individualization of the instructional program. Teachers with diagnostic/prescriptive competencies utilize all relevant human resources including both professional and staff personnel. For example, schoolbus drivers, secretaries, custodians, and lunchroom workers, in their observations of the pupil, may have developed special insights not clouded by professional myopia or detachment. The skilled teacher then synthesizes the information obtained into a program that best meets the individual educational needs of both handicapped and nonhandicapped pupils.

Gross Motor Skills   The development of gross motor skills may be facilitated through a variety of subtasks, including engaging the pupil in:

1. Active games and sports
2. Calisthenics
3. Gymnastics
4. Dance in all its various forms
5. Yoga and other body-mind development approaches

In the absence of anatomical anomalies and neurological disorders, the development of the body's strength, endurance, agility, flexibility, vitality, speed, coordination, rhythm, and grace may be accomplished in any one or more of the outlined ways.

The scope of the activities available may be fully appreciated by simply enumerating the many sports available for programming purposes. Extensive lists of active games and sports are available in widely used physical education textbooks. Sufficient selection may be made under most limitations imposed by the physical resources of the school and community, seasonal and climatic factors, community preferences, and the skills and imagination of teachers. Artificial limitations, however, may arise because of community biases and/or pervasive sexism. The imbalance in the use of school funds is particularly glaring as evidenced by the overwhelming diversion of resources into activities predominantly utilized by males. Special awareness is thus essential in reducing the impact of sexual bias on the choice of activities, methods, and materials, especially in the area of sports. A case in point is the teenage girl who yearns to play football but is denied the opportunity while a reluctant boy is forced to participate in little league activities where every game brings the agony of humiliation. However, when sexism is not operating and each pupil can engage in any safe and healthy gross motor activity, then teachers have abundant curriculum options for developing gross motor skills. Looking at the scope of gross motor skills available, one can more fully appreciate the nature of individualized instruction. A commitment to democracy means that all pupils are not expected to participate in the same activity. Pupils should have opportunities to participate in activities of their choice that contribute to a sound mind in a sound body. Biased or coercive approaches to programming are unpardonable, especially when countless programming options exist.

A special note must be made of the necessity for providing adequate gross motor movement experiences for all. The importance of learning to enjoy and develop one's body, to find exhilaration and health through pleasurable physical activity, is a universal need. This need is legitimized and highlighted in PL 94-142, which makes gross motor experiences a requirement for all individualized educational programs for the handicapped.

Academic Skills The curriculum has traditionally emphasized the development of academic skills as exemplified by the universal priority assigned the three Rs. Academics dominate the entire curriculum, and more attention has been directed toward identifying relevant methods and materials in this area than any other. Despite this greater attention, individualized academic programming is still far from realized in most classrooms. The proliferation of knowledge and skills in every academic area makes it impossible for every pupil to learn everything of importance. For teachers and/or administrators, communities, or parents to make that choice for all pupils in a school system is not only a harrowing task, but places the decision makers in an undesirable, omniscient position. On the other hand, a democratic approach is enhanced when the pupils are able to express and develop their individuality through choosing subcategories in, for example, reading, science and social science, and even mathematics.

Science For example, the general area of science has innumerable subcategories that keep multiplying (e.g., physics, biology, chemistry, biophysics). Under each category, the scientific method, i.e., problem identification, hypotheses formulation, and testing, may be learned and utilized. In choosing a subcategory a pupil may need help; however, he/she must ultimately take final responsibility for the decision. Whichever area is chosen provides the student with further choices in yet additional subcategories. For example, for the study of the principles of growth, traditionally subsumed under biology, many alternate approaches are available:

1. Taking care of classroom plants
2. Taking care of classroom pets
3. Taking care of terraria and aquaria
4. Displaying retrospective pictures of the pupil from infancy on
5. Showing a film(s) on plants that uses time action photography to depict the stages of growth
6. Studying charts that demonstrate the stages of growth in humans and animals
7. Using the microscope to study cell division
8. Viewing an especially developed exhibit or project, designed by the pupils, whenever possible, this exhibit may, for example, demonstrate the stages of embryonic growth and include plaster of Paris replicas, preserved specimens, charts, or pictures from magazines
9. Conducting nutrition experiments with plants and animals to demonstrate the effects of different substances and conditions on growth

For each pupil who does not have an understanding of the growth process, the teacher, together with the pupil, selects one or more of the above experiences, depending upon the pupil's interests, abilities, and needs. Whenever practical the pupil is then placed in an interest group or with a "buddy" for peer learning and reinforcement.

Arithmetic   It should be noted that the alternate approaches suggested for the teaching of one arithmetic concept, namely, addition, involve what is known as functional arithmetic. The dichotomization of arithmetic or any other subject into functional and traditional is absurd since this characterization implies that the traditional may indeed be nonfunctional or even dysfunctional. *All* instruction should be functional. The problem arises when functionality is conceived as merely being utilitarian in the present or in the near future. Functionality, however, refers to any skill or knowledge that aids the individual pupil in his/her present total functioning and as he/she might need to function in the distant and unpredictable future. Functionality also refers to that which is pleasurable, recreational, and supportive of mental and physical health.

Examples of alternative approaches to teaching addition include:

1. Begin with oral problems and with number games.
2. Teach addition as the process used to make change.
3. Help the student practice counting by 1s, 5s, 10s, and 25s.
4. Work on addition by manipulating real objects.
5. Practice addition by playing games involving dice, spinning wheels, and playing cards.
6. Use flashcards with basic addition facts, recognizing the fact that much of basic arithmetic is the revisualization of number facts.
7. Teach addition through the use of a number line.
8. Ask the pupil to total up bills or checks for accuracy.
9. Ask the pupil to prepare a shopping list from a brochure, throwaway, or newspaper advertisement.
10. Tell the pupil to indicate how much money is needed for the purchase.
11. Plan any functional task involving measurement in the construction, design, or preparation of an article of clothing, a food or a meal, or a piece of furniture.
12. Explain the sales tax indicating the amount of tax due. Give pupil bills where sales tax should be added. Ask the pupil to compute the final bill.
13. Assign the pupil a task involving the production of quantities of an object in an assembly line activity. Ask the pupil to indicate the total amount produced.
14. Take the pupil on a trip to a store. After a purchase, ask the pupil to verify the amount of change received.
15. Ask the pupil to use a dollar changing machine. Indicate that he/she is to verify receipt of the correct change.

16. Ask the pupil to return deposit bottles to a store. Tell the pupil to check to see whether he/she has received the amount due.
17. Challenge the pupil with problems involving the measurement of objects, distances, and heights.
18. Assign the pupil problems involving the use of measuring cups and spoons.

Reading   As with arithmetic, many of the approaches available to teachers of reading involve functional activities. A partial list of these functional reading subcategories includes:

1. Assist the pupil in responding appropriately to written information and markings found on watches, clocks, and other dials and gauges.
2. Help the pupil respond appropriately and accurately to written information found on safety signs, size labels, price tags, and other signs and labels.
3. Expose the pupil to instructions written in simple notes and on packages, machinery, equipment, toys, games, items to be assembled, and in manuals that accompany machinery and equipment.
4. Provide the pupil with experience in locating information from charts, diagrams, maps, directories, schedules, bulletin boards, menus, and reference books, including dictionaries.
5. Help the pupil to respond appropriately to employment applications and to a host of other applications, blanks, and forms.
6. Assist the pupil in interpreting the information found on checks, check stubs, market receipts, work timecards, and bills.
7. Provide the pupil with experiences in decoding and comprehending information found in travel and promotional brochures, information booklets, driving manuals, or other instructional materials.
8. Assist the pupil in unlocking the information found in help wanted ads, printed advertisements, and in real estate and other special sections of magazines and newspapers.
9. Help the pupil interpret reading materials in such a way that he/she is less likely to be victimized by propaganda and other manipulative techniques.
10. Provide the pupil with reading experiences that bring pleasure and excitement, thus enriching his/her life while providing a valuable leisure time activity to be used now and in the future.

If one examines this partial list of functional reading activities, it should be clear that each of the optional approaches offers alternatives within alternatives. Each optional approach further suggests the materials needed to implement the selected program.

Speech   Speech as a skill area to be developed need not be taught as a separate entity unless there are pupils who evidence significant problems with speech, hearing, and/or language development. The assistance of a speech-language and hearing therapist will be necessary to design therapeutic programs that can be implemented in the classroom as well as in the more formal therapeutic situation. However, for other pupils who are developing within normal limits, speech skill development should be part of every other curriculum area. Discussions arising out of the content of other academic, aesthetic, and affective programming can serve as the principal means for improving oral language skills. Speech skills are also facilitated through creative or aesthetic experiences where language plays an integral part. It should be noted that there is likely to be a transfer effect from learning experiences in the written language sphere. Listening, speaking, reading, and writing all reinforce each other. Therefore, speech development, necessarily, is an integral part of the language instructional gestalt. Some examples of ways to generate provocative and stimulating discussions follow:

1. Read a story together and discuss its characters, events, and implications.
2. Show a film or filmstrip as part of a history, social science, or science lesson. The film or filmstrip can serve as the impetus for an informative discussion that not only leads to concept development but to the practice and enrichment of oral language skills.
3. Discuss a television program of particular interest to the pupil. Not only may speech skills be developed but questions of aesthetics may be explored.
4. Hold a discussion on a recent event that is of special interest to the pupil. These current events discussions both develop an awareness of the sciences or social sciences as well as facilitate speech skills.
5. Prepare a choral reading as part of aesthetic development programming. The participation in this creative oral language experience may contribute to an appreciation for literature as well as improve expressive language skills.

Effective teachers should look beyond the traditional methods and materials to arrive at innovative approaches that may be the answer for particular pupils with special learning needs. The skilled diagnostician/programmer looks beyond labels as well, and uses methods and materials that zero in on the unique needs of the pupil regardless of diagnostic label. This is especially so when a label refers to a widely heterogeneous population and describes a trait in nonbehavioral, amorphous terms.

Operant Conditioning Management

No discussion of motivation would be complete that does not include operant conditioning. So much literature (Ullman and Krasner, 1965;

Ayllon and Azrin, 1968; Becker, Thomas, and Carnine, 1969; Smith and Smith, 1969; Buckley and Walker, 1970; Glaser, 1971; Agras, 1978) has been published on methods and research findings in regard to operant conditioning that the present review of methods is deliberately cursory.

Operant conditioning is based on the use of reinforcers to motivate behavior. A reinforcer is any environmental response to a behavior (or any environmental stimulus *viewed* as a response to a behavior) that is followed by an increase in the frequency or intensity of the behavior. Two tenets underlie all operant processes:

1. The frequency and intensity of all behavior, other than behaviors that are classically conditioned, are determined by the subsequent environmental response to that behavior. To control the environmental response to behavior, the teacher must consider a number of aspects:
    a. Available sources of response and their compatibility. Are peers, parents, and classroom aides responding in incompatible ways to the behavior to be modified?
    b. Types of reinforcement available. The reinforcement of attention may be stronger than the negative effect of reprimand, i.e., a reprimand may be a reinforcer to a pupil seeking attention. Reinforcers may gain or lose currency with the pupil over time. Reinforcer categories, i.e., food, tokens, and praise, are differently effective with individual pupils.
    c. Frequency of reinforcement. Reinforcement often starts on a one-to-one frequency or a regular and rapid frequency basis and gradually becomes irregular and less frequent.
    d. Negative reinforcement. The withdrawal of a noxious stimulus is as effective a reinforcer as the presentation of a desirable stimulus. Release from isolation is the type of negative reinforcement most widely used in schools.
2. Recording baseline behavior and behavior during interventions is essential in order to determine the success of the interventions.

No operant conditioning program can be implemented or evaluated without reference to charts that indicate changes in behavior. Behavior must be stated in measurable terms and intervention procedures must be described in explicit detail.

For those behaviors that cannot be modified totally, a shaping procedure is used. Small, partial accomplishments are reinforced at the beginning. As soon as this initial component of the behavior is mastered, reinforcement for it is withdrawn and offered again only when an additional component of the behavior is added on to it. This process is continued until the total behavior is demonstrated. For many tasks, a backward shaping procedure is used. Under such circumstances, the pupil is assisted with the entire behavior except for the final component. When the pupil finishes the task by completing the final component, he/she is reinforced. When the final component is consistently demonstrated, reinforcement is withdrawn and offered again only when the next earlier component is also demonstrated. This backward shaping is continued until the total task is mastered.

All behaviors require intermittent reinforcement on a continuing basis in order to be maintained. The ideal is for a large part of the reinforcement to be internalized, i.e., for the pupil to reinforce himself/herself.

ACTIVITIES AND EXPERIENCES

1. Select a key concept usually associated with science curricula. For this concept, enumerate the various approaches one could take in the logical development of that concept. Be sure to include relationships with other subject areas. For each approach identified, list the materials that might be used to help that instruction come alive.
2. Health and safety have received little attention in the curriculum. What methods would you recommend as ideally suited to the instruction of pupils in healthy and safe living? What subcategories of instruction are available?
3. A major goal of instruction in political science and government is acquainting pupils with the nature and dimensions of national, state, and local government. What are the subcategories of instruction and the methods and materials that are most likely to achieve this goal?
4. What are the primary goals of instruction in economics? What subcategories, methods, and materials are suggested by these goals?
5. What are the primary goals of instruction in sociology, anthropology, and psychology? How may these subjects best be taught as separate entities in the social sciences and as interrelated subjects?
6. Develop a unit of study that ignores traditional subject matter designations and deals exclusively with problem solving, the development of insights, and the facilitation of transdisciplinary concepts.
7. Write a position paper describing how you would design an educational program in which the pupil is provided with the opportunity to decide what he/she wants to learn, how he/she wishes to be taught, and how he/she wishes to be evaluated. Discuss the possible problems expected from this approach.
8. Discuss the ways in which parents can be helpful in selecting methods and materials appropriate to the instruction of their child.

9. Aesthetic education has received scant attention in the curriculum. What subcategories would you include in aesthetic development? What programming approaches are possible? What effect does age of the pupil have on programming alternatives?
10. Discuss the various subcategories that you would include in a comprehensive program designed to facilitate affective development.
11. After you have identified alternate subcategories, methods, and materials appropriate to the instruction of a particular subject or concept, select a pupil and arrive at a decision on the programming approach you will use. Justify your approach and report, orally and/or in writing, on the results of your program.
12. Once you have gained some experience in arriving at instructional options for a particular pupil, proceed to the task of selecting options in such a way that you can schedule several pupils in a group activity. Justify why you have set up the group in the way that you have.
13. Read one of the books on operant conditioning included in the references. Follow up by designing an operant conditioning program for one or more pupils.

CONCLUDING STATEMENT

A competent educator appreciates the critical professional responsibility involved in identifying programming alternatives. Only after motivating program options have been identified can meaningful programs be designed to assist pupils in broadening their skills and concepts. At the heart of the individualization process is a profound respect both for subject matter and for the individual pupil. Consequently, there should be a common-sense approach to the selection of methods of instruction, based upon the logic of the subject itself. For example, since spelling is a written language skill, it must never be taught exclusively or predominantly through auditory channels. Spelling bees should be written, not oral. Another case in point relates to the copying of written work from the chalkboard. Since writing depends largely on revisualization skills, copying must be shunned because that process only impedes the development of revisualization skills. Unfortunately, these examples of what not to do represent the rule rather than the exception for those teachers who have not thought out the relationship between the instructional process and the nature of the educational task. Yet another example involves asking a pupil to select a misspelled word from a list containing all other correctly spelled words. The process of selecting the misspelled word reinforces that misspelling. It appears obvious that a teacher must analyze the subject matter if he/she expects to become a competent programmer.

Once the teacher has identified programming options that are sensible because they are consonant with the nature of the subject, then the task becomes one of selecting a program option that will motivate and be appropriate to the learning patterns of a particular pupil. This second task requires an understanding of the individual pupil that comes through well-planned and well-executed interactions with the pupil and significant others and through careful and skilled observations. After engaging in the variety of informal assessment techniques available, the teacher, ideally with the help of the pupil, must choose an instructional approach(es) and materials that are most likely to facilitate learning because they are motivating, because they meet a need, and because they make epistemic sense.

POSTTEST

At this point retake the Pretest.

LITERATURE CITED

Agras, W. S. (ed.). 1978. Behavioral Modification: Principles and Clinical Applications. 2nd Ed. Little, Brown & Co., Boston.

Ayllon, T., and Azrin, N. H. 1968. The Token Economy. Appleton-Century-Crofts, New York.

Becker, W. C., Thomas, D. R., and Carnine, D. 1969. Reducing Behavioral Problems: An Operant Conditioning Guide for Teachers. ERIC Clearinghouse on Early Childhood Education, Urbana, Ill.

Buckley, N. K., and Walker, H. M. 1970. Modifying Classroom Behavior. Research Press, Champaign, Ill.

Glaser, R. (ed.). 1971. The Nature of Reinforcement. Academic Press, Inc., New York.

Smith, J. M., and Smith, D. E. P. 1969. Child Management: A Program for Parents and Teachers. Ann Arbor Publishers, Ann Arbor.

Ullman, L., and Krasner, L. (eds.). 1965. Case Histories in Behavior Modification. Holt, Rinehart & Winston, Inc., New York.

SUGGESTED READINGS

Abt, C. 1970. An evaluation model: How to compare curriculum materials. Nat. Schools 86:21–28.

Anderson, R. C., Faust, G. W., Roderick, M. C., Cunningham, D. C., and Andre, T. (eds.). 1969. Current Research on Instruction. Prentice-Hall, Inc., Englewood Cliffs, N.J.

Anderson, R. M., Greer, J. G., and Odle, S. J. (eds.). 1978. Individualizing Educational Materials for Special Children in the Mainstream. University Park Press, Baltimore.

Ashcroft, S. S. 1976. NCEMMH: A network of media/material resources. Audiovis. Instruct. 21:46–47.

Bender, M., Valletutti, P. J., and Bender, R. 1976. Teaching the Moderately and Severely Handicapped. Vol. III. Functional Academics for the Mildly and Moderately Handicapped. University Park Press, Baltimore.

Bloom, B. S., Hastings, J. J., and Madaus, G. F. 1971. Handbook on Formative and Summative Evaluation of Student Learning. McGraw-Hill Book Co., New York.

Bullough, R. U. 1974. Creating Instructional Materials. Charles E. Merrill Publishing Co., Columbus, Oh.

Gagné, R. M. 1970. The Conditions of Learning. 2nd Ed. Holt, Rinehart & Winston, Inc., New York.

Gagné, R. M., and Gephart, W. J. 1968. Learning Research and School Subjects. F. E. Peacock, Itasca, Ill.

Joyce, B., and Weil, M. 1972. Models of Teaching. Prentice-Hall, Inc., Englewood Cliffs, N.J.

Langdon, D. G. 1973. Interactive Instructional Designs for Individualized Learning. Educational Technology Publications, Englewood Cliffs, N.J.

Miller, J. P. 1976. Humanizing the Classroom. Praeger Publishers, New York.

Reeder, A. F., and Bolen, J. M. 1976. Match the materials to the learner. Audiovis. Instruct. 21:24–25.

Thomas, J. I. 1975. Learning Centers: Opening Up the Classroom. Holbrook Press, Boston.

Thomas, J. I. 1977. Options for learning: A process for accommodating individual differences. Educ. Leader 34:346–350.

Walberg, H. J. (ed.). 1974. Evaluating Educational Preferences: A Sourcebook of Methods, Instruments, and Examples. McCutchan, Berkeley.

Weinthaler, J., and Rotberg, J. M. 1970. The systematic selection of instructional materials based on an inventory of learner abilities and skills. Except. Child. 36:615–619.

Van Etten, C., and Van Etten, G. 1976. The measurement of pupil progress and selecting instructional materials. J. Learn. Disabil. 9:469–480.

Module 11

The teacher will evaluate the effects of classmates and of himself/herself on the attitudes, behavior, and learning of each individual pupil in the classroom and will modify these interactions when necessary.

PRETEST

1. What are some of the reasons for knowing the social forces at work in the classroom especially as related to peer influence?
2. In order to more effectively utilize the human resources and social forces in the classroom, what questions should teachers ask about each of their pupils before organizing instructional experiences?
3. From our knowledge of mental hygiene, what attitudes should be communicated by teachers in order to build the self-confidence of their pupils?
4. What are some of the informal ways in which teachers may evaluate themselves as being significant in the total social process in the classroom?
5. Describe briefly the Flanders System of Interaction Analysis. In your discussion, report on several of the measurements possible through the use of this system.
6. What are some of the weaknesses attributed to the Flanders System of Interaction Analysis?
7. The Flanders System is a system for the analysis of verbal communication. According to Amidon and Flanders, what are some of the most important verbal skills?

INTRODUCTION AND OVERVIEW

Earlier modules explored the effects of community and parental attitudes, values, and goals (Modules 1 and 2) and the effects of the classroom and school's physical environment (Module 3) on pupil behavior and learning. This module focuses on methods of affecting the attitudes, behavior, and learning of individual pupils through teacher and peer interactions. Undesirable pupil behaviors and learning problems are frequently attributed to pupil characteristics and conditions rather than to external factors, e.g., failure to learn a skill is misdiagnosed as a sign of the pupil's lack of intelligence when, in reality, the dimensions of the task have been poorly or improperly explained or demonstrated by the teacher. The search for cause or etiology when restricted to the pupil, unfortunately, serves to divert attention from other likely problem causes such as deleterious physical and social environments, inappropriate media and materials, illogical and faulty instructional programming, and unharmonious teacher-pupil interactions.

Once teachers appreciate the effect on learning and behavior of the classroom's social climate, they will then consciously intervene to assist in the development of an interpersonal milieu in the classroom that provides fertile soil for learning. In such a milieu, peers interact and act in each other's best interests and form, with the teacher, a cohesive team striving together toward mutually agreed upon and supported educational goals.

It is clear, at least in contemporary American society, that peers significantly influence and reinforce the attitudes and behavior of group members (Bronfenbrenner, 1970). People quickly incorporate into their own life-style the attitudes, values, and behavior of respected and/or feared peers. The paradoxical conformity of nonconformists to a preferred or socially mandated subgroup furnishes graphic testimony to the power of peer influence. The contagion or ripple effect of hostile or disruptive pupils on their classmates supplies continuous evidence of the adverse human interaction effects that shape behavior and learning in the classroom (Christoplos and Valletutti, 1979). Pressures from respected or feared others are difficult to resist, especially when one hopes to avoid being ridiculed, ostracized, or punished. Because of the significant effects of peer modeling on behavior and learning, teachers must discover and come to understand fully the social forces at work in the classroom and to identify and utilize those pupils who are most likely to be modeled by their classmates.

The management of learning experiences in all curriculum areas demands that teachers understand *and* expertly use the social environment of the classroom. The ideal arrangement is one that includes in the classroom peer models whose behaviors and attitudes toward learning motivate other pupils to behave in cooperative and constructive ways and to approach learning with enthusiasm. Through utilization of *positive* models, the influence of negative models (those with power to disrupt the class and reduce teaching effectiveness) is diminished. Consideration of modeling factors must become an essential element in administrative decisions relevant to class composition.

As the mainstreaming movement gains in momentum and greater pupil heterogeneity increasingly becomes a classroom reality, the organization and management of the classroom's human environment become a more arduous task. Wide-range heterogeneity can be stimulating, enlightening, motivating, and challenging. However, with greater heterogeneity, the danger of negative ripple or contagion effects increases and is compounded when pupils with serious behavioral problems are present in the class. Unfortunately, when teachers do not possess special skills of educational diagnosis and of classroom management, the presence of pupils with behavioral deviations and disorders can lead to the disruption of the class and the corruption of educational goals (Christoplos and Valletutti, 1979).

Attention, thus far, has been directed principally to the possible harmful ripple effects of antisocial, anti-intellectual, anti-achievement, and anti-teacher behaviors of peer models. The major impetus to modify and/or diminish their disruptive impact must be to provide or help develop positive models in the planning of individualized educational programs for each pupil. In order to more effectively utilize human resources as behavior models and learning facilitators in the classroom, teachers should be able to answer the following questions for each pupil in their class:

1. Who has a positive, motivating influence and serves as a model of constructive behavior on (pupil's name)? How can I utilize this influence to facilitate growth and development in both parties?
2. Who has a negative influence on (pupil's name)? How can I diminish that influence or help to metamorphize that influence into a positive one?
3. Who can (pupil's name) work with cooperatively in small group activities? Large group activities?
4. Who can (pupil's name) be tutored by in the various skill areas?
5. Who can (pupil's name) tutor in the various skill areas?
6. How can I make sure that (pupil's name) feels that he/she is an essential part of the class team, working toward his/her own development and the growth and progress of classmates?

Answers to these questions are essential to the diagnostic/prescriptive process and are a prerequisite to the organization of classroom activities, the facilitation of constructive behaviors, and the encouragement of learning.

While recognizing that the major influence of peers on the behavior and learning of classmates is critical to the planning and organization of instructional experiences, teachers must not overlook or underestimate the effect of their own personality and behavior on their pupils. It is unlikely that pupils model their teachers to the same extent that they model peers (Bandura, 1969). It should be obvious, however, that to maximize pupil modeling of teachers, teachers must behave in a manner that earns pupil respect and admiration.

Earning the respect and admiration of pupils depends, undoubtedly, on a host of personal variables, including interest and enthusiasm for teaching, knowledge of subject matter, creative skill in providing stimulating learning experiences, a sense of humor, and a genuine and natural respect for the individual worth of each pupil. Building the self-confidence of pupils so that they come to realize a heightening sense of self-worth must be consistently communicated in the countless interactions between teacher and pupils. Not only does building self-confidence help engender a positive view of teachers, it also results in improved pupil performance that, naturally, will lead to further valuing of self.

> Conditions and consequences that are *universal positives* are . . . experiences that acknowledge success, insure a variety of stimulation, lead to an increase of self-esteem or improved self-image, and lead to an increase in confidence (Mager, 1968, p. 58).

Teachers' communication of their perceptions, in positive terms, of pupils' skills, knowledge, abilities, and potential is a primary factor in building self-concept.

A particularly successful way of building self-concept is through praising each pupil as an individual and on an individual basis. Teachers must encourage praise from a variety of sources, including admired peers, other teachers, parents, classroom aides, and classroom volunteers. It is essential that praise be in keeping with the pupil's own self-perception, or else it may be perceived as artificial and manipulative.

Teachers may chart their comments to pupils to: 1) determine the frequency of praise, criticism, and neutral comments and 2) ascertain the distribution of praise to various class members during a particular time segment. A sample chart to record rewarding, critical, and neutral comments is shown in Table 1.

A positive self-concept may also be encouraged by helping the pupil gain a sense of belonging, e.g., assisting the pupil to realize that he/she

Table 1.   Evaluation of teacher's comments to pupils

Date _____   Time Segment _____

Curriculum Area or Class Activity _____

Directions: Place the applicable symbol (+), (−), or (0) in the column next to the name of the pupil to whom the comment was made. After you have written down the nature of each comment for the time segment specified, analyze your comments to each pupil for quality and quantity. Are you criticizing too much? Are you ignoring some pupils and lavishing praise on others?

Pupil's Name	Praise (+)	Criticism (−)	Neutral (0)
1.			
2.			
3.			
4.			
5.			

shares with classmates attributes including those of a cultural, social, and community nature. A positive self-concept is further stimulated through the development of pupil awareness and appreciation that each classmate shares common as well as unique problems. Assisting pupils to realize that no one is perfect physically, intellectually, or in performance capability is vital to the acquisition of a healthy and realistic self-concept in which one can examine oneself with an objective eye balanced by gentle humor. Positive self-image is enhanced by arriving at a psychological state where individual differences are viewed as desirable rather than as ego destructive. In addition, pupils must be assisted in accepting uncertainty and lack of knowledge as a natural and common state and not as evidence of individual deficit or failure. Finally, teachers must engage in small step instruction to assure success while each pupil is encouraged to set his/her own reasonable learning goals that are success oriented and self-reinforcing.

It seems probable from our knowledge of mental hygiene that teachers who communicate the attitudes undergirding the following statements are more likely to have a positive impact on the behavior and learning of their pupils:

1. I value you as a unique, special, total human being with individual needs and differences.
2. I am deeply committed to helping you grow and develop as a total person.
3. I believe that you are capable of learning, and I will help you to do so despite any problems you encounter.

4. I will constantly strive to help you realize and appreciate your worth and value.
5. I will provide you with learning experiences that are exciting, valuable, challenging, and within your ability.
6. While I provide you with learning experiences that are within your ability, I will always encourage you to believe the next higher level is within your ability to master.
7. I will never ridicule, humiliate, belittle, or label you.
8. I will recognize your individual needs for rest and leisure.
9. I will provide an environment that is responsive and rewarding to your attempts as well as your successes.

Feelings and attitudes may be communicated both verbally and non-verbally. Recognizing the importance of teacher communications, various procedures have been advocated for their analysis. A prerequisite to formal techniques for evaluating these communications is the careful analysis and precise identification of what is to be communicated, thus making the task of evaluating the communications markedly simpler. Formal techniques are particularly advantageous in that they force teachers to consider what they hope to communicate to pupils in addition to knowledge and skills. Several methods of interaction analysis are available to teachers. Videotaping lessons and later analyzing them to determine whether one has communicated, both verbally and nonverbally, desired attitudes are central to the evaluation task. Audiotaping, or the use of audio cassettes, also may help. However, the use of audio techniques prevents the analysis of nonverbal communication. Nonverbal communication is potentially more powerful than verbal communication since gesture and other body language, facial expressions, and vocal inflections and tones are capable of negating the words being said. In addition to the use of recording techniques, teachers may evaluate their own success by measuring pupil growth and development. Fellow teachers may be asked to evaluate typical lessons according to previously formulated guidelines. In conferences with pupils, teachers may share their philosophy of education, including their goals of communication, asking the pupils for their perceptions of the relative success of these communications.

Teachers may develop and/or select different methods of classroom interaction analysis. An awareness of some already developed techniques would assist in modifying or developing a method to meet individual needs, situations, and preferences. Interaction analysis refers to any technique used to study the chain of classroom events so that each event is taken into consideration. A frequently used technique in educational research and in pre- and inservice teacher education is the Flanders System of Interaction Analysis (Amidon and Flanders, 1967). The

Flanders System is concerned with verbal interaction only, undoubtedly because it can be observed with greater reliability than nonverbal behavior. In this system, the observer/recorder measures the social climate of the classroom by classifying all teacher verbal interactions as either direct or indirect, giving central attention to the amount of freedom the teacher grants pupils. Indirect teacher influence categories are: 1) accepting feeling, 2) praising or encouraging, 3) accepting ideas, and 4) asking questions. Direct teacher influence categories include: 5) lecturing, 6) giving directions, and 7) criticizing or justifying authority. The Flanders System also provides categories of student talk: 8) responding to the teacher and 9) initiating talk. Flanders has established that indirect teacher talk is followed by significantly more pupil talk than direct teacher talk. The system also includes a tenth notation, which refers to silence or confusion or time spent in behaviors other than those classifiable by any of the other numbers in the system. All of these categories are claimed to be mutually exclusive and are said to be inclusive of all verbal interactions occurring in the classroom.

The observer/recorder, when using this system, listens and records the category number of interactions occurring every 3 seconds. The method of recording these interactions consists of entering the sequence of numbers into a 10 row by 10 column table or matrix. From an analysis of the matrix, a description of the classroom interaction may be developed. The percentage of teacher talk is found by dividing the total of tallies in Columns 1 through 7 by the total number of tallies in the matrix, while the percentage of pupil talk is computed by dividing the total of tallies in Columns 8 and 9 by the total of tallies in the matrix. A frequently cited index of teacher behavior is the I/D ratio, the ratio of indirect to direct teacher talk. This measure is arrived at by adding the total number of teacher behaviors, both indirect and direct. A revised I/D ratio that seeks to determine motivation and control is computed by dividing the total of tallies in Columns 1–3 by the total of tallies in Columns 1–3 and 6–7. Other indexes used are: the teacher response ratio (TRR), which measures the teacher's tendency to react to the ideas and feelings of the pupils; the teacher question ratio (TQR), which measures the tendency of the teacher to use questions during the content-oriented part of class discussions; and the pupil initiation ratio (PIR), which indicates the proportion of pupil talk judged to be an act of pupil initiation.

While the Flanders System is apparently the most widely used formal system of interaction analysis, it has been criticized for a number of reasons. The most frequently cited weaknesses include:

1. Lack of explicitness in that there is uncertainty about the most appropriate category to be used for particular teacher-pupil interactions

2. Use of time as the basic unit of coding and the attendant difficulty in recording behaviors at 3-second intervals, while they are happening (the system was not intended to be used retrospectively from recordings)
3. Failure to emphasize the specific cognitive or curriculum aspects of the classroom interaction
4. Failure to measure cognitive achievement before the lesson in order to determine whether cognitive levels following a lesson have changed
5. Lack of a component that attempts to measure nonverbal communication or the nonverbal components of the verbal elements
6. Tendency to view talk as transmission rather than communication
7. Inability to use this system during teacher-pupil interactions that are less formal than the typical question-answer sequence emphasized by the Flanders System
8. The limited applicability to more innovative classroom practices and settings (for example, innovations such as the open classroom and the open space school)

Despite the documented and publicized shortcomings and limitations of the Flanders System, its true value is that its use has alerted teachers to the importance of their interactions with pupils, to the need to develop more effective classroom behavior as part of the total social process in the classroom, and to the fact that desired communication skills may be experimented with and practiced. Among the most important verbal skills, according to Amidon and Flanders (1967, p. 3), are the following:

1. Ability to accept, clarify, and use ideas
2. Ability to accept and clarify emotional expression
3. Ability to relate emotional expression to ideas
4. Ability to state objectively a point of view
5. Ability to reflect accurately the ideas of others
6. Ability to summarize ideas presented in group discussion
7. Ability to communicate encouragement
8. Ability to use criticism with the least possible harm to the status of the recipient

ACTIVITIES AND EXPERIENCES

1. Select a class and for at least three of the pupils answer each of the following six questions:
   a. Who has a positive, motivating influence and serves as a model of constructive behavior on (pupil's name)? How can I utilize this influence to facilitate growth and development in both parties?

b. Who has a negative influence on (pupil's name)? How can I diminish that influence or help to metamorphize that influence into a positive one?

c. Who can (pupil's name) work with cooperatively in small group activities? Large group activities?

d. Who can (pupil's name) be tutored by in the various skill areas?

e. Who can (pupil's name) tutor in the various skill areas?

f. How can I make sure that (pupil's name) feels that he/she is an essential part of the class team, working toward his/her own development and the growth and progress of classmates?

2. For each of the following statements, discuss in paragraph form the underlying emotional concomitants.

a. I value you as a unique, special, total human being with individual needs and differences.

b. I am deeply committed to helping you grow and develop as a total person.

c. I believe that you are capable of learning, and I will help you to do so despite any problems you encounter.

d. I will constantly strive to help you realize and appreciate your worth and value.

e. I will provide you with learning experiences that are exciting, valuable, challenging, and within your ability.

f. While I provide you with learning experiences that are within your ability, I will always encourage you to believe the next higher level is within your ability to master.

g. I will never ridicule, humiliate, belittle, or label you.

h. I will recognize your individual needs for rest and leisure.

i. I will provide an environment that is responsive and rewarding to your attempts as well as your successes.

3. Prepare a brief position paper that explains your philosophy of education and the basic values you wish to communicate to pupils. From this position paper, design a system and/or approaches that you might use to determine whether you are successful in your communications.

4. Make a videotape of an actual or simulated lesson, and ask several of your peers to analyze your interaction with pupils. Encourage them to avoid judgmental terms such as good or bad and desirable or undesirable. Emphasize that the task is to identify the nature of the interaction, not the quality.

5. Obtain a copy of the Flanders System of Interaction Analysis (see Amidon and Flanders, 1967). Carry out the system acting as an observer/recorder for a peer or classmate. Then ask the peer to observe and record for one of your lessons. Afterward, hold several

meetings to analyze and discuss the results, drawing implications for instructional practices.

6. Write a brief term paper that explores both the strengths and weaknesses of the Flanders System. Compare it with other formal systems that have been developed. The paper should be well documented.

7. Use the chart included in the body of the module to record the evaluative comments you make to a class of pupils. Then write a report on modifications you plan to make as a result of your analysis of the chart.

8. In examining classroom environments and teacher behavior, how can you measure the values and attitudes being modeled in relation to the following issues?
   a. Sexism versus equality
   b. Racism versus equality
   c. Ageism versus equality
   d. Materialism versus spiritualism/idealism
   e. Elitism versus democracy
   f. Competition versus cooperation
   g. Conformism versus independence
   h. Escapism versus realism
   i. Violence versus pacifism
   j. Indifference to others versus sensitivity to others
   k. Indifference to beauty versus sensitivity to beauty
   l. Impetus to change versus fatalism
   m. Perfection versus coping

CONCLUDING STATEMENT

For too long, teachers have failed to assume a holistic approach to evaluation. They typically seek atomized explanations for single pupil behaviors. Explanations further tend to fix on the pupil's innate or acquired characteristics, emphasizing past occurrences, genetic characteristics, and familial environmental factors. This approach, conditioned and reinforced by many teacher training practices, unfortunately mitigates against an analysis of social influences active in the present milieu, particularly those occurring in the classroom itself. The current social processes, including peer as well as teacher influence, if ignored, overlooked, or not controlled, can only result in problems in classroom organization, behavior management, and in the improper and unsuccessful design of learning experiences. Pupils will learn better in responsible, responsive, and rewarding classroom environments where social forces and processes are designed and utilized for maximal positive effects.

POSTTEST

At this point retake the Pretest.

LITERATURE CITED

Amidon, E. J., and Flanders, N. A. 1967. The Role of the Teacher in the Classroom: A Manual for Understanding and Improving Teacher Classroom Behavior. Rev. Ed. Association for Productive Teaching, Inc., Minneapolis.

Bandura, A. 1969. Principles of Behavior Modification. Holt, Rinehart & Winston, Inc., New York.

Bronfenbrenner, U. 1970. Two Worlds of Childhood: U.S. and U.S.S.R. Russell Sage Foundation, New York.

Christoplos, F., and Valletutti, P. J. 1979. Education. In P. J. Valletutti and F. Christoplos (eds.), Preventing Physical and Mental Disabilities: Multidisciplinary Approaches. University Park Press, Baltimore.

Mager, R. F. 1968. Developing Attitude Toward Learning. Fearon Publishers, Belmont, Cal.

SUGGESTED READINGS

Amidon, E. J., and Giammatteo, M. C. 1965. The behavior of superior teachers. Elem. School J. 65:283–285.

Amidon, E. J., and Hough, J. B. (eds.), 1967. Interaction Analysis: Theory, Research and Application. Addison-Wesley Publishing Co., Inc., Reading, Mass.

Amidon, E. J., and Hunter, E. 1967. Improving Teaching: The Analysis of Classroom Verbal Interaction. Holt, Rinehart & Winston, Inc., New York.

Anderson, J., and Hansford, B. C. 1974. An informal processing procedure for scoring Flanders Interaction Analysis categories. J. Exper. Educ. 43:6–7.

Bandura, A., Blanchard, G. B., and Ritter, B. 1969. The relative efficiency of desensitization and modeling approaches for inducing behavioral, affective, and attitudinal changes. J. Pers. Soc. Psychol. 13:173–179.

Bandura, A., and Kupers, C. A. 1964. Transmission of patterns of self-reinforcement through modeling. J. Abnorm. Soc. Psychol. 69:1–9.

Bandura, A., Ross, D., and Ross, S. 1963. Imitation of film mediated aggressive models. J. Abnorm. Soc. Psychol. 66:3–11.

Bennett, N. 1976. Teaching Styles and Pupil Progress. Harvard University Press, Cambridge.

Bledsoe, J. C. 1967. Self-concepts of children and their intelligence, achievement, interests and anxiety. Childhood Educ. 43:436–438.

Bondi, J. C. 1970. Feedback from interaction analysis: Some implications for the improvement of teaching. J. Teach. Educ. 21:189–196.

Brophy, J. E., and Good, T. L. 1974. Teacher-Student Relationships. Holt, Rinehart & Winston, Inc., New York.

Canfield, J., and Wells, H. C. 1976. 100 Ways to Enhance Self-Concept in the Classroom. Prentice-Hall, Inc., Englewood Cliffs, N.J.

Charles, C. M. 1976. Individualizing Instruction. C. V. Mosby Co., St. Louis.

Coopersmith, S. 1967. The Antecedents of Self-Esteem. W. H. Freeman & Co., San Francisco.

Coulthard, M. 1974. Approaches to the analysis of classroom interaction. Educ. Rev. 22:229–232.

Csapo, M. 1972. Peer models reverse the 'one bad apple spoils the barrel' theory. Teach. Except. Child. 39:321–327.

Davies, I. K. 1973. Competency Based Learning: Management, Technology, and Design. McGraw-Hill Book Co., New York.

Epstein, E. 1973. The self-concept revisited: On a theory of a theory. Am. Psychol. 28:404–416.

Felker, D. W. 1974. Building Positive Self-Concepts. Burgess Publishing Co., Minneapolis.

Flanders, N. A. 1966. Interaction Analysis in the Classrrom: A Manual for Observers. School of Education, University of Michigan, Ann Arbor.

Flanders, N. A. 1970. Analyzing Teaching Behavior. Addison-Wesley Publishing Co., Inc., Reading Mass.

Gearheart, B. R., and Weishahn, M. W. 1976. The Handicapped Child in the Regular Classroom. C. V. Mosby Co., St. Louis.

Gergen, K. 1971. The Concept of Self. Holt, Rinehart & Winston, Inc., New York.

Good, T. L., and Brophy, J. E. 1973. Looking in Classrooms. Harper & Row Publishers, New York.

Haddan, E. E. 1970. Evolving Instruction. Macmillan Publishing Co., Inc., New York.

Hamachek, D. E. 1969. Characteristics of good teachers and implications for teacher education. Phi Delta Kappan 50:341–345.

Hartup, W. W., Glazer, J. A., and Charlesworth, R. 1967. Peer reinforcement and sociometric status. Child Dev. 38:1017–1024.

Harvey, O. J., Prather, M., White, B. J., and Hoffmeister, J. K. 1968. Teachers' beliefs, classroom atmosphere and student behavior. Am. Educ. Res. J. 5:151–166.

Kagan, J. 1971. Personality Development. Harcourt Brace Jovanovich, Inc., New York.

Kounin, J. S., and Gump, P. V. 1958. Ripple effect in school discipline. Elem. School J. 59:158–162.

La Benne, W. D., and Greene, B. I. 1969. Educational Implications of Self-Concept Theory. Goodyear Publishing Co., Pacific Palisades, Cal.

Measel, W., and Wood, D. W. 1972. Teacher verbal behavior and pupil thinking in the elementary school. J. Educ. Res. 66:99–102.

Michaelis, J. U., Grossman, R. H., and Scott, L. F. 1975. New Designs for Elementary Curriculum and Instruction. McGraw-Hill Book Co., New York.

Miller, J. P. 1976. Humanizing the Classroom. Praeger Publishers, New York.

Morse, W. 1964. Self-concept in the school setting. Child. Educ. 41:195–198.

Pickett, L. A. 1970. Can the level of instruction be raised through the use of interaction analysis? Educ. Leader 3:597–599.

Psencik, L. F. 1969. Interaction analysis improves classroom instruction. Clearing House 43:555–561.

Purkey, W. W. 1970. Self Concept and School Achievement. Prentice-Hall, Inc., Englewood Cliffs, N.J.

Roberts, M. C., Santogrossi, D. A., and Thelan, M. H. 1977. The effects of model imitation on affect. Pers. Soc. Psychol. Bull. 3:75–78.

Roush, R. E., and Kennedy, V. J. 1971. Changing teacher behavior with interaction analysis. Education 91:220–222.

Sanders, N. M. 1966. Classroom Questions: What Kinds? Harper & Row Publishers, New York.

Stuck, G. B., and Wyne, M. D. 1971. The study of verbal behavior in special and regular elementary school classrooms. Am. J. Ment. Defic. 75:463–469.

Walker, J. J. 1976. Gifted Teacher, Know Thyself. Department of Special Education, Appalachian State University, Boone, N.C.

Worrell, J., and Nelson, C. M. 1974. Managing Instructional Problems. McGraw-Hill Book Co., New York.

Module 12

(with Florence Christoplos)

The teacher will accommodate educational programs to pupil temperament and learning style characteristics.

PRETEST

1. There are several pupils in your class with short attention spans. What are the ways in which you can manage your instructional program to accommodate these pupils?
2. How does perseverance differ for pupils with short concentration spans? For pupils with long concentration spans?
3. What relevant external factors influence the concentration/perseverance levels of pupils?
4. Define what is meant by high distractibility.
5. Explain why being distracted by important stimuli is a necessary human trait.
6. What elements should be considered in deciding whether to allow distractible pupils to set aside an unfinished task to pursue a new task?
7. What arrangements are of assistance to pupils who are easily distracted by petty and irrelevant stimuli?
8. Why should pupils themselves control the use of environmental protections against distractibility?
9. Describe a shaping technique used to remediate nonproductive distractibility.
10. What modifications in the educational program may be necessary for a high activity pupil? For a low activity pupil?
11. How can the withdrawn pupil be helped to accept new situations?
12. What is the only significant problem that high approach pupils may have?
13. How can teachers help pupils who experience difficulty with transitions?
14. What effect can a high intensity teacher have on a low intensity pupil? A low intensity teacher on a high intensity pupil?
15. With what kinds of tasks are impulsive learners most efficient?
16. With what kinds of tasks are impulsive learners at a disadvantage?
17. What can a teacher do to help impulsive learners with tasks that are causing them difficulty?
18. Define verbal mediation.
19. What can a teacher do to help reflective learners with tasks that are causing them difficulty?
20. List several educational tasks that are more suitable to a reflective mode of learning.
21. List several educational tasks that are more suitable to an impulsive mode of learning.

22. Define the terms *field dependency* and *field independency*.
23. Identify four key issues yet to be resolved relevant to learning modality.
24. Why should reported sex and ethnic differences in learning style be considered by educators to be a function of cultural expectations?

INTRODUCTION AND OVERVIEW

An evaluation of a pupil's educational programming needs and the design of individualized educational programs are incomplete unless attention is paid to that pupil's learning style. The teacher's task, as proposed in this module, is to become familiar with each pupil's learning style and to use that knowledge to create and structure learning experiences and to manage the learning environment. The teacher's temperament and learning style are, of course, of equal importance with that of the pupil. It is the interaction between the temperament of teacher and pupils that more heavily determines learning outcomes rather than the temperament of either one in isolation. In this module, understanding pupil learning styles includes understanding a pupil's response style in learning.

Teachers should also be aware that, in testing situations, a pupil's performance varies on different types of tests, all purporting to measure the same knowledge and skills. Identifying *how* a pupil tests best, e.g., multiple choice or essay, oral or written, is as important as identifying how a pupil learns best. Designing appropriate testing experiences that accommodate individual pupil temperament[1] and cognitive style is as much part of individualizing programs as is designing learning experiences.

Concentration

Learning styles reflect basic personality patterns. For example, there are pupils who are able to concentrate for relatively long periods of time while other pupils are able to concentrate only for short periods. For those pupils with short concentration characteristics, task assignments should be shorter *or* pupils should be allowed to leave and return to tasks periodically. Under the latter circumstances, pupils may be given all assignments for the day at once and told that they must be finished by a set time later in the day. During the day, gentle reminders are given to help the pupils return to the task, but the pupil is never required to finish any one task at one sitting. Self-regulation is the long-term objective. Therefore, perseverance for pupils with short attention spans means the ability to keep going back to a task until it is finished. For other pupils, perseverance means staying with the task for one sitting until it is finished. In most classrooms, however, the method of perseverance promulgated, expected, and rewarded usually depends on the teacher's attitude toward finishing a task at one sitting, e.g., a teacher and/or school administrator may feel that pupils are being overindulged if

---

[1] The most comprehensive descriptions of temperament characteristics are presented in the work of Thomas, Chess, and Birch (1968) and Thomas and Chess (1977).

allowed to complete a task at several sittings rather than at one. Further-more, teachers may view shorter concentration spans as highly disruptive to classroom management. High concentration, however, can also be a liability to classroom management. A pupil who concentrates with great intensity for long periods becomes irritated by the necessity for changing to a new task as required by most class schedules. A teacher committed to individualized instruction, however, arranges for all pupils with all degrees of concentration span to function smoothly and without penalty in the classroom.

Since so much of education requires pupil concentration on an educational task, teachers need to determine concentration/perseverance levels before they design instructional experiences for pupils. A particu-larly cogent example of the effects of short concentration on learning is with the hard-of-hearing pupil with a short concentration span. This type of pupil is highly dependent on speechreading for language development. The pupil who concentrates fleetingly on the speaker's face is likely to be deficient in the acquisition of comprehension, interest, and speechreading skills as a result of the inability to concentrate visually. With such pupils, teachers must repeat and review information more so than with those not so multiply handicapped. Without these precautions, minimal motivation toward learning is likely to occur with further decreasing concentration levels and increasing distractibility. The acquisition of academic and other skills depends greatly on concentration skills and the acceptability of one's style of concentration in the classroom. When only one style is expected, pupils with another style cannot help but be adversely affected. The pupil who cannot complete a task at one sitting is invariably penalized under traditional circumstances.

Learning styles vis-à-vis concentration are evaluated primarily through observing pupils as they work on a variety of tasks, under various conditions, at different times of the day, and in the several sub-ject or subskill areas of the curriculum. Concentration/perseverance is a multidimensional characteristic further influenced by other relevant fac-tors, including the motivating influence of subject matter, the size and composition of the instructional group, and the nature, type, and fre-quency of the reinforcement provided by the teacher. Whenever possible, pupils should be encouraged to establish their own schedules of work completion and the sequence of learning events compatible with their own learning style. Different concentration/perseverance styles may require the scheduling of shorter learning segments, frequent rest periods, the alternation of quiet tasks with active curriculum experiences, and/or the design of special educational schedules. Teachers need to plan special instructional sequences for pupils with concentration/perseverance levels so short that they interfere with the acquisition of academic and other higher level skills. In severe cases of this nature, the immediate objective is to increase concentration for specific tasks, most successfully beginning with those with greatest emotional impact. Since a minimal span of concentration is prerequisite to all educational tasks, as minimal concentration levels are identified, they should be added to descriptions of needed competencies in task analyses.

Distractibility

Distractibility may appear, at first glance, to be another way of characterizing level of concentration. However, the two terms refer to separate entities, although both refer to aspects of attention. Pupils with either long or short concentration spans may be easily distracted by irrelevant stimuli or may be indifferent to irrelevant stimuli. High distraction refers to a person's predilection to orient toward petty, irrelevant stimuli and away from the task at hand. Distractibility is an attribute possessed by all to varying degrees. To be distracted by important stimuli irrelevant to the task at hand is, of course, necessary for survival, as for example, responding to a fire alarm. To be distracted by stimuli that promise more provocative, stimulating, and enriching tasks is normal behavior that, rather than interfering with learning, facilitates it in the direction of the new task. Many teachers become disconcerted when pupils are attracted to new stimuli, feeling threatened by what appears to them to be a loss of control and a departure from the holy writ of the lesson plan. The intensity, educational value, and emotional impact of the distraction must be considered in determining the relative priority of the distraction task and the task at hand. Pupils must be allowed, whenever feasible, to pursue new tasks or tangents prompted by dramatic and novel external stimuli with an understanding that, by an established time, they will return to the uncompleted task.

An especially vivid instance of the distracting effect of content with greater emotional intensity than the planned lession is recalled:

> On the occasion of a visit from her college supervisor, a student teacher was conducting a well-planned pre-Thanksgiving lesson traditional to mid-November social studies curricula. During the early stages of the lesson, a coal truck, moving directly under the classroom window, was delivering to the school basement what appeared to be a powdered black substance that vaguely resembled coal. Suddenly, the truck overturned in its maneuvering, followed by much noise, a cloud of black smoke, and the excited voices of several workers and passersby. The pupils, immediately tuning out talk of Miles Standish and Priscilla, jumped up and ran to the windows for a better view. The student teacher reprimanded the pupils, attempting to round them up like so many errant chicks, while struggling to resume her lesson. Although forced to remain in their seats, the pupils nevertheless continued listening to the outside noises, twisting and elongating their necks and

bodies to catch an occasional view. After what seemed an interminable and fruitless effort to pursue the task at hand, the college supervisor asked permission to intervene. He then invited the pupils to quietly join him at the window for a discussion. Once they were at the window, he asked them to look at what was happening and to notice as many relevant elements as possible. After the comparative quiet of observation and analysis, the supervisor led a discussion on the following questions:

1. How do you think they will be able to get the truck right side up again?
2. Why did the truck overturn?
3. How might the accident have been prevented?
4. How well do you think the black powder they are delivering will burn? How long do you think it will last compared to other fuel? To other grades of coal?
5. How much money do you think this grade of coal costs the city? What do we mean by grades of coal? What are the grades of coal?
6. Who makes the decisions necessary to purchase coal for the schools?
7. How are the decisions made concerning from whom to buy the coal and how to determine price?

The pupils became intensely involved in the unexpected drama and in the questions and answers that touched on knowledge of science, economics, and government. They were especially excited by the unanswered questions and eager to search for the answers at a later time. The distraction of the real-life drama contained too much emotional impact for the teacher to have even considered carrying out her lesson on long-dead Pilgrims. A time for the Pilgrims was then set aside by the college supervisor for a later and less distracting interlude.

Failure to consider interrelated elements contributes to the view that distractibility is a sign of disability or pathological state, as evidenced by its inclusion in the minimal cerebral dysfunction and specific learning disorder syndromes. Regardless of environmental, psychological, or neurological cause, to be distracted by petty and random stimuli is a learning problem responsive to careful teacher intervention. The pupil who is easily distracted by petty and irrelevant stimuli needs an environment structured to protect him/her against distracting stimuli. For example, if the pupil is markedly distracted by visual stimuli, he/she should be given the option of facing away from the window, the door, and other sources of visual distraction, or even facing a colorless and unadorned wall. Pupils who experience problems of distractibility from irrelevant auditory stimuli should be given the option of wearing ear plugs. Unfortunately, programs have been established for pupils who are easily distracted without considering whether they are dealing with normal distractibility or with distractibility that prevents effective and efficient learning. Also, most programs structured to reduce random stimuli fail to give the pupil the option to use a device or special arrangement to assist him/her with the problem. Failure to involve the pupil in the therapeutic process and in therapeutic decisions is a professional mistake. When pupils control the use of environmental protections against distractions, they also become sensitive to their own problem and learn how best to regulate and overcome the problem by slowly discarding the protections. If the teacher maintains control, he/she is guessing at the pupil's need and fostering unnecessary pupil dependency. People have varying degrees of distractibility and are distracted by different sensory stimuli. A pupil whose parent has had a traumatic experience with gas leakage from a household appliance may be more sensitive to the distracting presence of unusual or suspicious odors. Other pupils may have been conditioned or are innately more responsive to either auditory or visual stimuli. Recognizing the presence of a specific stimulus' distraction potential is the critical first step in reducing its impact. For example, an inconsequential noise ignored by most people may be devastating to one pupil, e.g., the ticking of a clock. Sensitivity to the fact that a pupil is being distracted should lead to a search for or questioning about the source of the distraction. Starting with the elimination of the distraction's source, the teacher, if possible, should gradually reintroduce the distraction using shaping procedures (see Module 10). Eliminating the distraction source may involve allowing pupils with this problem to change their seats so that they are far away from the offending stimulus. The clock may need repair or its sound may be softened. The pupil may have to wear ear plugs. Again, an important dimension is involving the pupil in the problem resolution.

One of the best ways of dealing with nonproductive distractibility is to discuss with the pupils involved their tendency to overreact, scatter, or daydream when there are competing auditory or visual stimuli, giving them strategies, materials, and options for protecting themselves against the allure and fascination of inconsequential stimuli.

Increasing the resistance to distractibility may indeed become a general lesson plan of value to an entire class. To do this, a teacher may initiate a class-wide shaping technique by gradually introducing competing stimuli during lessons, encouraging pupils to ignore these distractions. Once pupils are able to continue working or resume working quickly even though there are highly stimulating interruptions, such as a classmate (an actor) having a noisy and turbulent temper tantrum, review the idea that there are stimuli such as a fire drill gong that must not be ignored. The use of simulated experiences can be most helpful in program planning since distracting stimuli are omnipresent.

Activity Level

Much recent literature deplores the high activity level of school children implying a pathological etiology. However, activity level differences are more profitably viewed on a continuum of a temperament dimension. Some pupils require far more energy outlets than others. Not only do they need more than average activities of a gross motor nature, they also require continual energy release possibilities during quiet activities. For example, a high activity pupil may listen to a story with more interest and comprehension if allowed to manipulate quiet materials, e.g., pipe cleaners, or doodle on paper while listening. A high activity pupil who is forced to keep hands and feet quiet while listening will need to concentrate so heavily on remaining quiet that attention to and comprehension of the story will be diminished considerably. On the other continuum extreme, the low activity pupil may need encouragement to move about more frequently in order to assure healthy physical development. Teachers must be especially sensitive that their classroom scheduling does not encourage the low activity pupil to remain immobile for such long periods that health and social problems may arise. The teacher's own activity level also serves, in one way or another, as a model in modifying pupil activity.

Approach and Withdrawal

Some pupils respond to new situations with pleasurable anticipation whereas others respond with suspicious reserve. Recognizing these variations in response to novelty as temperament variations and not as personality disorders allows greater accommodation of programming. Allowing pupils to bring familiar objects with them to new situations or showing them how new material to be learned incorporates or grows from material already covered helps the withdrawn pupil accept the new situation somewhat more rapidly. However, allowing sufficient time for familiarity to turn withdrawal around is a key to proper programming for this type of pupil. The only significant problem that the high approach pupil may have is in demonstrating insufficient caution in approaching potentially dangerous situations.

Adaptability

Some pupils are able to switch easily from one task to another. Other pupils find transitions most difficult. As with approach/withdrawal, variations on the adaptability continuum of behavior should not be viewed in terms of pathology or lack of normalcy but as benign and innate differences in human behavior. Pupils who manage transitions easily present no educational management problem. Pupils who find transitions more difficult may need assistance from the teacher and must eventually learn to assist themselves. The major assistance technique is preparing for the transition before it arrives. A teacher may verbally signal the approaching transition at intervals. The pupil may be taught to use a stopwatch to indicate the imminence of a transition. As with other temperament characteristics, the teacher's facility in adapting to change has a strong modeling impact on pupils.

Intensity of Reaction

Some pupils consistently react strongly to environmental stimuli whereas others rarely exhibit more than mild reactions. Intensity of reaction is unrelated to intensity of feeling. A pupil may be very moved without giving any indication of this depth of feeling. On the other hand, a pupil may respond with apparent outrage to a situation that in reality affects him/her little. Teachers must identify the pattern of intensity of all pupils in order to know when to treat a high intensity reaction casually (for example, with a pupil for whom high intensity is the style) and when to be particularly concerned with a mild or no display of emotion (for example, with a pupil for whom low intensity is the style). Different cultural expectations for males and females are often intervening elements, as are differences among ethnic groups. The modeling impact of a teacher's intensity is again a factor. However, a more important interaction possibility is that of misunderstanding and intolerance between individuals with widely varying intensity reaction characteristics. For example, a low intensity pupil may be frightened and overwhelmed by a high intensity teacher. A high intensity pupil may see a low intensity teacher as disinterested or boring. Understanding differences as temperamental in origin helps to alleviate any misunderstandings and encourages greater acceptance of variations.

Impulsivity and Reflection

Two further response styles that both characterize and influence learning are impulsivity and reflection. Impulsivity refers to a pattern of rapid responses to stimuli. Impulsive learners are most efficient with learning tasks requiring rapid responses, as, for example, riding a bicycle. Most motor learning requires that muscle coordination be rapidly integrated into the individual's kinesthetic patterns and kinesthetic memory. Other factors being equal, impulsive or rapid response learners tend to learn motor tasks more efficiently than more hesitant, reflective, and/or cautious individuals. In motor and other tasks requiring rapid response learning patterns, reflective learners need encouragement to take risks, make guesses, and in other ways increase their speed of response.

On the other hand, much academic material requires thoughtful and delayed responses to ensure accuracy and understanding. For these tasks, impulsive learners are at a disadvantage and need to be encouraged to slow down, review before responding, and to use verbal mediation. Verbal mediation means talking to oneself about the task, labeling essential clues, describing possible responses, indicating why they are right or wrong. Cognitive efficiency is considerably advanced when the pupil utilizes verbal mediation in problem solving, i.e., when the pupil engages in an internal monologue in attempting to solve a problem. Social studies questions involving evaluation and judgment are typical of tasks best responded to in a reflective rather than an impulsive manner.

Both reflective and impulsive styles of learning are highly modifiable by environmental engineering. Teachers can be effective models of rapid pacing in an effort to stimulate more impulsive learning; teachers also can use an exaggerated slowness and model verbal monologues in instructional pacing and in their various interactions with pupils to stimulate reflective learning.

Obviously teachers must be skilled in changing their pace to suit task needs as well as pupil needs. Teachers must respect impulsivity and reflection as equally valuable means of learning. They must especially value and reward the pupil who adjusts his/her response style to the nature of the task. Typical of tasks for which a reflective mode is more suitable are science experiments, social relations, oral math problems, and written expression. Typical of tasks for which an impulsive mode is more suitable are foreign language learning, drills in spelling and number facts, most fine and gross motor activities, and safety habits. Other tasks require combinations of both reflective and impulsive learning styles at different points in the development of skills, e.g., the learning of number facts requires rapid response while the solving of written problems requires reflection, power reading, and speed of response as well. Teachers must analyze single tasks so as to be prepared to encourage an impulsive or reflective style in pupils as needed.

Field Dependence and Field Independence

For purposes of working with handicapped pupils and young elementary school children, a useful learning style diagnosis concerns what is often referred to as task-centeredness. A pupil who is highly task-centered does not look for clues in the expressions or comments of others. All attention is focused on the elements of the task. Such a pupil is sometimes labeled field independent. Other pupils are often referred to as people-oriented or field dependent. These pupils seek the reactions of others in making decisions as to their accuracy. A people-orientation is productive and helpful in tasks requiring a sensitivity to others but counterproductive in other situations. For example, when group decisions are needed, the pupil who is oriented toward people is more likely to see the need for compromise and adjustment. In a math problem, a people-oriented pupil is likely to depend less on the requirements or the correctness of the task and more on the approval of others, thus not learning the task as well as someone who is task oriented. In group discussion tasks, teachers may need to deliberately call the attention of the task-centered or field independent pupils to the feelings, values, and needs of the others. For academic tasks requiring field independence or task-centeredness, teachers must be careful not to show their approval or disapproval and must avoid external reinforcement of any kind. In this latter case, requiring pupils to evaluate themselves, having them set their own standards of evaluation, and using self-checking programmed instruction material will help to develop greater task-centeredness.

Modalities

Learning modality refers to auditory, visual, kinesthetic, or tactile channels of learning. Some researchers (Kirk, McCarthy, and Kirk, 1968) believe that differences in auditory or visual learning skills (in terms of reception, association, and expression) must be taken into consideration in planning learning experiences. Research findings, with regard to modality learning, however, are highly controversial. Whether to stress building up weak modalities or ignoring weak modalities to build on strong modalities is one of the several key issues that remain unresolved. Additional issues are:

1. The value of a multisensory versus a single modality approach
2. The relationship of subject matter elements to modality of instruction
3. The changing modality dominance as the pupil matures

No suggestions relevant to modality training or the relationship of modality preference to programming are offered here because the state of knowledge is too primitive.

Miscellaneous Aspects of Learning Style

Additional questions a teacher may want to ask in order to accommodate pupil learning styles are:

1. Does the pupil work best alone? one-to-one? in small groups? in large groups?
2. If reinforcement is to be used,
    a. what type of reinforcement is likely to be most successful?
    b. what frequency of reinforcement is likely to get the best results?
    c. what sources of reinforcement are likely to be the most effective?
3. What subject areas are most motivating to the pupil?
4. Can highly motivated learning tasks incorporate less motivated knowledge and skills? That is, can skills traditionally assigned to be

developed in one subject be assigned to subject areas of greater pupil interest?

A brief word on learning style and sex and ethnic differences is necessary. It is more productive to think of reported sex or ethnic differences as being a product of cultural expectations rather than of genetic factors. Looking at individual differences for traits discussed in this module leads to more educational alternatives than looking at group differences. This pedagogical approach seems especially warranted because there are more differences within subgroups than there are among groups. For example, differences in math ability among girls is greater than differences between girls and boys.

Finally, testing style must be considered in evaluating pupil progress. Pupils demonstrate their knowledge and skills differently depending on their test style: oral or written examination, essay, true or false, sentence completion, or multiple choice. Variations in success may not be a function of knowledge but rather a result of test response style. Teachers must assist pupils in acquiring skills in taking the various types of tests that they will be exposed to throughout their years of school and in vocational and other adult pursuits. Test-taking skills must be an integral part of educational programming with attention paid to variations among individual pupils.

ACTIVITIES AND EXPERIENCES

1. Plan learning activities for two different subject areas. Prepare behavior frequency charts for measuring three different learning style traits. Use these charts during both activities to determine the learning style of at least five pupils. Answer the following questions about your findings:
    a. Was learning style consistent between the two subject areas?
    b. What were some external factors influencing these learning style traits?
    c. How would you modify future lessons to make sure your measurements are valid?
    d. How would you modify future lessons to accommodate learning styles?
2. Prepare and submit a report on research findings related to modality learning.
3. Read and report on the nine personality dimensions developed by Thomas, Chess, and Birch (1968) in *Temperament and Behavior Disorders in Children*.

4. Prepare two lessons to teach the same information and skills to two equivalent groups of pupils. One lesson plan should be multisensory and the other unisensory. Carry out the lessons and test both groups with the same test. Report on the results.
5. Write three test questions for a single curriculum area. Then rewrite these questions (to obtain the same information) in a different question format, e.g., if the first question was written in essay form change it to a series of sentence completion, multiple choice, or matching items.

CONCLUDING STATEMENT

A selected number of pupil temperamental and learning style traits have been discussed. Teachers must realize, however, that the interaction of their own temperament and learning style with that of the pupil has considerable influence on pupil learning and behavior. Any particular trait has little predictability for learning and behavior, except when viewed in its interaction with the characteristics of others and with the nature of tasks.

Value issues may arise, as may be appreciated from the following example: A field-dependent or people-oriented pupil may learn a task better when taught by a highly structured and controlling teacher. However, the dependency traits of this pupil would be reinforced, and thus would be most likely to eventually impede later learning that requires independent thought.

Teachers do not always have the ability to adjust and change their learning and teaching styles to match the needs of pupils. Teacher limitations should be identified and *respected* and administrators should recognize that, in most cases, the wisest procedure is to match, in a nonjudgmental way, teacher traits with pupil traits.

POSTTEST

At this point retake the Pretest.

LITERATURE CITED

Kirk, S. A., McCarthy, J. J., and Kirk, W. D. 1968. Examiner's Manual. Illinois Test of Psycholinguistic Abilities. University of Illinois, Urbana.

Thomas, A., and Chess, S. 1977. Temperament and Development. Brunner/ Mazel, New York.

Thomas, A., Chess, S., and Birch, H. 1968. Temperament and Behavior Disorders in Children. New York University Press, New York.

SUGGESTED READINGS

Anapolle, L. 1967. Visual training and reading performance. J. Reading 10:372–382.

Arena, J. I. (ed.). 1969. Teaching Through Sensory-motor Experiences. Academic Therapy Publications, San Rafael, Cal.

Bateman, B. 1964. Learning disabilities—Yesterday, today, and tomorrow. Except. Child. 31:167–177.

Bateman, B. 1965. The Illinois Test of Psycholinguistic Abilities in Current Research: Summaries of Studies. University of Illinois, Urbana.

Behrmann, P. 1971. Activities for Developing Visual Perception. Academic Therapy Publications, San Rafael, Cal.

Borys, S. V., and Spitz, H. H. 1978. Reflection-impulsivity in retarded adolescents and nonretarded children of equal mental age. Am. J. Ment. Defic. 82:601–604.

Bryan, T. 1972. The effect of forced mediation upon short-term memory of children with learning disabilities. J. Learn. Disabil. 5:605–609.

Bryan, T., and Wheeler, R. 1972. Perception of learning-disabled children: The eye of the observer. J. Learn. Disabil. 5:484–488.

Bush, W. J., and Giles, M. T. 1969. Aids to Psycholinguistic Teaching. Charles E. Merrill Publishing Co., Columbus, Oh.

Carroll, J. B. 1972. Review of the Illinois Test of Psycholinguistics. In O. K. Buros (ed.), The Eighth Mental Measurements Yearbook. Vol. II., pp. 819–823. Gryphon Press, Highland Park, N.J.

Chaney, C. M., and Kephart, N. C. 1968. Motor Aids to Perceptual Training. Charles E. Merrill Publishing Co., Columbus, Oh.

Fernald, G. 1943. Remedial Techniques in Basic School Subjects. McGraw-Hill Book Co., New York.

Flavell, J. H., Beach, D. R., and Chinsky, J. M. 1966. Spontaneous verbal rehearsal in a memory task as a function of age. Child Dev. 37:283–299.

Freides, D. 1974. Human information processing and sensory modality: Cross-modal functions, information complexity, memory and deficit. Psychol. Bull. 81:284–310.

Frostig, M. 1964. The Frostig Program for the Development of Visual Perception. Follett Publishing Co., Chicago.

Frostig, M. 1972. Visual perception integration functions and academic learning. J. Learn. Disabil. 5:1–15.

Gibson, J. J., and Gibson, E. J. 1965. Perceptual learning: Differentiation or enrichment. Psychol. Rev. 62:32–44.

Gorelick, M. C. 1965. Effectiveness of visual form training in a pre-reading program. J. Educ. Res. 58:315–318.

Gould, L. M. 1967. Visual perception training. Elem. School J. 67:381–389.

Hallahan, D. P., and Kauffman, J. M. 1976. Introduction to Learning Disabilities: A Psycho-Behavioral Approach. Prentice-Hall, Inc., Englewood Cliffs, N.J.

Hammill, D. 1972. Training visual perceptual processes. J. Learn. Disabil. 5:552–559.

Hammill, D. D., and Larsen, S. C. 1978. The effectiveness of psycholinguistic training: A reaffirmation of position. Except. Child. 44:402–414.

Harris, A. J. 1965. Individualizing First Grade Reading According to Specific Learning Aptitudes. Office of Research and Evaluation, Division of Teacher Education, City University of New York, New York.

Harris, A. S. 1969. Visual and auditory modalities: How important are they? Con-challenger. In N. B. Smith (ed.), Current Issues in Reading, pp. 184–190. International Reading Association, Newark, Del.

Hellmuth, J. (ed.). 1965. Learning Disorders. Vol. I. Special Child Publications, Seattle.

Kagan, J. 1965. Reflection-impulsivity and reading ability in primary grade children. Child Dev. 36:609–628.

Kagan, J., and Kogan, N. 1970. Individuality and cognitive performance. In P. H. Mussen (ed.), Carmichael's Manual of Child Psychology. Vol. I., pp. 1273–1365. John Wiley & Sons, Inc., New York.

Kagan, J., Rosman, B. L., Day, D., Albert, J., and Phillips, W. 1964. Information processing in the child: Significance of analytic and reflective attitudes. Psychol. Monogr. 78.

Kass, C. E. 1966. Psycholinguistic disabilities of children with reading problems. Except. Child. 32:533–539.

Keogh, B. K., and Donlon, G. 1972. Field dependence, impulsivity, and learning disabilities. J. Learn. Disabil. 5:331–336.

Laycock, V. K. 1978. Assessing learner characteristics. In R. M. Anderson, J. G. Greer, and S. J. Odle (eds.), Individualizing Educational Materials for Special Children in the Mainstream, pp. 29–55. University Park Press, Baltimore.

Maryland State Department of Education. (undated). Parameters of Individualization. Part I. Cognitive Style/Abstracts of Educational Research. Vol. IV, No. 1. Division of Planning, Research, and Evaluation, Baltimore.

McCarthy, J. J., and McCarthy, J. F. 1969. Learning Disabilities. Allyn & Bacon, Boston.

Meichenbaum, D. H., and Goodman, J. 1971. Training impulsive children to talk to themselves: A means of developing self-control. J. Abnorm. Psychol. 77:115–126.

Mercer, C. D., Cullinan, D., Hallahan, D. P., and La Fleur, N. K. 1975. Modeling and attention-retention in learning-disabled children. J. Learn. Disabil. 8:444–450.

Messer, S. B. 1976. Reflection-impulsivity: A review. Psychol. Bull. 83:1026–1052.

Muehl, S., and Kremen, K. S. 1966. Ability to match information within and between auditory and visual sense modalities and subsequent reading achievement. J. Educ. Psychol. 57:230–239.

Peter, L. J. 1975. Competencies for Teaching: Therapeutic Instruction. Wadsworth Publishing Co., Belmont, Cal.

Ross, D. M., and Ross, S. A. 1972. The efficacy of listening training for educable mentally retarded children. Am. J. Ment. Defic. 77:137–142.

Roswell, F., and Natchez, G. 1971. Reading Disability: Diagnosis and Treatment. Rev. Ed. Basic Books, Inc., New York.

Salvia, J., and Ysseldyke, J. E. 1978. Assessment in Special and Regular Education. Houghton Mifflin Co., Boston.

Smith, C. M. 1971. The relationship of reading method and reading achievement to ITPA sensory modalities. J. Spec. Educ. 5:143–149.

Stott, D. H. 1978. The Hard-to-Teach Child: A Diagnostic-Remedial Approach. University Park Press, Baltimore.

Stuart, I. R. 1967. Perceptual style and reading ability: Implications for an instructional approach. Percept. Mot. Skills 24:135–138.

Sullivan, J. 1972. The effects of Kephart's perceptual-motor training on a reading clinic sample. J. Learn. Disabil. 5:32–38.

Thelen, H. A. 1967. Classroom Grouping for Teachability. John Wiley & Sons, Inc., New York.
Valett, R. E. 1978. Developing Cognitive Abilities: Teaching Children to Think. C. V. Mosby Co., St. Louis.
VanWitsen, B. 1967. Perceptual Training Activities Handbook. Columbia University Press, New York.

Test Answers

1. Steps employed in determining individual educational objectives that benefit each pupil are the:
   a. Establishment of national or universal priority listing of educational goals and objectives
   b. School district's priority listing reflecting community (as well as other elements) educational goals and objectives
   c. Filtering of school district and community goals through the individual teacher's perceptions and value system
   d. Modification by the teacher of school district and community educational goals and objectives
   e. Implementation of various teacher directed diagnostic strategies
   f. Individually identified educational goals and objectives (IEOs)
(Mastery Criterion: All six in the order listed)

2. Hierarchical ordering of educational objectives is a difficult task due to the:
   a. Shifting demands by society for new objectives
   b. Impossibility of consensus
(Mastery Criterion: Two)

3. "What to teach" is the most important objective of teacher preparation programs.
(Mastery Criterion: One)

4. Teachers play a significant role in the development of curriculum goals and objectives by:
   a. Serving on a systemwide steering committee for those purposes
   b. Voting on the school district's goals and objectives before their official publication
   c. Developing curriculum guides through inservice workshops
(Mastery Criterion: Three)

5. Community educational goals and objectives are unofficially communicated by:
   a. Local newspapers and magazines
   b. Local radio and television shows

    c.   Social and community groups
    d.   Religious organizations and meetings
    e.   Meetings of political organizations
    f.   Fraternal and sororal groups
    g.   Meetings of special interest groups
    h.   Public symposia
    i.   Informal and formal meetings with parents and other family members

(Mastery Criterion: Six)

6.   The teacher must have developed his/her own power base so that he/she can work toward alternate objectives that conflict with community- and/or school district-supported ones.

(Mastery Criterion: One)

7.   Teachers are subject to pressure from:
    a.   Internal (school and school system) forces
    b.   External (community) forces

(Mastery Criterion: Two)

8.   Teachers owe a degree of responsibility to:
    a.   International or panhumanistic needs and values
    b.   National goals and expectations
    c.   State goals and expectations
    d.   Local governmental goals and expectations
    e.   Community goals and expectations
    f.   Local board of education values and objectives
    g.   School district's (central administration's) goals and objectives
    h.   Regional administrators' goals and objectives
    i.   School principal's values and objectives
    j.   Other school administrators and supervisors
    k.   PTA and other parent-sponsored advocacy groups
    l.   Parents of their pupils
    m. Pupils' needs, interests, goals, and values
    n.   Goals and objectives of the profession
    o.   Goals and objectives of professional associations or teachers' unions
    p.   Own needs, interests, goals, attitudes, and values

(Mastery Criterion: 10)

9.   School district and community educational goals and objectives are identified by:
    a.   Local Board of Education directives and other publications
    b.   School district selected or developed curriculum guides
    c.   State Department of Education (Instruction) directives and other publications

    d.   State Department of Education (Instruction) curriculum guides

    e.   Local teacher associations and/or union publications

(Mastery Criterion: Three)

10.   Unofficial sources that influence community and school district educational goals and objectives are:

    a.   Local newspapers and magazines

    b.   Local radio shows

    c.   Locally produced television shows

    d.   Social and community groups

    e.   Churches, temples, and other religious organizations and meetings

    f.   Meetings of political organizations

    g.   Fraternal and sororal groups

    h.   Meetings of special interest groups

    i.   Lecture and lecture series (public symposia)

    j.   Parents of pupils

(Mastery Criterion: Six)

11–13.   There are no set answers for these questions. Responses to be self-evaluated or teacher-evaluated.

(*Overall* Mastery Criterion: Questions 1–8: Six
                                             Questions 11–13: Three)

MODULE 2

1. Factors that inhibit individualized instruction are:
    a. The absence of diagnostic skills or diagnostic skill training for preservice and inservice teachers
    b. The assignment of diagnosis to other professionals, such as psychologists, whose tests are of little value in defining instructional programs
    c. Pressures from the school system, the community, and from families that discourage teachers from individualizing instruction
(Mastery Criterion: Three)

2. School policies and procedures violate an appreciation for individual differences by:
    a. Expecting all pupils to be ready for academic instruction by the first grade or six years of age
    b. The use of curriculum guides
    c. The use of standardized texts for all students in a particular grade
(Mastery Criterion: Two)

3. Possible effects of relative inactivity are that:
    a. Pupils may self-stimulate
    b. Pupils may move about distracting and annoying their classmates
(Mastery Criterion: Two)

4. They may become frustrated and confused because they cannot leap over one or more vital steps prerequisite to the accomplishment of a specific task.
(Mastery Criterion: Accept all reasonable answers.)

5. Pupils may be embarrassed because they cannot obtain the money for class trips, class parties, for lunches, live in a poor section of town, etc.
(Mastery Criterion: Accept all reasonable answers.)

6. The pupil might be restless, irritable, inattentive, hyperactive, and fail to learn.
(Mastery Criterion: The answer should indicate some concern with the effect of malnourishment on pupil learning and behavior.)

7. The pupil might be restless, irritable, argumentative, hyperactive, and fall asleep during your most exciting teaching.
(Mastery Criterion: The answer should indicate in some way that a tired pupil cannot be expected to behave or learn satisfactorily.)

8. This is a good question. Unfortunately, there are no good answers. Do you have one?

9. The halo effect occurs when a pupil has some positive traits, e.g., is attractive, docile, smiles frequently, or conforming. The viewer then somehow adds all sorts of additional positive traits to the individual's personality.
(Mastery Criterion: Accept any reasonable answer.)

10. Characteristics of pupils and their families used in making judgments about learning and behavior are:
    a. Racial background
    b. Ethnic background
    c. Religious preference
    d. Socioeconomic class
    e. Neighborhood or section of town
    f. Family status and history in community
(Mastery Criterion: Four)

11. Being treated as inferior often leads to self-hatred, apathy, indifference, hatred of others, aggression, and hostility. It may also motivate the devalued pupil to prove his/her worthiness.
(Mastery Criterion: Answer should include both elements.)

12. The answer should indicate that low grades are demoralizing, causing many pupils to devalue themselves and to give up trying for success.
(Mastery Criterion: Accept any reasonable answer.)

13. The answer should indicate that the basics are more than the three Rs.

14. When pupils are active learners, participating in the learning experiences, manipulating objects, touching, smelling, sensing, they will learn better than if they merely watch and listen to the teacher.
(Mastery Criterion: The answer must provide an example of an action setting versus a passive setting.)

15. While the example in the module refers to conflicts in language usage and speaks of the difference between formal (school) and informal (family) language, the answer may refer to any other significant area of behavior. Make sure that the conflict is evident and that it seriously interferes with the pupil's acquisition of new skills because these new skills are not valued by the family.

(*Overall* Mastery Criterion: 13)

MODULE 3

1.	True	14.	False
2.	True	15.	True
3.	False	16.	True
4.	True	17.	False
5.	True	18.	True
6.	False	19.	False
7.	True	20.	True
8.	False	21.	True
9.	False	22.	True
10.	True	23.	False
11.	True	24.	True
12.	False	25.	True
13.	True	26.	False

(*Overall* Mastery Criterion: 23)

MODULE 4

Part A

1. *True.* A teacher analyzes the pupil's level of functioning so that he/she may take the pupil from the level of performance to a higher level.
2. *False.* The teacher's task is not to assign labels but rather to describe behaviors and, whenever possible, interpret them in terms of developmental patterns and expectations.
3. *False.* A teacher should compare a pupil's behavior only to the behaviors previously demonstrated by that pupil.
4. *True.* This statement makes sense because, developmentally, this is what occurs. Later skills are built upon the earlier acquired ones.
5. *False.* The teacher's choice of materials should reflect the interests of the pupil which, in turn, are determined by the pupil's chronological age.

(Mastery Criterion: Five)

Part B

1. c, a, b
2. CORRECT
3. c, b, a
4. a, c, b
5. b, a, c
6. CORRECT
7. c, a, b
8. c, b, a
9. b, c, a
10. a, c, b

(Mastery Criterion: Nine)

Part C

The answers to Part C (Questions 1–10) can be found in the listings of developmental milestones found in the module.

(Mastery Criterion: Eight)

(*Overall* Mastery Criterion: Must meet criterion on each Part.)

MODULE 5

1. Teachers must realize that a heightened awareness of medical problems will aid them in making decisions about:
    a. The need for medical and paramedical diagnosis and/or treatment
    b. Appropriate referral services
    c. Logical individual educational objectives
    d. Effective and efficient learning activities and experiences
    e. Suitable classroom organization practices and procedures
    f. Perceptive behavior management strategies and techniques
    g. Facilitative methods, materials, and specialized equipment
    h. Skillful and productive teacher-parent interactions
(Mastery Criterion: Six)

2. The so-called residual diathesis or the imponderable X factor explains variations in performance between and among pupils with similar conditions, knowledge, and abilities. The unknown factor, undoubtedly, includes such intrapsychic variables as interest, motivation, accommodation, and adaptability.
(Mastery Criterion: Both elements.)

3. Behavioral clues suggesting the presence of a hearing loss and their alternate feasible explanations are:
    a. The pupil responds better when closer to the sound source.
        AFE (Alternate Feasible Explanation): The pupil has attention problems and is less distracted when nearer the sound source.
    b. The pupil's ability to respond increases markedly when there are only slight decreases in distance from speaker and vice versa.
        AFE: The pupil attends better when closer to the speaker and benefits from nonverbal clues such as body language.
    c. The pupil responds to sound but is unable to follow simple commands or answer simple questions.
        AFE: The student has difficulty in comprehending individual words and phrases although he/she hears the sounds.
    d. The pupil may distort or omit sounds, especially consonants. This may be particularly true for final sounds and word endings.
        AFE: The pupil speaks that way because his/her parents and peers speak that way.
    e. The pupil's voice quality, pitch, resonance patterns, and volume may be poor. (Problems in speech and voice production are highly symptomatic of hearing impairment.)

AFE: The pupil is speaking at too low a pitch for his/her vocal apparatus resulting in a hoarse voice.

f. The pupil may stare closely at the speaker's face in order to benefit more fully from visual clues to supplement defective hearing.

AFE: The student is having problems with auditory processing, e.g., auditory discrimination, and is seeking visual clues to what is being said.

g. The pupil may suffer a lag in speech and language development despite a higher level of general overall intellectual functioning.

AFE: The pupil has a problem with speech production, i.e., an expressive aphasia in which, despite satisfactory auditory skills, he/she is unable to carry out the motor plan to speak with facility.

h. The pupil may present behavioral problems resulting from frustration and confusion due to an inability to comprehend the auditory cues and general behavior of others. He/she may be inattentive, hyperactive, uncontrollable, and even destructive.

i. The pupil may fail to respond or responds inappropriately to oral directions or questions.

AFE: The teacher speaks too softly.

j. In response to oral questions, the pupil uses expletives such as "Huh?" and "What?"

AFE: The pupil has problems processing speech when it is spoken at too fast a rate and says "Huh?" while he/she is still processing the information.

k. The pupil may complain about an inability to hear.

AFE: The pupil is confusing poor ability to discriminate or comprehend with the inability to hear.

l. The pupil may tilt his/her head to one side.

AFE: The pupil is tillting his/her head to one side because of a visual defect.

(Mastery Criterion: Nine. Please note there are many other AFEs for each behavior enumerated. Consult with your instructor or colleagues for other AFEs that are logical.)

4. Some of the pupil behaviors that suggest the presence of ocular pathology include the following:

a. Rubbing his/her own eyes frequently

b. Squinting

c. Closing one eye and tilting the head to one side

d. Assuming unusual reading and writing postures when working with books or at chalkboards

    e.   Sitting too close to a television set or movie screen

    f.   Performing academically at an inadequate level despite general intellectual functioning

    g.   Complaining of blurred vision

    h.   Pupil's eyes seem to be "crossed," i.e., misalignment of the eyes, for example, one eye deviates toward the nose

    i.   Rapidly moving the eyes especially in the horizontal plane

    j.   Complaining of ocular discomfort when exposed to bright lights

    k.   Complaining that he/she cannot see at night or in dim light

    l.   Experiencing difficulty catching a ball or reaching for objects

    m. Exhibiting a lack of physical coordination and problems with mobility

    n.   Complaining of a dark or black spot in the center of his/her eye(s)

    o.   Inability to see small letters and requiring large print books and/or magnifying equipment

    p.   Complaining of ocular pain or headache

    q.   Complaining of double vision

    r.   Is handicapped in athletics and other physical activities

(Mastery Criterion: 12)

5.   During a grand mal seizure, the pupil should be removed from dangerous areas (e.g., a woodworking shop). Hard surface furniture should be removed to prevent damage to extremities. The pupil should be placed in a position where he/she is lying on his/her side with any confining clothing loosened. The pupil's mouth and nose should be uncovered and, if possible, food and gum removed from the mouth. If movements are vigorous, the pupil should be restrained gently and comforted. A padded object, such as a stick, prepared in advance, should be gently inserted between the teeth to prevent a pupil from biting his/her tongue during a seizure. A comfortable, private place should be provided in which the pupil may rest after the seizure is over. When a pupil fails to come out of the seizure, emergency medical help should be obtained. Strategies for obtaining medical help should be established beforehand.

(Mastery Criterion: Eight elements)

6.   The pupil appears to lose control momentarily or appears to drift away. If speaking, speech will be interrupted, staring into space will occur, and his/her eyelids will flutter. After a brief moment, the vacuous look will disappear, and the conversation will be resumed where previously left off. Lapses in behavior during active learning as opposed to passive learning may be indicative of petit mal seizure activity.

(Mastery Criterion: Both elements)

7. Associated dysfunctions frequently found in persons suffering from cerebral palsy include a high incidence of:
    a. Seizures
    b. Hearing loss
    c. Visual loss
    d. Visual field defects
    e. Sensory impairment, including diminished ability to recognize an object by touch and a reduced awareness of light touch and pain
    f. Mental retardation
    g. Speech disorders
    h. Dental abnormalities
    i. Perceptual and other learning disabilities
    j. Behavior correlates associated with cerebral dysfunction, including hyperactivity, perseveration, impulsivity, and distractibility
    k. Social and emotional problems
(Mastery Criterion: Eight)

8. Labels used to identify individuals with minimal cerebral dysfunction are:
    a. Strauss syndrome
    b. Hyperkinetic syndrome
    c. Minimally brain damaged
    d. Psychoneurological learning disabled
    e. Specific learning disabled
    f. Perceptually impaired
(Mastery Criterion: Four)

9. The symptoms included in the MCD syndrome include the following:
    a. Short attention span or distractibility
    b. Perseveration or an inability to shift attention and to persist in a particular thought or action
    c. Hyperactivity (hyperkinesis) (drivenness)
    d. Hypoactivity
    e. Poor impulse control (impulsivity)
    f. Low frustration tolerance
    g. Emotional lability
    h. Clumsiness, awkwardness, incoordination (fine and gross motor)
    i. Reading problems (dyslexia)
    j. Writing problems (agraphia)
    k. Oral language problems (the aphasias)
    l. Arithmetic problems (acalculia)

m. Social imperception
n. Poor response to reward and punishment
o. Antisocial behavior
p. Incompetent learning through pictures
q. Perceptual problems
r. Memory deficits
s. Body image difficulties
t. Spatial orientation inadequacy
u. Confusion in laterality or lack of cerebral dominance
v. Problems with left-right orientation
w. Paradoxical response to stimulant drugs
(Mastery Criterion: 15)

10. The common signs of an orthopaedic problem include:
a. Pain in the spine, the extremities, and/or the hips
b. A limp, with or without pain
c. Deformity
d. Restriction of movement
e. Peculiarities of gait
f. Swelling, locking, or buckling of joints
(Mastery Criterion: Five)

11. The classic symptoms of diabetes are:
a. Excessive urination (polyuria)
b. Excessive thirst (polydipsia)
c. Excessive appetite or hunger (polyphagia)
d. Dry skin
e. Sweet or fruity odor to breath
f. Weight loss
(Mastery Criterion: Five)

12. The symptoms generally associated with hypoglycemia (abnormally low blood sugar level) are:
a. Restlessness and irritability
b. Sweating
c. Pallor
d. Throbbing headache
e. Sudden changes in behavior
f. Excessive hunger
g. Convulsions
h. Twitching of the arms and legs
i. Coma
(Mastery Criterion: Six)

13. As with many other handicapped individuals, students who are too short, tall, or fat may become bitter, hostile, aggressive, depressed, and angry because of the ridicule and ostracism of peers and significant adults. Frustration may also be engendered in the short individual who has practical problems because of architectural barriers to the use of equipment that is sized according to average size. In later life, difficulties arise in finding mates and in obtaining jobs since many employers and search teams, consciously or unconsciously, reject candidates who are too short or too obese.

(Mastery Criterion: General idea should be stated that society penalizes those who deviate from the normal in size and weight, perhaps throughout their lifetimes. These adverse societal reactions invariably result in psychologically critical conditions in those persons so discriminated against.)

14. Some of the most commonly occurring life-threatening or fatal diseases in pupils are:
    a. Cystic fibrosis
    b. Congenital heart disease
    c. Kidney failure
    d. Leukemia
    e. Tumors
    f. Juvenile muscular dystrophy
    g. Hemophilia
    h. Sickle cell anemia

    In establishing IEOs for students with fatal illnesses, teachers have two major concerns: providing an educational program for these pupils because school is the normal work of childhood and young adulthood, and dealing with the emotional responses of these pupils to their illnesses. Anxiety, regression, loss of appetite, apathy, restlessness, guilt, depression, anger, bitterness, and acting-out behavior may be characteristic. Teachers often will have to work with parents and siblings whose behaviors frequently mirror those of the ill child.

(Mastery Criterion: Five. You may identify other fatal diseases. Check your answer with your teacher, a colleague(s), a medical journal, or a family physician.)

15. A list of the more severe indicators of emotional problems occurring in students include:
    a. Excessive lethargy, or its opposite, hyperactivity
    b. Noncommunicative behavior, such as elective mutism
    c. Frequent use of the toilet for evacuation

    d. Tics and ritualistic behaviors
    e. Extreme withdrawal, apathy, depression, and grief
    f. Self-destructive behavior
    g. Sexual exhibitionism, sexual assaults, and sexual aberrations
    h. Extreme somatic complaints in the absence of physical causes
    i. Recurrent hypochondriasis
    j. Stealing
    k. Pathological lying
    l. Cruelty to animals
    m. Cruelty to the defenseless and weak (the young, the elderly, and the handicapped)
    n. Firesetting
    o. School phobia and truancy

(Mastery Criterion: 12)

16. Hyperactivity is a subjective phenomenon. What might be considered normal behavior by some teachers might be hyperkinetic to others. Assuming agreement by several professionals that a given pupil is hyperactive, the following explanations for this behavior might be correct for the specific pupil under study.

He is hyperactive because:

    a. He has suffered obvious brain damage.
    b. He has the minimal cerebral dysfunction syndrome.
    c. The class is boring.
    d. The teacher is overstimulating.
    e. The teacher rewards hyperactive behavior.
    f. He is hungry.
    g. He is fatigued.
    h. He has intestinal worms.
    i. His underwear is too tight.
    j. He has body lice.
    k. He has been sitting still too long in the classroom.
    l. He has been given too much seatwork and not enough active learning experiences.
    m. He is showing off to attract the attention of a peer.
    n. The work is too easy or too difficult.
    o. He does not know the appropriate behavior for a quiet lesson as opposed to outdoor play.
    p. He has ingested too much junk food and drink.
    q. He has been abusing drugs.

(Mastery Criterion: 10)

(*Overall* Mastery Criterion: 13)

MODULE 6

Part A

1.	True	12.	True
2.	True	13.	False
3.	True	14.	False
4.	True	15.	True
5.	False	16.	False
6.	True	17.	True
7.	True	18.	False
8.	True	19.	False
9.	False	20.	True
10.	True	21.	True
11.	True	22.	True

(Mastery Criterion: 18)

Part B

1. *Unacceptable Referral Request*
   To: Ms. Jones, Principal
   From: Mr. Tyrone, First Grade Teacher
   Re: Sarah Macauley, Pupil

   Sarah has been behaving in a bizarre fashion lately. She is disrespectful, inattentive, and rude. She has been such a problem that I feel she must be seriously emotionally disturbed. Her relationship with classmates is strained, and she is often hostile, apparently due to her lack of self-esteem resulting from the poor quality of her academic performance. She should be referred for psychiatric help because I believe she is pre-psychotic.

   (The above referral is unacceptable first because it uses ambiguous, subjective words, e.g., bizarre, disrespectful, inattentive, rude, problem, strained, hostile, and poor. Second, it is a poor request because it interprets behavior: "she is often hostile due to her lack of self-esteem resulting from the poor quality of her academic performance." Third, it is not an effective recommendation because it places a label on the pupil, i.e., "seriously emotionally disturbed" and "pre-psychotic." Finally, it is an inferior sample because it does not provide documentation for the recommendation.)

   Acceptable Referral Request
   To: Ms. Jones, Principal
   From   Mr. Tyrone, First Grade Teacher
   Re: Sarah Macauley, Pupil

I am requesting that the Referral and Placement Committee consider the referral of Sarah Macauley to a mental health agency or private mental health professional. I am making this request based on the following observations:

1. On February 28, Sarah, in lining up to board the school bus, began barking like a dog and "snapped" at several of her classmates. When asked by me to stop, she continued in the behavior for approximately 5 minutes until she boarded the bus.

2. On March 1, 2, and 3, Sarah continued the behavior described in item 1 above. On March 3, however, she actually bit the ankle of a classmate (see report of March 3).

3. On Monday, March 6, during a subtraction activity, at approximately 11:10 am, Sarah arose from her seat, tore up the ditto sheet, threw the pieces on the floor, and began banging her forehead against the blackboard ledge. I went to her and restrained her from hurting herself.

4. Since Monday's episode, Sarah has spent most class time (Tuesday through Friday, March 7–10) staring out of the window. She mumbles to herself (I have been unable to hear any intelligible words) and occasionally snarls. She has not completed any assigned work given out in class.

I am very concerned about the above behaviors and believe that they are serious enough to warrant immediate attention. Thank you.

(Mastery Criterion: If your referral request has one example of an ambiguous, subjective, judgmental word, *or* of an interpretation, *or* of labeling, it does not meet criterion.)

2. The answer to this question depends upon the community you have chosen. You must either self-evaluate or ask your instructor to do so. To meet criterion, you must identify all the *major* agencies in the community and answer items a–g for each agency identified.

3. a. *Dermatology* is a branch of medicine that deals with the skin, its structure, functions, and diseases.

   b. *Endocrinology* is a branch of medicine that deals with the endocrine glands, their structure, functions, and diseases.

   c. *Internal Medicine* is a branch of medicine that deals with the diagnosis and treatment of nonsurgical diseases.

   d. *Neurology* is a branch of medicine that deals with the diagnosis and treatment of diseases of the nervous system.

   e. *Ophthalmology* is a branch of medicine that deals with the structure, functions, and diseases of the eye.

   f. *Orthopaedics* is a branch of medicine that deals with the correction or prevention of skeletal deformities.

g.   *Otolaryngology* is a branch of medicine that deals with the structure, functions, and diseases of the ear, nose, and throat.
h.   *Pediatrics* is a branch of medicine that deals with children, their development, care, and diseases.
i.   *Psychiatry* is a branch of medicine that deals with mental, emotional, or behavioral disorders.
j.   *Urology* is a branch of medicine that deals with the urinary or urogenital tract.
(Mastery Criterion: 10. Accept any reasonable definition.)

4.   a.   *Art Therapy* is a professional discipline concerned with the purposeful use of art to meet the psychological needs of individuals and groups.
b.   *Dance Therapy* is a professional discipline that uses movement and movement interaction to meet the psychotherapeutic needs of individuals and groups.
c.   *Music Therapy* is a professional discipline that uses music as the basic tool in efforts to attain prescribed behavior changes.
d.   *Occupational Therapy* is a professional discipline concerned with the development and maintenance of functions and skills necessary to general functioning, the prevention, deterioration, or loss of life functions and skills, and the remediation of functional deficits.
e.   *Physical Therapy* is a professional discipline concerned with the treatment of disease by the use of physical and mechanical means, including heat, cold, light, water, electricity, massage, ultrasound, exercise, and functional training.
f.   *Speech and Language Therapy* is a professional discipline concerned with the development, correction, or restimulation of speech and language function so that individuals may successfully communicate with each other.
(Mastery Criterion: Six. Accept any reasonable definition.)

5.   a.   *Nutritionists* are professionals concerned with the act or process of nourishing or being nourished that encompasses one's relationship to food biologically, culturally, socially, and psychologically.
b.   *Orthotists* are professionals concerned with the fitting of devices known as orthoses to patients with disabling conditions of the limbs and spine.
c.   *Prosthetists* are professionals concerned with the fitting of devices known as protheses to patients with partial or complete absence of a limb or limb segment.
d.   *Rehabilitation counselors* are professionals concerned with the evaluation of the needs of disabled clients and the coordination of the rehabilitation process by way of the purchase of services with the

primary purpose of assisting the disabled individual in obtaining employment.

e. *Social workers* are professionals concerned with helping individuals, groups, or communities to improve or restore their ability to function in socially optimal ways. Social workers also are concerned with creating social conditions supportive of this goal.

f. *Therapeutic recreation specialists* are professionals concerned with the utilization of recreational experiences for the correction, remediation, or modification of behavior.

(Mastery Criterion: Six. Accept any reasonable definition.)

(*Overall* Mastery Criterion: Must meet criterion on each question.)

MODULE 7

Part A   Test Inventories

For a suitable inventory of noun plurality, see the body of this module.
(Mastery Criterion: Accept any reasonable approximation.)

Part B   Observation and Documentation of Pupil Behaviors

1. If you are a student, ask your college instructor to evaluate your observation report.
2. If you are student teaching, ask your college supervisor and/or cooperating teacher to evaluate your observation report.
3. If you are a teacher, ask a colleague or a supervisor to review your report.

(Mastery Criterion: Accept the evaluation of the instructor, college supervisor, cooperating teacher, supervisor, and/or colleague. However, if you feel that you are not being judged fairly, seek another opinion.)

Part C   Sampling Behaviors

1. *Skills*
    a. The pupil has spelled 51 words correctly out of a total of 63 different words.
    b. The pupil has written three simple declarative sentences.
    c. The pupil has written a simple interrogative sentence.
    d. The pupil has written two simple imperative sentences.
    e. The pupil has written a compound sentence.
    f. The pupil has used the following adjectives: most, pretty, lovely, red, pink, blue, yellow, purple, some, special, two.
    g. The pupil has used the following pronouns correctly: you, it, me, they, her, I.
    h. The pupil has written the following prepositional phrases: of seasons, for a walk, with me, to the park, at the two lovely swans, for mother, around the corner, to Ocean City, for bluefish, in September.
    i. The pupil has used the following infinitive phrases: to come, to swim.
    j. The pupil has written the following verbal phrase (adjectival): swimming in the lake
    k. The pupil has written a series, separating them correctly with commas: red, pink, blue, yellow, and purple.
    Knowledge and Concepts
    a. The pupil has indicated that spring is a season.

b. The pupil has indicated that blooming flowers and trees are part of spring.
c. The pupil has indicated that summer follows spring.
d. The pupil has indicated that Ocean City is a nearby place to go for swimming and fishing during the summer.
e. The pupil has indicated that school will resume in September after summer vacation.
f. The pupil has indicated that flowers come in the following colors: red, pink, blue, yellow, and purple.

2. Problems demonstrated by the pupil in the sample are:
a. Faulty comparison of adjective—"most beautifulest"
b. Misspelling of the following words:

seasons	→ seesons
flowers	→ flours (two out of three times)
two	→ too
lovely	→ lovley
blue	→ blew
purple	→ puprle
mother	→ mothre
surprise	→ suprize
and	→ an (spelling or word usage error)
also	→ allso
would	→ wood
because	→ becaus
September	→ Setpember

c. Failure to use the plural of swan
d. Failure to use the apostrophe in summer's
e. Failure to capitalize City in Ocean City
f. Capitalization of Blue in bluefish
g. Use of sentence fragment—"And so are the trees."
h. Failure to use a question mark in fourth sentence
i. Use of a run-on sentence in next to last sentence
j. Failure to use commas before and after "maybe" in next to last sentence
k. Writing of "maybe" as if it were two separate words

3. Patterns that exist among the problems are:
a. Misspellings involving homophones: flowers → flours, blue → blew, two → too, would → wood
b. Misspellings involving letter reversals: September → Setpember, mother → mothre, purple → puprle, lovely → lovley
c. Misspellings involving phonetic rules or analogies: surprise → suprize, seasons → seesons
d. Confusion in capitalization: Ocean City → Ocean city, bluefish → Blue fish

4. Before making educational programming decisions, diagnostic
    information is needed relevant to the:
    a. Pupil's use of apostrophe in contractions, e.g., summer is →
        summer's
    b. Pupil's total skills vis-à-vis capitalization (see Module 7)
    c. Pupil's pronunciation of the word and (Does he/she say "an?")
    d. Pupil's total skills vis-à-vis commonly used homophones
5. The following teaching objectives are recommended for the pupil:
    a. The pupil will correctly spell the following pairs or sets of homo-
        phones in written communications:

        flower—flour
        blew—blue
        two—to—too
        wood—would

    b. The pupil will capitalize correctly both words of proper nouns
        that are comprised of more than one word, e.g., Ocean City, Salt
        Lake City, Catskill Mountains, Pikes Peak, and Grand Canyon
(Mastery Criterion: You must have approximated the answers as outlined above.)

Part D   Interviewing and Interacting
With the Pupil and the Pupil's Parents

1. If you are a student, ask your college instructor to evaluate the tape.
2. If you are a student teacher, ask your college supervisor and/or
    cooperating teacher to evaluate the tape.
3. If you are a teacher, ask a colleague or a supervisor to review the
    tape.
(Mastery Criterion: Decide beforehand with the evaluator the criterion
level of performance. If you do not meet criterion on the pretest, read the
materials and engage in the suggested activities and experiences before
taking the posttest.)

(*Overall* Mastery Criterion: Must meet criterion on each part of the test.)

MODULE 8

1. Fundamental questions that a teacher should ask himself/herself before establishing a required mastery level for each objective are:
    a. How valued is mastery of the skill to the pupil?
    b. How valued is mastery of the skill to the pupil's parents?
    c. Is the mastery level of the skill consonant with the developmental progression of the pupil?
    d. How necessary is mastery of the skill to acceptance and/or reinforcement by others, including peers and significant adults?
    e. How important is mastery of the skill to the physical and mental health and safety of the pupil?
    f. How critical is mastery of the skill to the daily life functioning of the pupil?
    g. How significant is mastery of the skill to the future life functioning of the pupil including vocational, leisure, and recreational pursuits?
    h. How essential is each subskill to the acquisition of important higher level skills?
    i. How much do the local community and the greater community value mastery of the skill?

(Mastery Criterion: Seven)

2. Pupils should incorporate the following questions in their self-evaluation:
    a. What skills and knowledge do I currently possess?
    b. What problems am I experiencing that are interfering with my learning progress?
    c. Why am I having these problems, and what can I do to improve my performance?
    d. How can I help others continuously evaluate my progress, and how can I, gradually, take an increasingly active role in evaluating my growth and development?

(Mastery Criterion: Four)

3. Pupils are given the opportunity to:
    a. Become more fully acquainted with instructional objectives especially the rationale for their inclusion in the instructional experience
    b. Have an input into determining mastery levels that are realistic and motivating

Both of these accomplishments are significant to the teaching/learning process because appreciating the necessity for learning specified skills and participating in determining required mastery levels may provide the motivation for achievement of these desired levels of mastery.

(Mastery Criterion: Accept any reasonable approximation.)

4.   For a sample Teacher-Pupil Evaluation of Progress Contract, see the body of the module.

(Mastery Criterion: Accept any reasonable approximation or improvement on the sample form.)

5.   For samples of self-rating forms appropriate to younger pupils, see the body of the module.

(Mastery Criterion: Accept any reasonably motivating and well designed pupil self-rating form.)

(*Overall* Mastery Criterion: Four)

MODULE 9

Part A

Items 1, 5, 6, 9, 13, 14, 17, and 20 are stated in behavioral terms.
(Mastery Criterion: 18)

Part B

The phrase or clause that provides information about conditions under which the learner is expected to perform is:

1. After being shown several pictures of common tools
2. Given a ruler, ribbon, and scissors
3. When shown a sample of a completed pattern of beads strung on a piece of yarn
4. Without the assistance of a cane
5. With a specially designed spoon

(Mastery Criterion: Five)

Part C

The following sentences describe a criterion of acceptable performance:

1. The pupil, after being shown several pictures of common tools, will select the tool each picture matches in five out of five trials for 100% accuracy.
2. Given a ruler, ribbon, and scissors, the pupil will measure and then cut six pieces of ribbon, measuring 10 inches each, in 5 minutes with no greater than 1/16 inch deviation.
3. When shown a sample of a completed pattern of beads strung on a piece of yarn, the pupil will reproduce the pattern exactly within 2 minutes.
4. The pupil will walk up the practice stairs in physical therapy without the assistance of a cane, in less than 1 minute, without falling.
5. With a specially designed spoon, the pupil will eat the applesauce without spilling or causing the applesauce to dribble down his/her chin.

(Mastery Criterion: Five. Accept any reasonably completed behavioral statement.)

Part D

See Figures 1 and 2 in the body of the Module.
(Mastery Criterion: Accept any reasonable approximation.)

(*Overall* Mastery Criterion: Must achieve mastery on each part of the test.)

MODULE 10

1. The diagnostically oriented teacher must:
    a. Thoroughly analyze each instructional area, completely investigating the underlying rationale for including each instructional experience in the curriculum
    b. Thoroughly analyze which methods and materials are logical and appropriate to the instructional process for each area of the curriculum
(Mastery Criterion: Both tasks must be described.)

2. Fine motor skills may be practiced and developed by:
    a. Playing a musical instrument(s)
    b. Producing a crafts project
    c. Creating a painting, sculpture, or other work of fine art
    d. Building and/or repairing models, toys, and projects
    e. Drawing architectual plans and designs
    f. Constructing and/or repairing furniture, household equipment, and furnishings
    g. Designing and creating clothing
    h. Preparing foods
    i. Carrying out vocationally oriented fine motor tasks, such as sorting, assembling, and packing
    j. Executing a host of other avocational and recreational pursuits
(Mastery Criterion: Seven)

3. When there are pupils in a classroom whose disorders interfere with fine motor skill development, the teacher must establish:
    a. The appropriateness of each subcategory of activities suitable for fine motor development
    b. The identification of possible resource people to assist in the development and implementation of a therapeutic program
(Mastery Criterion: Both elements must be included in the answer.)

4. Advice and counsel should be sought from the following individuals:
    a. First and foremost, the pupil
    b. Second, the pupil's parents or surrogate parents
    c. Third, other teachers who teach or who have taught the pupil
    d. Fourth, teacher aides, class parents, and classroom volunteers
    e. Fifth, other relevant school staff, including secretaries, lunchroom workers, schoolbus drivers, and custodians
(Mastery Criterion: Four of the five major categories of relevant human resources.)

5. Gross motor skills are developed and practiced by participating in:
    a. Active games and sports
    b. Calisthenics

    c.   Gymnastics
    d.   Dance in all its various forms
    e.   Yoga and other body-mind development approached
(Mastery Criterion: Five)

6.   Special attention should be given to gross motor movement experiences for all pupils since learning to enjoy and develop one's body and to find exhilaration and health through pleasurable physical activity is a universal need. PL 94-142 requires that gross motor experiences be included in all individualized educational programs for the handicapped.

(Mastery Criterion: Both elements must be included in the answer.)

7.   Approaches to teaching the principles of growth are:
    a.   Taking care of classroom plants
    b.   Taking care of classroom pets
    c.   Taking care of terraria and aquaria
    d.   Displaying retrospective pictures of the pupil from infancy on
    e.   Showing film(s) on plants that use time action photography to depict the stages of growth
    f.   Studying charts that demonstrate the stages of growth in human and animals
    g.   Using the microscope to study cell division
    h.   Viewing an especially developed exhibit or project, designed by the pupils, whenever possible. This exhibit may, for example, demonstrate the stages of embryonic growth and include plaster of Paris replicas, preserved specimens, charts, pictures from magazines.
    i.   Conducting nutrition experiments with plants and animals to demonstrate the effects of different substances and conditions on growth

(Mastery Criterion: Seven)

8.   To generate stimulating discussions in the classroom:
    a.   Read a story together and discuss its characters, events, and implications.
    b.   Show a film or filmstrip as part of a history, social science, or science lesson. The film or filmstrip can serve as the impetus for an informative discussion that not only leads to concept development but to the practice and enrichment of oral language skills.
    c.   Discuss a television program of particular interest to the pupil. Not only may speech skills be developed but questions of aesthetics may be explored.

    d.   Hold a discussion on a recent event that is of special interest to the pupil. These current events discussions both develop awareness of the sciences and social sciences as well as facilitate speech skills.

    e.   Prepare a choral reading as part of aesthetic development programming. The participation in this creative oral language experience may contribute to an appreciation for literature as well as improve expressive language skills.

(Mastery Criterion: Five)

9.   The following are alternate approaches to teaching addition:

    a.   Begin with oral problems and with number games.

    b.   Teach addition as the process used to make change.

    c.   Help the pupil practice counting by 1s, 5s, 10s, and 25s.

    d.   Work on addition by manipulating real objects.

    e.   Practice addition by playing games involving dice, spinning wheels, and playing cards.

    f.   Use flashcards with basic addition facts, recognizing the fact that much of basic arithmetic is the revisualization of number facts.

    g.   Teach addition through the use of a number line.

    h.   Ask the pupil to total up bills or checks for accuracy.

    i.   Ask the pupil to prepare a shopping list from a brochure, throwaway, or newspaper advertisement.

    j.   Tell the pupil to indicate how much money is needed for a purchase.

    k.   Plan any functional task involving measurement in the construction, design, or preparation of an article of clothing, a food or a meal, or a piece of furniture.

    l.   Explain the sales tax indicating the amount of tax due. Give pupil bills where sales tax should be added. Ask the pupil to compute the final bill.

    m.   Assign the pupil a task involving the production of quantities of an object in an assembly line activity. Ask the pupil to indicate the total amount produced.

    n.   Take the pupil on a trip to a store. After a purchase, ask the pupil to verify the amount of change received.

    o.   Ask the pupil to use a dollar changing machine. Indicate that he/she is to verify receipt of the correct change.

    p.   Ask the pupil to return deposit bottles to a store. Tell the pupil to check to see whether he/she has received the amount due.

    q.   Challenge the pupil with problems involving the measurement of objects, distances, and heights.

r.   Assign the pupil problems involving the use of measuring cups and spoons.

(Mastery Criterion: 12)

10. The following are some of the functional reading approaches to teaching reading:

a.   Assist the pupil in responding appropriately to written information and markings found on watches, clocks, and other dials and gauges.

b.   Help the pupil respond appropriately and accurately to written information found on safety signs, size labels, price tags, and other signs and labels.

c.   Expose the pupil to instructions written in simple notes and on packages, machinery, equipment, toys, games, items to be assembled and in manuals that accompany machinery and equipment.

d.   Provide the pupil with experience in locating information from charts, diagrams, maps, directories, schedules, bulletin boards, menus, and reference books, including dictionaries.

e.   Help the pupil to respond appropriately to employment applications and to a host of other applications, blanks, and forms.

f.   Assist the pupil in interpreting the information found on checks, check stubs, market receipts, work timecards, and bills.

g.   Provide the pupil with experiences in decoding and comprehending information found in travel and promotional brochures, information booklets, driving manuals, and other instructional materials.

h.   Assist the pupil in unlocking the information found in help wanted ads, printed advertisements, and in real estate and other special sections of magazines and newspapers.

i.   Help the pupil interpret reading materials in such a way that he/she is less likely to be victimized by propaganda and other manipulative techniques.

j.   Provide the pupil with reading experiences that bring pleasure and excitement thus enriching his/her life while, at the same time, providing a valuable leisure time activity to be used now and in the future.

(Mastery Criterion: Eight)

11. The individualization of instruction is consonant with democratic principles because it:

a.   Depends on the interests and motivation of each pupil

b.   Allows the pupil choices in selecting subcategories of curriculum areas and methods and materials desired

    c.   Provides the pupil's parents or surrogate parents with a role in the selection of methods and materials and in the identification of subcategories of curriculum areas

    d.   Does not require all pupils to participate in the same activity

    e.   Avoids biased or coercive approaches to educational programming

    f.   Identifies countless programming options

(Mastery Criterion: Accept any reasonable answer that includes the elements outlined above.)

12.   Functionality refers to any skill or knowledge that aids the individual pupil in his/her present total functioning and as he/she might need to function in the distant and unpredictable future. Functionality also refers to that which is pleasurable, recreational, and supportive of mental and physical health.

(Mastery Criterion: Accept any reasonable approximation.)

13.   A reinforcer is any environmental response to a behavior (or any environmental stimulus *viewed* as a response to a behavior) that is followed by an increase in the frequency or intensity of the behavior.

(Mastery Criterion: Accept any reasonable approximation.)

14.   The two tenets that underlie all operant processes are:

    a.   The frequency and intensity of all behavior, other than behaviors that are classically conditioned, are determined by the subsequent environmental response to that behavior.

    b.   Recording baseline behavior and behavior during interventions is essential to determining the success of the interventions.

(Mastery Criterion: Accept any reasonable approximation.)

15.   In shaping a behavior, small, partial accomplishments are reinforced at the beginning. As soon as this initial component of the behavior is mastered, reinforcement for it is withdrawn and offered again only when an additional component of the behavior is added on to it. This process is continued until the total behavior is demonstrated.

    In backward shaping, the pupil is assisted with the entire behavior except for the final component. When the pupil finishes the task by completing the final component, he/she is reinforced. When the final component is consistently demonstrated, reinforcement is withdrawn and offered again only when the next earlier component is also demonstrated. Backward shaping continues until the total task is mastered.

(Mastery Criterion: Accept any reasonable approximation.)

(*Overall* Mastery Criterion: 12)

MODULE 11

1. Reasons for knowing the social forces at work in the classroom are:
   a. Pupils are significantly influenced by the behavior and attitudes toward learning demonstrated by peers.
   b. The contagion or ripple effect rapidly transmits deviant attitudes and behaviors of one or more pupils to classmates.
   c. The teacher must understand and expertly use peer models whose behaviors and attitudes toward learning motivate classmates both to behave in cooperative and constructive ways and to pursue with eagerness the acquisition of knowledge and skills.
   d. The teacher must attempt to modify the behavior or diminish the influence of disturbed or disturbing peer models.
   e. Teachers must assist in the development of an interpersonal milieu in the classroom that encourages peers to interact and act in each other's best interests and form with the teacher a cohesive team striving toward mutually agreed upon and supported educational goals.

   (Mastery Criterion: Four)

2. Before organizing instructional experiences, teachers should ask the following questions:
   a. Who has a positive, motivating influence and serves as a model of constructive behavior on (pupil's name)? How can I utilize this influence to facilitate growth and development in both parties?
   b. Who has a negative influence on (pupil's name)? How can I diminish that influence or help to metamorphize that influence into a positive one?
   c. Who can (pupil's name) work with cooperatively in small group activities? large group activities?
   d. Who can (pupil's name) be tutored by in the various skill areas?
   e. Who can (pupil's name) tutor in the various skill areas?
   f. How can I make sure that (pupil's name) feels that he/she is an essential part of the class team, working toward his/her own development and the growth and progress of classmates?

   (Mastery Criterion: Six)

3. The following attitudes should be communicated by teachers in order to build pupil self-confidence:
   a. I value you as a unique, special, total human being with individual needs and differences.
   b. I am deeply committed to helping you grow and develop as a total person.

c. I believe that you are capable of learning, and I will help you to do so despite any problems you encounter.
d. I will constantly strive to help you realize and appreciate your worth and value.
e. I will provide you with learning experiences that are exciting, valuable, challenging, and within your ability.
f. While I provide you with learning experiences that are within your ability, I will always encourage you to believe the next higher level is within your ability to master.
g. I will never ridicule, humiliate, belittle, or label you.
h. I will recognize your individual needs for rest and leisure.
i. I will provide an environment that is responsive and rewarding to your attempts as well as your successes.

(Mastery Criterion: Accept any reasonable approximation or any others offered that are consonant with approved mental hygiene practices. The answer may be done in paragraph form and may deal with the feelings underlying the statements used in the body of the Module.)

4. Teachers can evaluate themselves in the following informal ways:
    a. Use videotapes
    b. Use audio cassettes or tapes
    c. Ask fellow teachers to evaluate typical lessons
    d. Measure success as a direct function of pupil growth and development
    e. Hold conferences with pupils and asking them to evaluate the success of the teacher-pupil interaction

(Mastery Criterion: Four)

5. For a brief description of the Flanders System review the body of the Module.

(Mastery Criterion: Accept any reasonable approximation of the content.)

6. Weaknesses attributed to the Flanders System are the:
    a. Lack of explicitness in that there is uncertainty as to the most appropriate category to be used for particular teacher-pupil interactions
    b. Use of time as the basic unit of coding and the attendant difficulty in recording, at 3-second intervals, behaviors while they are happening
    c. Failure to emphasize the specific cognitive or curriculum aspects of the classroom interaction
    d. Failure to measure cognitive achievement prior to the lesson to determine whether cognitive levels following a lesson have changed

e.   Lack of a component that attempts to measure nonverbal communication or the nonverbal components of the verbal elements
f.   Tendency to view talk as transmission rather than communication
g.   Inability to use this system during teacher-pupil interactions that are less formal than the typical question-answer sequence emphasized by the Flanders System
h.   The limited applicability to more innovative classroom practices and settings (for example, innovations such as the open classroom and the open space school)

(Mastery Criterion: Six)

7.   Important verbal skills of the Flanders System include the ability to:
a.   Accept, clarify, and use ideas
b.   Accept and clarify emotional expression
c.   Relate emotional expression to ideas
d.   State objectively a point of view
e.   Reflect accurately the ideas of others
f.   Summarize ideas presented in group discussion
g.   Communicate encouragement
h.   Use criticism with the least possible harm to the status of the recipient

(Mastery Criterion: Seven)

(*Overall* Mastery Criterion: Six)

MODULE 12

1. In order to accommodate the learning style of pupils with short attention spans, teachers can:
   a. Make task assignments shorter
   b. Periodically allow pupils to leave and then return to tasks during the school day
   (Mastery Criterion: Both elements must be included.)

2. Pupils with short attention spans who are able to persevere keep going back to a task until it is finished. Pupils with long attention spans stay at the task for one sitting until it is finished.
   (Mastery Criterion: Accept any reasonable approximation.)

3. Relevant external factors that influence the concentration/perseverance levels of pupils are:
   a. The motivating influence of subject matter
   b. The size and composition of the instructional group
   c. The nature, type, and frequency of reinforcement
   (Mastery Criterion: Three)

4. High distractibility refers to a person's ease in orienting toward petty, irrelevant stimuli and away from the task at hand.
   (Mastery Criterion: Accept any reasonable approximation.)

5. Being distracted by important stimuli may be necessary for survival.
   (Mastery Criterion: Accept any reasonable approximation.)

6. The elements to consider in deciding whether to allow pupils to set aside an unfinished task to pursue a new task include:
   a. Intensity of the distracting stimuli
   b. Educational value of the new task
   c. Emotional impact of the distracting stimuli
   (Mastery Criterion: Three)

7. The teacher can help pupils who are easily distracted by structuring a protective environment. For example, if the pupil is markedly distracted by visual stimuli, he/she should be given the option of facing away from the window, the door, or other sources of visual distraction or of being seated so that he/she is facing a colorless and unadorned wall. Pupils who are distracted by irrelevant auditory stimuli should be given the option of wearing ear plugs.
   (Mastery Criterion: Accept any reasonable approximation.)

8. When pupils control the use of environmental protections against distractions, they also become sensitive to their own problem and

learn how best to regulate and overcome the problem. Eventually they discard the protections. If the teacher maintains control, he/she is guessing at the pupil's need and fostering unnecessary pupil dependency.
(Mastery Criterion: Accept any reasonable approximation.)

9. If the teacher has time and sufficient assistance, a shaping technique may be initiated by gradually intruding competing stimuli during lessons, encouraging pupils to ignore these distractions.
(Mastery Criterion: Accept any reasonable answer that includes the essence of behavioral shaping.)

10. High activity pupils require more energy outlets than other pupils. Not only do they need more than average activities of a gross motor nature, they also require continual energy release possibilities during quiet activities. On the other hand, a low activity pupil may need encouragement to move about more frequently.
(Mastery Criterion: Accept any reasonable approximation.)

11. Allow withdrawn pupils to bring familiar objects with them to new situations or show them how new material incorporates or grows from old material.
(Mastery Criterion: Accept any reasonable approximation.)

12. The only significant problem that high approach pupils may have is in demonstrating sufficient caution in approaching potentially dangerous situations.
(Mastery Criterion: Accept any reasonable approximation.)

13. The major assistance teachers can provide pupils who experience difficulty with transitions is by preparing them for transitions before they arrive. A teacher may verbally signal the approaching transition at intervals. Teachers may teach pupils to use stopwatches to indicate the imminence of transition.
(Mastery Criterion: Accept any reasonable approximation.)

14. A low intensity pupil may be frightened and overwhelmed by a high intensity teacher. A high intensity pupil may see the low intensity teacher as disinterested or boring.
(Mastery Criterion: Accept any reasonable approximation.)

15. Impulsive learners are most efficient with tasks requiring rapid responses.
(Mastery Criterion: Idea of rapid response must be articulated.)

16. Impulsive learners are at a disadvantage with tasks that require thoughtful and delayed response.

(Mastery Criterion: Idea of slow, deliberated response must be articulated.)

17. Teachers can help impulsive learners with tasks that are causing them difficulty by encouraging them to slow down, to review before responding, and to use verbal mediation.
(Mastery Criterion: Three)

18. Verbal mediation refers to a cognitive process wherein one talks to oneself about a task, labeling essential clues, describing possible responses, indicating why they are right or wrong, etc.
(Mastery Criterion: Accept any reasonable approximation.)

19. Teachers can help reflective learners with tasks that are causing them difficulty by using exaggerated slowness in instructional pacing and in their various interactions.
(Mastery Criterion: Idea of exaggerated slowness must be articulated.)

20. Educational tasks suitable to a reflective mode of learning include:
    a. Science experiments
    b. Social relations
    c. Oral math problems
    d. Written expression
(Mastery Criterion: Four)

21. Educational tasks suitable to an impulsive mode of learning include:
    a. Foreign language learning
    b. Spelling
    c. Number facts
    d. Most fine and gross motor activities
(Mastery Criterion: Four)

22. Field dependency refers to pupils who are people-oriented and seek the reactions of others in making decisions as to task accuracy. Field independency refers to pupils who are highly task-centered and do not look for clues in the expressions and comments of others.
(Mastery Criterion: Accept any reasonable approximation.)

23. Four key issues yet to be resolved relevant to learning modality include:
    a. Should building up weak modalities be stressed? Should weak modalities be ignored to build on strong modalities?
    b. What is the value of a multisensory versus a single modality approach?
    c. What are the relationships of subject matter elements to modality of instruction?

d.   What are the effects of changing modality dominance on instruction as the pupil matures?

(Mastery Criterion: Four)

24. Reported sex and ethnic differences in learning style should be viewed by educators as a function of cultural expectations because looking at individual differences is more productive, in terms of educational programming, than looking at group differences. In addition, there are more differences within subgroups than there are among groups.

(Mastery Criterion: Both elements must be included.)

(*Overall* Mastery Criterion: 20)